Riding the Ox Home

Riding the Ox Home

A History of Meditation from Shamanism to Science

Willard Johnson

Beacon Press
Boston

Beacon Press
25 Beacon Street
Boston, Massachusetts 02108

Beacon Press books are published under the auspices
of the Unitarian Universalist Association
of Congregations in North America.

First published in 1982 by Rider & Company
An imprint of the Hutchinson Publishing Group
Copyright © by Willard Johnson 1982
First published by Beacon Press in 1986 by arrangement with the author

92 91 90 89 88 87 86   5 4 3 2 1

Library of Congress Cataloging-in-Publication Data

Johnson, Willard L.
    Riding the ox home.

    Reprint. Originally published: London : Rider, 1982.
    Bibliography: p.
    Includes index.
    1. Meditation—Comparative studies. 2. Meditation—
History.   I. Title.
BL627.J6   1987   158'.12   86–47752
ISBN 0–8070–1305–6 (pbk.)

To Liv, Liz, Helen, Ben and Fritz
who help so much
And to meditators everywhere –
may we transform our world!

For these too are foods, as much needed
by the psyche as proper diet is for the
body. The mental and spiritual need
spiritual food, seeking the quiet,
meditation and considering spiritual
matters.

'Look into that closed room, the
empty chamber where brightness is
born! Fortune and blessing gather
where there is stillness. But if
you do not keep still – this is what
is called sitting but racing around.'

(Chuang Tzu, *Basic Writings*,
Burton Watson, transl., New York:
Columbia University Press, 1964, p. 54)

Contents

The kung-an *of Po-chang Huai-hai solved!*
(Illustrated opposite)

According to Ch'an (meditative) Chinese Buddhism, Po-chang Huai-hai (AD 720–814) presented his followers with the enigma or *kung-an* (Japanese *kōan*) of the dilemma of looking for the ox (or Buddha-nature) which is already underneath oneself. This Japanese scroll picture shows the solution in the upturned gaze of the ox-tamer. Po-chang, when asked what the Buddha is, answered, 'It is like seeking for an ox while you are yourself on it'. When asked what use knowing the ox could serve, the master replied, 'It is like going home riding on it'. Here, the ox has been discovered and tamed, allowing an important shift of attention. The rider no longer seeks the ox in vain, which was under him all the while. His dilemma dissolves, enabling him to ride the ox home, harmonized with its powerful nature. The ox-tamer looks upwards, 'staring up at the sky and breathing', as Chuang Tzu described it. Ox and meditator seem suspended in space in a delicate, transcending harmony which allows ecstasy. In this state, one can attend to other facets of reality, beginning like a discoverer to venture out into the world.

The picture derives from the centuries-old 'ox and herdsman' series which depict the stages of meditative development. These sets of six, eight or ten scenes were popular among meditation students as training manuals and commentaries on the contemplative life. In this book, I comment on one such set of ten which shows the herdsman, or more properly the ox-tamer (since tamers do more than just herd), going through the process of self-transformation which brings the animal and spiritual minds into balance.

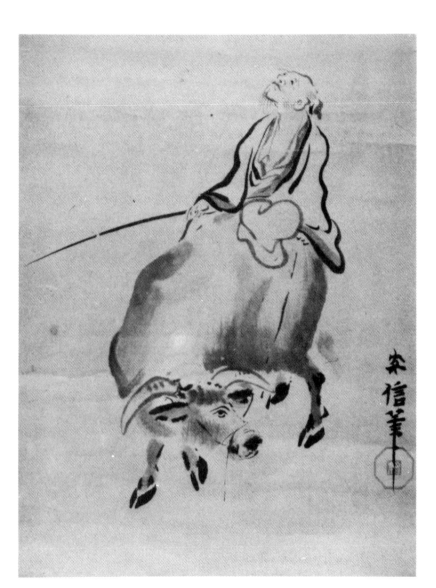

Introduction

In this book, I seek to re-interpret meditation for our present day and its needs. For too long meditation has been identified as a withdrawal form of religious pursuit, and for too long we have allowed it to escape us. The problem is that we have failed to recover from traditional literature and practice the meaning of meditation for our own times and lives. Accounts, though adequate in representing some meditative traditions, severely fail to bring out their meaning for us now, preferring to leave it unrecovered from the doctrines and uses of the past. Or, when we do seek to apply the traditional teachings, as in the case of Indian yoga or Sino-Japanese Ch'an/Zen, they remain locked in their traditional mould, unadapted and largely uninterpreted for relevance to the style and dilemmas of our own lives or suitability to our situations, our aspirations and our seekings for the something more. Without recovering what human beings have learned about meditation in the past, we shall never be able to advance it; and, without opening it to new interpretation and further expansion, it will never possess meaning and possibility in our own lives.

Since I seek in this exposition to interpret meditation for our own times, I need to specify at the outset the meaning I attribute to certain key terms I shall be using. Though these terms carry the usual baggage of their past meanings, they function in this account in a specialized sense. Otherwise, I shall be condemned from all sides for not according with this or that sense of my key terms, while this will not be my

1

intent. Books aplenty seek to describe the past meanings of meditation, and these I have used as material for my own, but it is not my intention to repeat them. Rather, to re-invent the spectrum of possibilities which meditation offers to us today, I will use this term, along with the words 'ecstasy', 'mysticism', 'spirituality' and 'maturity' (or greater degrees of self-knowledge), in the following special meanings. Anyone who seeks, as I do, to found a new knowledge must extricate its key terms from the matrix of the past, so that they indeed shine forth in all their new possibility. And this will mean that the reader, for the sake of argument, must suspend the old meanings, so that my account of meditation for our own times will make proper sense.

First comes the word I use to designate the subject of my exposition itself. 'Meditation' as a term calls up negative, cultish, vague or strictly religious associations when used in English. The encyclopedia (*Britannica* in this case) considers it the 'profound and generally peaceful consideration of truths' by which to order one's life, especially for those dedicated to religious pursuits. Ordinary dictionary definitions consider it simply to be reflective or contemplative thought, while other sources in our Euroamerican cultural mainstream fail to include it among subjects of interest or importance. Schools and churches alike fail utterly to include it, and only fringe innovative groups take it seriously. At the popular level, as well as in intellectual circles, meditation is considered in primarily negative terms, as a form of passivity, withdrawal or, ironically, a kind of self-preoccupation! Our cultural impoverishment clearly lies bare when we consider how we use and understand this term.

In this book, I mean by 'meditation' a wide variety of activities which seek to expand and enhance the reach of the mind and its possible functioning, generally produced by forms of sensory-motor discipline which include sitting quietly, relaxing, closing the eyes, breathing deliberately, and taking a meditative object to still the ordinary, anxious functioning of consciousness. With such a broad definition, I seek to liberate meditation from cultish connotations and even religious associations, since meditation can just as well be a secular practice. In effect, meditation has no intrinsic goal or meaning; it is rather a technique, a way of developing consciousness. We think it has a goal because almost all those involved in or teaching meditation use it for what they intend it to produce, while this is not intrinsic but extrinsic to the technique of meditation itself. It is, rather, a widespread human technique which trains consciousness. We can see the common features of this technique in the great diversity of human activities that fall under my definition. I prefer to leave meditation with the broadest possible meaning, since I want our cultural activity and preferences to be able to evaluate and adapt it to be used for what it is – a mental technique or praxis, neutral and devoid of any specific application or goal other than that it be successful as a means of consciousness transformation. Although I suggest in this book how it might be used, and has been used in the past, anyone can use meditation for consciousness enrichment of a vast variety of specific forms and uses. We are just beginning to discover these, and I expect the process of this discovery to accelerate rapidly in the near future.

An even more difficult term is 'ecstasy', which I use here to designate the state reached or achieved in meditation. This word has so many specific meanings in diverse contexts, mainly religious, that I use it with trepidation, and specify here as carefully as I can how I redefine the term for use in this book. In the broadest etymological sense, ecstasy means departure from one's original or ordinary condition, thus some abrupt change of mind or mood. From this, specific senses of the term developed, none of which I intend! In Greek, its source, it meant departure into disturbed states of mind, insanity or bewilderment; it could designate hysteria, diabolical possession, or astonishment (as when Jesus disputed with the doctors and the onlookers were amazed). With the meaning of being 'beside oneself', it can designate entrance into states of frenzy or stupor, anxiety, fear or passion (*Oxford English Dictionary*), of all kinds or 'morbid states' of consciousness, such as a swoon, a trance or catalepsy. I grant that these meanings are not common today, but even our ordinary usage of the word to designate an exalted, extremely happy state of mind, or rapturous delight, is not what I mean by the term. Finally, I wish also to exclude the traditional religious uses of the term, as in mysticism, where it indicates the state of mental rapture when the soul leaves the body to participate in the blessed state of divine transcendence (as in St Teresa's ecstasy, so beautifully portrayed by Bernini in marble). Rather, I seek to use this term with its etymological meaning of departing from one's ordinary state of mind, or being 'beside oneself', but specifying that the state entered has very few, if any, of the qualifications put on it in the examples above. Instead, I intend by this term the wide variety of peaceful, quiet, perceptive, learning, extended and expanded mental states which can be produced by regular meditative discipline. The primary feature of all of these is that they transcend our ordinary mental condition, which is usually characterized by changeable, sensory-dominated self-consciousness, coloured by affect tones related to negative intrapsychic conflict and anxiety. One enters through meditation into another form of consciousness, which can be thought-filled or thought-transcending, but which goes beyond restrictive affect or negative feeling. In this state, 'beside ourselves', we learn, mature, grow, and develop the mind's reach and depth of experience. To a great extent the content of ecstasy cannot be determined from outside, but must be discovered in one's own experience. I offer this discussion only to specify how I am, and how I am not, using this key term. Meditation is the technique which deliberately produces forms of ecstasy, experimental states of consciousness which can be used to learn about self and world and to develop one's mental potential and extend its possibilities. Science, our dominant system of cultural knowledge, seeks different extensions, and produces a different reality with its appropriate reality experience.

Introduction

In any discussion of these terms, the subject of mysticism will surely arise. In this book, 'mysticism' does not mean any of the usual things, especially not as a substitute for the word 'religion' (often used to dismiss the subject of both), nor does it refer only to lofty-sounding saints and yogis of ancient times. Mysticism seems best described as a particular form of direct knowledge. Mystics repeatedly claim to know by becoming the object of knowledge (a tree, or God, for instance). For this to be possible, they maintain, one must transcend one's ordinary, limited identity, the surrendering of attachment to this usual selfhood being the primary requirement for having the experience, which is particularly characterized by a sense of 'oneness'. My view of mysticism understands it as a much broader form of knowledge, in which traditional mystics have specialized in one particular manner, namely towards the realization of doctrinally inter-preted absolutes, like the unity of all phenomenal diversity, or the presence of the Divine. For the following chapters, I will define mysticism as indicating a broad range of deliber-ately altered states of consciousness used to realize something about spiritual reality. This could even include working with dream images, accepting them as means of approaching spiritual reality (as visionary dreams used to reach ecstatic experiences). I think we need, at this point at least, to make no restrictions on what mysticism should be. In this decade, we have reached the cultural threshold for innovation in all the areas covered by these terms. By leaving them broad and open, we can use our own original voices creatively to identify and study these states of consciousness, just as we have recently developed whole fields of thought which analyse the 'language of self' as in the examples of the psychology of narcissism and self-deception. So again, experience finally must define all these difficult terms, not by historical precedent or stipulated content, but in terms of how we experience them. This content can be put to further analysis later.

Another concept which concerns me in this book is

spirituality, and the development of spiritual maturation. Generally, society today concerns itself with successive forms of maturation, from physical, to social, to intellectual, but we have, particularly outside religion, forgotten to concern ourselves with developing spiritual forms of maturity. This raises the question of my definition of 'spiritual' in the discussion of meditation. To answer this, I have to return to the beginning of spirituality, using the analogy of the contemporary myth of physical evolution as my model to explain how we arrived where we are today. I think the first datable event in the evolution of spiritual consciousness was eight hundred thousand years ago, when proto-humans domesticated fire. This event constitutes one of the great achievements of our genus before the much later elaboration of civilization. Before that time, I imagine hominid consciousness to have evolved solely as a means of adaptation and survival in a threatening, hostile world whose sole rule was eat or be eaten, kill or be killed. Consciousness then provided survival value by adapting hominids to external threat. Its fight-flight structure had supreme survival value for literally thousands of millennia. But then, hominids adopted fire, the first ally in their quest for survival. It is no wonder that many religions remember this alliance by divinizing fire, or making it a primary symbol! A fight-flight consciousness is sensorily dominated, that is, it survives by constant alert attention to external threat, deciding either to stand and fight or to take flight before danger. With fire, the first opportunities for a radically new evolution in consciousness became possible. Seated in their caves or huddled around the primeval fire in the jungle, hominids began to evolve a qualitatively new form of consciousness, since by providing security and warmth, the fire allowed their sensory-dominated survival consciousness to relax. Literally 'entranced' by the fire (as we all have been, in part remembering that deep past), they began to experience 'ecstasy', or the mind's standing outside its ordinary fight-flight readiness. I suggest that this began as an inner, spiritual parallel to the hominid's increasingly enhanced consciousness of the external world, seen for example in early tool development. Certainly other experiences also caused consciousness to stand outside its primal fight-flight form, as love, or the vigil of the hunter, but we can date the domestication of fire, so I take this as my landmark.

We have come a long way in both physical and spiritual evolution since that time, but the sense of 'spiritual' which I intend goes all the way back to the first breakthrough of qualitatively different consciousness. 'Spiritual' in this book means the forms of consciousness we have evolved beyond the sensory-dominated, physically adaptive forms of awareness which we must use every day to avoid injury and death as well as to succeed in the complex tasks which assail us as soon as we wake. This definition frees spirituality from religion, though it has been in the matrix of religion (which for most of its history has not in the main been spiritual but rather largely another means of adaptation to the material world) that spirituality has been nurtured. It is time to liberate it from the evolutionary structure which gave it birth, and to cultivate our generic, human spirituality, whether we choose to be religious or secular in our commitment to seeking the ultimate meanings in our existence. 'Spirituality' is thus the consummation rather than the means of bringing about our consciousness forms and acts, to love rather than (however subtle it may be) to act as if life were still a matter of kill or be killed, to participate in the fullness of the Other (in I-Thou relations), rather than to take the Other solely as an object for instrumental survival actions (I-It forms).

From this too, finally, stems my definition of maturity, which I have used the Asian 'ox-taming' pictures to explain in the context of meditative self-exploration and development. Maturity contrasts with fight-flight, kill or be killed, and infantile adaptive patterns. The heritage from our distant ancestry is the success of the fight-flight form of consciousness, something which our infancy makes even more obstinate in us (like a mean ox). Infantile adaptation, like our primeval adaptive patterns, achieves its goals by not spiritual, but coercive, immature' mechanisms. To mature, to become fully adult, means to be able to stand outside these patterns, thus to learn who we really can be. In this lies the promise of spirituality, of love, and our flowering as *Homo sapiens*, the last surviving hominid form. If we are truly 'knowing' humans, we need to know not in our infantile, primeval persona, but as truly human, lovingly empathetic individuals who care for creation and all its creatures. Meditation will serve this potential in us, but we have to free it from its own past and from our own ignorance of it. To this goal I dedicate my book, *Riding the Ox Home*.

Willard Johnson

1

The Original Meaning of the Word 'Yoga'

To begin this investigation of the trans-cultural meaning of meditation, let us look at the true meaning of one of the oldest terms for meditation: the Sanskrit word *yoga*. In meaning it resembles its cognate English word 'yoke', the action which brings together two or more burly, powerful animals so as to make use of their strength. Ordinarily, *swamis* and *gurus* coming from India give a theistic interpretation of the meaning of the word when they say, without hesitation, that *yoga* means 'union'. Actually, this translation does not do justice to the term at all. For one, metaphysically, since one's spirit is already one with the Absolute, as the Upaniṣads declared, what is there to achieve the union? (see Chapter 4). Furthermore, another Sanskrit term, *samādhi*, is a much better candidate for the notion of meditation's aim of unifying the distracted, diverse parts of one's mental equipment, and is an accepted word for the goal of yoga practice which unifies consciousness. In fact, yoga is more properly the means to *samādhi*, which in turn is the state wherein the goals to which yoga may be put are realized.

This can be clarified if we look at the original meaning of the term 'yoga', along with its verbal root, √*yuj*, from which it derives in Sanskrit grammar. The Sanskrit dictionary lists over thirty different meanings for these terms, but the original, first use of the verb clearly meant 'to harness horses to a chariot'. It would be inappropriate, even, to say that it means 'to yoke', since the old Vedic age meaning of the word had nothing at all to do with lumbering oxen.

To understand this original meaning of the word 'yoga' we

have to go back to the Vedic age in north-west India, probably sometime before 1500 BC, when semi-barbaric, nomadic, cattle-herding, Indo-Aryan groups came over the Khyber Pass on to the plains of the Indus river valley. Roughly the same process brought related Indo-European peoples into northern Europe, Greece, the Middle East and Iran. It must have resembled the coming of the cowboys into the American West, mounted on their horses, wielding death-dealing firearms. The Indo-Aryans harnessed their horses to battle chariots, with which they terrorized the remaining peoples of the declining, pacifistic Harappan civilization, plundering and subjugating and killing those who resisted. These ancient Indo-Aryan battle chariots belonged to warrior-aristocrats (something like the cattle barons of the old West) who financed their construction and fought from them, usually with bows and arrows. However, at that time a sophisticated harness and horse collar had not yet been invented, making the horse and chariot very difficult to handle. So who harnessed the horses and drove the chariot? Not the owner-aristocrat, but his *sūta*, or charioteer, a figure so important in later Hindu culture that, when Viṣṇu incarnated to help the forces of righteousness to defeat evil on earth, he chose to be Kṛṣṇa, Arjuna's charioteer (see Jean Varenne, *Yoga*, Chapter 6).

The charioteer's actions in the highly skilled process of harnessing his master's horses were described by the verb √*yuj*, 'to harness'. The guild of charioteers developed such skill that tremendous prestige accrued to them. This skill constituted their yoga, their self-discipline which led to achieving their professional goal, the harnessing and driving of their masters' battle chariots.

Thus the original meaning of the term 'yoga' had as its basis an achieved skill, which one masters in preparation for an adventure or an activity in the world, the yoga's goal. By its very ancestry, yoga meant the preparations for departure, readying for an expedition or adventure. Many of the later meanings of the term flow from this ancestry. Even in the earliest texts, it had come by extension to designate such things as 'war', 'conquest', 'skill', and even 'warrior'. Finally, it came to designate also any means or device, such as a remedy, a magical charm, a trick, any undertaking, or the result of any of these. I find this quite revealing as we search, at the outset, for the basic meaning of meditation. Therefore, 'yoga', the oldest word still in use for meditation, means a skill in which one trains oneself, harnessing some previously uncontrolled forces, in order for their powers to enhance the success of some undertaking or adventure. This contrasts strongly with the widely held notion of meditation as some kind of a withdrawal into an inner fastness, from which one undertakes no outward, worldly action, but loses oneself in another state of being totally divorced from the concerns of daily life and this world. In fact, meditation, like the earliest yoga of these highly skilled charioteers, more than an end in itself is a means to whatever end one chooses. When thinking of meditation, recall this archaic image of the first *yogins* (practitioners of yoga), who had to harness powerful horses with inadequate equipment, thus eliciting from themselves the best of their own skill, for the goal of preparing to set off for a journey of conquest in the world.

As it happened, the term 'yoga' could not be applied metaphorically to meditation during the time of the *Ṛg Veda* (1500 BC) because meditation had not yet become a discipline. This meaning does not occur in a text until the time of the middle early Upaniṣads and early Buddhism, around 400 BC. However, already in the earlier text, 'yoga' did take on metaphorical meanings, as in the verse from the *Ṛg Veda* (5.81.1): '[Priests] harness their mind, indeed, harness their sacred thoughts.' Here the underlying meaning of discipline leading to a special skill comes forth clearly. In this case, the harnessing or disciplining of the mind's creative verbal abilities leads to better praising of the god to whom the priests address their chants. Thus, the word came to be one of the major Sanskrit terms for the discipline of the metaphorical horses (the senses and mental faculties; see Chapter 4). And this is meditation, which after centuries emerged as a major feature of the creative merging of Indo-Aryan and indigenous Indus civilizations.

One might ask the question, as some have, 'wasn't meditation a part of the earliest, Indus Valley based Harappan civilization?' The question arises because we see in Harappan representations of deified figures that the figures sit with their legs crossed. These images have led some people to conclude that Indus Valley peoples practised some form of early 'yoga'. However, we have no evidence to substantiate the speculation (for one thing, the sparse language of the civilization resists convincing deciphering), and a better explanation is simply that this way of sitting, later developed into the yogic 'lotus posture' (*padmāsana*), was just the most common way of sitting in that part of the world. Then, when later people sat in meditation, they adopted the most natural, comfortable way of sitting known to them. In ancient China another way of sitting was adopted (see Chapter 3), and when, today, Westerners decide to meditate, it is to my mind best to sit as we find it most comfortable, in a chair, or with some kind of backrest.

So we have no written evidence that formalized meditative disciplines evolved in explicit form, both in India and in ancient China, until around 500 BC (Chapter 3). However, in the writings of Chuang Tzu, some of the first (*c.* 300 BC) to describe early Chinese meditative practices, we find the same emphasis on meditation as a skill which one cultivates and acquires to achieve ambitions. The following passage, like many in Chuang Tzu's writings, metaphorically describes meditation in the image of the skill of a cicada catcher (who probably gathers these insects to sell in the market):

When Confucius was on his way to Ch'u, he passed through a forest where he saw a hunchback catching cicadas with a sticky pole as easily as though he were grabbing them with his hand.

Confucius said, 'What skill you have! Is there a special way to this?'

'I have a way,' said the hunchback. 'For the first five or six months I practice balancing two balls on top of each other on the end of the pole and, if they don't fall off, I know I will lose very few cicadas. Then I balance three balls and, if they don't fall off, I know I'll lose only one cicada in ten. Then I balance five balls and, if they don't fall off, I know it will be as easy as grabbing them with my hand. I hold my body like a stiff tree trunk and use my arm like an old dry limb. No matter how huge heaven and earth, or how numerous the ten thousand things, I'm aware of nothing but cicada wings. Not wavering, not tipping, not letting any of the ten thousand things take the place of those cicada wings – how can I help but succeed?'

(Chuang Tzu, Basic Writings, Watson, pp. 120–1)

Here, very much as in the case of the original meaning of the term 'yoga', Chuang Tzu describes meditation as a skill which brings success in a difficult task, in this case the catching of flighty insects on the end of a sticky pole. His meaning lies in the metaphor – one acquires meditative skills in steps, or stages, resulting in a concentration of the senses (five balls = five senses) and mental faculties so that they remain on one point or object (the meditative object, or the goal of the skill), this discipline resulting in sure success. From Plato we similarly learn that around the same time, Socrates drew such lessons from the skills of craftsmen whom he observed.

At the outset, then, one might answer the question 'why meditate?' by saying that meditation is a skill which one acquires, to enhance one's powers and abilities to pursue one's life goals. Meditation is unlike many of the other skills we acquire in the course of our education, since it radically reverses our ordinary modes of awareness. Usually, we use the senses to observe the world, and our powers of action to shape and control it to our advantage. In fact, our contemporary rationalistic-scientific civilization excels as no others ever have in such manipulatory skills. We fly, even to the moon, dive deep under the oceans, create vast cities and communicate instantaneously over great distances. One set of human skills, pertaining largely to the physical, visible world and our survival in it, produces this marvellous technology. Meditation does something completely different in that it reverses its outward, sensory orientation, directing the meditator to calm the body, to regulate the breath and, by temporarily closing the eyes and shutting off the other senses, to turn attention inward, exploring another dimension of consciousness. This dimension, as opposed to the sensory, involves being conscious of the other side of awareness, the non-sensory.

At this point, most people ask, 'well, what worth could a non-sensory awareness have, since we know the world only through our senses?' Meditation challenges the assumption that we know only through the senses, opening up the whole possibility of 'extra-sensory perception', and its correlate of influencing the world through non-motor means, or psychokinesis. Physiological psychology tells us, furthermore, that we have not one brain but two. The left brain, apparently, functions to analyse the world rationally, allowing the wonderful power over the physical universe which we have achieved. This brain leads us to think about the world and to act within it in certain ways, unfortunately to the exclusion of others which might be equally interesting and challenging. I think as I observe Western civilization that I detect what might be called a sensory domination of consciousness produced by the functioning of this left brain. By this I mean that we find almost all our satisfactions through the senses; we have convinced ourselves that sensory experience holds all the pleasures we could possibly seek, and thus we search for our entire life's experience in the sensory world. The adverse consequences of this essentially moral choice come out in our motivations and their consequences. The Achilles heel of our civilization is that the sensory domination of consciousness causes us to want more and more physical, sensory experience; this results in a voracious greed which motivates us to strip the environment and to exploit less developed areas of the world to satisfy our ever increasing desires for sensory satisfaction. This causes us to seek production of more goods to satisfy our desires, as environmentalist David Brower says, 'more *gross* national product', while meditators might seek 'more *subtle* national product', and growth only to support a modestly comfortable standard of living.

Now, what about the alternative consciousness which is reached through meditation, deriving from the right brain? This brain knows through 'intuition', feels satisfaction not through sensory experience as much as by sensing a-rationally what the underlying wholeness of life is. Because we have become so fascinated by the rational powers which lead to control of the physical environment, we have lost touch, largely, with this right hemispheric functioning of the brain. Religion, art and experiences of nature and music, for example, evoke this other sense of reality, but we have largely failed to deepen our experience of them because they have fallen under the all-pervading sway of our rationalistic, secularized civilization's choices to satisfy ourselves entirely through the physical world. Spiritual teachings have repeatedly warned that gold holds less value than spirit, and that the meek shall inherit God's earthly kingdom. What they have meant really involves this alternative mode of experiencing 'reality' through a-rational, feeling or intuitive modes of the right brain's functioning. Religions repeatedly stress that the realm of the spiritual is 'invisible', the object primarily of our non-sensory awareness, recommending prayer and meditation over sensory modes of awareness to come into touch with the ultimate values of spirit or the 'divine'. Whether one conceives this non-sensory right brain awareness as spiritual or not, it remains a largely unexplored *terra incognita* to us today, as vast and as fascinating as outer space and the galaxies, but much more accessible. Meditation proposes, in the most challenging of its potentials, that we might be able to experience realms of consciousness as fascinating as the world which confronts us every day through the senses; or alternatively that, through meditation, we can open up our experiences of this our physical world in ways of which we have never before dreamed. Meditators need not deny the physical world, but rather can know it through both rational-active and intuitive-perceptive modes of conscious functioning. By leading directly to the function- ing of the right brain, meditation could balance us, the rational-sensory domination of consciousness being modified and our life awareness coming to include intuitive functions.

Meditation serves this goal by harnessing the senses and the mental functions, so that the mind might itself become skilled at knowing and experiencing the world as a two-sided unity. Just as the mind is bicameral, so too is the world in which we must balance the benefits of environmental exploitation with the disadvantages of environmental pollution. At a personal level, we can experience the world as a means of satisfying our desires and as a consummatory experience in itself. If a person's life is all work and no play, what is the use of living? Work serves as an instrument to our creative activities and to our gaining a living, but play balances our being, serving no function but to engage us in the pleasurable activity for itself alone.

These sorts of goals, developing and balancing consciousness, constitute the overall goal of meditation. Still, however, meditation is not the goal, but merely a means, a skill one acquires applicable to any goal. Throughout this book, we shall be seeing the great diversity of goals which this means has been used to achieve. Some people have sought through meditation to relax, and to enhance their health and feeling of well-being. Others have used meditation to further their pursuit of wealth, or to enhance their adventures through the world. In devotional meditation (as in India's *bhakti-yoga*), some have sought to become aware of the Divine's presence in life; in this sense, they seek 'union' with the Divine, but this does not make meditation or yoga itself the 'union'. 'Union' is the goal they have chosen for their practice of meditation. Other people have used meditation to deepen their awareness of sexual experience, to help to create and appreciate art and beauty, to become aware of omens and signs, to acquire psychic powers, to heal or to lessen pain, and to make things go better during daily life.

Finally, meditation is neutral; it produces a mental discipline, a skill, which can be applied to whatever goal the practitioner seeks. For the duration of this exploration we need to suspend whatever preconceptions we hold about meditation, especially its goals. With this attitude we can survey how meditation developed in the Shamanism which is characteristic of archaic human communities (Chapter 2), and what civilizations have done with it (Chapters 3–6); then, we shall look at what science is learning about meditation (Chapter 7) and review what we might use it for (Chapters 8–10). So this book surveys the entire field of meditation, using evidence from all human cultures and civilizations, taking no one point of view but seeking to sketch a map of its entire human meaning. Its trans-cultural approach is intended to free us from limited viewpoints on meditation, so that we may better understand it, and make our own choices about it. I am sure that many will read this book and decide not to do anything with meditation, but at least that will be a choice based on knowledge rather than on ignorance. Others may already be involved in meditation, and see more clearly what they are doing against the backdrop of human experience, while still others will discover somewhere on the map of meditation where they would fit in, and begin to practise some form of it. I have no axe to grind in this investigation in the sense of having a meditation sect or sectarian inter-pretation to represent, though I do heartily affirm the possi-bilities of learning and creating through its powers. I also include opinions and value formulations about other matters, from how we should understand human history to how we should relate to it and how we might better mature to take care of our earth and of each other. As a writer, I deliberately try to push through to new knowledge, to answer original questions, and I engage in controversy, but none of my claims or pronouncements is intended to place itself above critical examination or refutation. This book reports the state of my thinking about meditation at this time (1981). Also, I myself am still learning about meditation in my own practice of it and have undertaken to teach and write about this subject as a consequence of my desire to know about it, not because I am convinced about it in some special or secret way. I have sought to learn about it to enhance my practice of it, but am still learning, and the very writing of this book is intended to further my knowledge and, indirectly, my meditation practice. Somehow, meditation beckons to me. I feel it can balance my life, deepening my experience of the world and its mysteries. I think meditation can make my life better, and prepare me for my death, so it behoves me to learn about it, and to apply what I learn to my attempts to meditate. And what I have learned already I wish now to share with you.

Ox Taming 1   *In the Beginning, Struggling to Emerge From Confusion*

At the end of each chapter, I will comment on one picture in the 'ox-taming' series of the Chinese Ch'an and Japanese Zen meditation tradition. In their original context, these pictures formed a visual parable of the stages of achieving the Buddhist enlightened mind, a subject also of poems and sets of verses, some of which used the pictures as their inspiration. Ch'an and Zen specialized in meditation as a means of achieving enlightenment or spiritual maturation in Sino-Japanese Buddhism. In this series, the artist interprets the stages of progression on the way to becoming a mature meditator. Naturally, they allow diverse interpretations, which to this day are being published. Westerners also have begun creating sets in ink brush, print, collage and other media (see Bibliography). I shall use these pictures to discuss the different stages of a maturing course of meditative self-transformation. My interpretations will not try to reproduce meanings already published by the Buddhist commentators, but will rather try to discover in them how meditation and other correlate activities change the self, resulting in greater degrees of self-knowledge and spiritual maturity.

First, though, preliminary observation of the entire set (see the end of each chapter for the sequence) finds all the pictures in a wide, free brush stroke delineating a circle. Perhaps the circle symbolizes the mind itself, each picture a different experience type; the allegorical progression shows the transformations which occur. The Ch'an/Zen tradition adopted, furthermore, the enigma first propounded by Po-chang Huai-hai (720–814) of the person riding an ox, interpreting it as a means of representing the search for Buddhahood. The insight of the *kōan* or riddle-image involved its instruction that when one realizes one already rides on the ox, and tames it, one can 'ride it home' (attain the goal of one's mental training or meditation). This goal comes in the eighth picture (ecstasy), with further development in the ninth; the tenth picture shows the consequent new person. Because in the original a 'boy' tames the ox, I will use 'boy' to mean 'immature person' of either sex.

The heritage of this allegory extends far back to the origins of civilization. In ancient Babylon, between the Tigris and the Euphrates, settled agriculture and cities first arose. Their development accelerated greatly, based in part on a dynamic force leashed to the service of human survival resulting from the domestication of the ox for transportation, and later for ploughing. This event produced a major turning point in the course of civilization, since it was the first extension made by human beings into controlling and using a motive power other than their own. The yoking of the ox, and later the harnessing of the horse, supplied the image base of this allegory, which remembers this domestication that took place throughout Asia. But in Ch'an and Zen, the allegory has been reapplied to show the liberating of spiritual power. Already the oldest Upaniṣads of early classical Sanskrit (sometime prior to 400 BC in the case of this image, found in *Bṛhad-āraṇyaka Upaniṣad* I.4.7) applied the ox-finding metaphor in a spiritual sense, when the author compared finding the essence of reality to tracing the ox's footprints. The text says that creation's diversity may be tracked back to the essence in all its forms. The person who meditates on the diversity sees only that, it claims, but that, and here is the image in its first spiritual application, 'the self [essence of all and one's inner essential self] is the track by which all this [reality may be found], since by it one knows all [creation], just as one finds [a stray animal] by its track.' This is Upaniṣadic affirmation of the self as source of gnōsis; for our interest, the metaphor of finding the lost animal as equivalent to gaining enlightenment is an important addition to the image's heritage. In early Pali Buddhism, too, this image occurs where comparisons with tending cows demonstrate various forms of self-transformative discipline. Probably the Ch'an tradition picked up this image from India via Central Asia. The Chinese too had their equivalent of the ox in the use of the water buffalo as their means of extending human power in the material world, a standard feature of Asian agrarian civilizations.

Each of the pictures in this set of ten shows the next stage of meditative development, along with the spiritual maturation process that goes along with it in the Ch'an/Zen tradition. These sets, which Japanese artists and poets produced in visual and lyric forms, provide us with an analysed portrait-description of the process of meditation in the symbolism of each subsequent picture. In this first, the boy, rope in hand, appears to be looking around for the ox, still completely out of sight. He appears to be about to cross the river by the bridge, but first looks back, perhaps troubled, over his shoulder. His new intention is definite as we see in his readied rope, but he has not sighted his quarry. That he looks back, over his shoulder, might mean that his past dominates him; since he has embarked on a new venture, he looks back, but his steps show the full resolve to change, to go across the stream. Or we can imagine that in the previous moment the boy thought he was leading the ox, which had in reality slipped behind him on the path to go out of sight in the dust, or round a nearby corner. The boy searches everywhere, wandering farther and farther away from home, becoming more and more lost and confused, wondering how to recover the ox and return home once again.

How should we regard this symbolic image? Interpretation requires that we be faithful to the original image, but allows us to help it to reveal meanings which perhaps did not occur to traditional interpreters, or which perhaps they knew very well. To elucidate my meditative maturity interest, this image represents immature chasing around and looking for something one needs or, worse, something one is attached to which is temporarily lost. We all have experienced the distress of such situations. Though the boy may be looking anxious, he also has a firmness of intention which will change the situation (or the mind which creates it). All nature stands ready for the boy's appreciation, but at this point is neglected. Whether from anxiety or desire to change, the boy looks round, ready to begin a special venture. He accepts responsibility both for what has already occurred (the ox is lost), and for what will happen in the future (once the ox is found, for which the rope is ready in hand). What has already happened is clear: the boy, turning away from himself, has estranged or alienated himself from the ox – a bad state.

The symbolism of the major actors in this allegory holds the key to its interpretation. The boy represents a person's ability to choose and act, but more, to observe and understand; perhaps even the boy is the nascent, still immature personality seeking for its proper place in the mental economy. The ox in turn represents the self or selves from which the person is separated or alienated. In the Sanskrit term *karma* these meanings occur, for like the ox, *karma* starts wild and untamed (in its infantile adaptive patterning especially), and can 'run away' from one's budding spiritual consciousness. In this respect, the escaped ox portrays out of control, habituated or stereotyped forms of behaviour which dominate and escape the boy (or his self-awareness). Meditative transformation begins when one realizes there is something more to living than just what early experience conditions into us all. Our contemporary psychologists have described its more extreme forms, like neuroticism and excessive narcissism (both infantile forms adopted in adult lives). In this sense, the boy must look over his shoulder to identify the burden on him so that he might divest himself of it (or 'tame' the ox). Finally, the boy and the ox represent the two possibly balancing minds, the animal which can be tamed and provides physical power and survival value in the world, and the spiritual, which provides other sources of reality experience and happiness. Here, the boy observes and takes reponsibility for the search, the subject of which we already know in his rope.

Classical Greek called this contest the *agōn*. Hence the ox-tamer is the agonist, and agony is our term for the process, though we understand the term in a much narrower sense today, isolating perhaps too much of the roughness of the struggle ahead, or the suffering it inflicts. The boy, or agonist, can be likened to the hero who ventures into the unknown (Gilgamesh, Buddha, Confucius), knowing that success requires coming to terms with the ox nature. *Karma* never relaxes, but fights by every devious means to survive, which conversely dooms spiritual consciousness against which *karma* works. Like the natural ecstatic, our own Socrates, the boy seeks to hear his inner voice, the *daimōn*, or spirit, within. To realize this spirituality, he must first find the ox to tame it. In the next picture, at least he sees it, albeit indirectly. It is not as easy as one might expect.

2

Who Invented Meditation?

Can we even meaningfully ask the question 'who invented meditation?' Surely the answer must be highly speculative, that is, not subject to falsification, since no hard physical evidence remains to use as evidence to describe the mental states or transformations of our earliest ancestors. Unlike bones, which do not decay, their ecstasies leave not a trace. Evolution shows us that the brain has gone through a massive and complex development accumulating mental possibilities gradually by the addition of successively more complex brain functions on to the primal reptilian brain of our most distant forerunners. But the physiological mechanisms necessary for meditative ecstasies to occur have been part of pre-hominid brains for millennia. Sometime while human consciousness evolved as allowed by these successively developed brain structures, ecstasy – the primary state to result from meditative discipline – must have been 'invented' or 'discovered' or 'evolved'; only then did it become part and parcel of our humanness, a portion of the human heritage. Can we speculatively determine when this happened, and how?

Far from being impossible to answer, this question at least makes sense. First, we can still speculate about matters which we cannot observe because they have left no physical remains. But secondly, we can observe primal human communities, peoples who still live in archaic human times – Stone Age peoples, such as the inhabitants of the Kalahari desert or New Guinea highlanders, hunting and gathering peoples whose cultures remain shamanistic. These people show us how things were in the distant past, since they are like living fossils. We have learned to observe such human communities and extrapolate from them clues to our own hidden, mysterious past. Using both these sources, we can attempt to answer the question concerning the human origins of meditation.

In this sense I do not believe that meditation and the ecstasy it produces came from some extra-terrestrial source, neither from God nor from flying saucer peoples (even though it may resemble forms of consciouness developed on planets other than our own), nor is meditative ecstasy somehow built into every human consciousness, as some essential feature of it. Rather, at some point in time man must have learned to become ecstatic, and persons must learn it, adding it as any skill to their mental experience.

How then, taking the speculative question first, did human beings learn to be meditative? Probably many opportunities or situations led to the discovery that doing certain things result in altered states of consciousness, including ecstasies. Even though archaeologists claim that human beings have had the same brain capacity for only the last fifty thousand years or so of their evolution, I think that at least the possibility of ecstasy has existed for a considerably longer time. One datable event in this speculative pre-history must be the domestication of fire, thought to have occurred around eight hundred thousand years ago. When proto-human groups had fires around which to huddle during long, cold, threatening nights in caves or other sheltered areas, they may have experienced the first ecstasies. Surely, we have all felt drawn into the dancing flames of campfires and fireplaces. For such primal peoples, fires meant security, protection from roaming wild beasts and warmth against the cold. The psychological effects of sitting for long hours before such fires must have been pronounced. The fire could become a mysterious presence, as comforter and protector, even a 'divine' being. Focusing for long hours on its dancing flames to the exclusion of all other sensory stimuli could well have produced ecstatic states, the flames drawing consciousness away from its fight-or-flight set into a calmed, altered state, not of anxiety but of repose.

Meditative states exhibit just such a calmness, and can be induced by long concentration on a single object of attention, the 'meditative object'. I imagine these long-distant proto-human ancestors of ours being drawn into the dancing flames of their fires, being entranced by their protector and falling into the first ecstatic states, the first 'meditatively' altered states of consciousness. That so many early religions used fire in ritual and symbolism confirms the powerful sway this element holds over human consciousness, a remnant of those first confrontations with this mystery revealing 'substance'. In fact, the French phenomenologist philosopher Gaston Bachelard devoted an entire book to the analysis of the psychological impact of fire (*The Psychoanalysis of Fire*, Boston: Beacon Press, 1964), during the course of which he concluded:

We are almost certain that fire is precisely the first object, the *first phenomenon*, on which the human mind *reflected*; among all phenomena, fire alone is sufficiently prized by prehistoric man to wake in him the desire for knowledge, and this mainly because it accompanies in him the desire for love. No doubt it has often been stated that the conquest of fire definitely separated man from the animal, but perhaps it has not been noticed that the mind in its primitive state, together with its poetry and its knowledge, had been developed in meditation before a fire.

(Bachelard, p. 55)

Perhaps the word 'invented' in my question conveys the wrong impression, since surely meditative states must have developed over long periods of time rather than having been invented at one specific, fateful juncture in prehistory. But the role of sitting before fires seems, as Bachelard agrees, somehow crucial to such a development. Other primal human experiences contributed too. The poet Gary Snyder started me on this line of questioning when he remarked once that he thought meditation's birth came in the archaic hunter's experience. He went on to explain that these early hunters had no powerful bows with which to fell game, so they had to approach their quarry very closely. Anyone who has ever hunted or stalked game knows that to approach wild animals is difficult. Snyder perceptively understood that to do this one needs to quiet the mind of all 'human' thoughts, in effect, entering into an ecstasy in which one 'stands outside' one's ordinary humanness. Consider the Eskimo hunter, who sits motionless for long hours at a seal hole in the ice, unmoving but ever ready to thrust his harpoon deep into the animal in that crucial moment it surfaces to breathe! Granted, archaic hunters did other things to aid their goal of close approach; evidence from Lamb's *Wizard of the Upper Amazon* indicates that jungle hunters also undertook body purges, rubbed herbs on themselves to lessen human scents, and so forth, but also prepared psychically for the hunt. This included identifying with the animals to be hunted so as to become inconspicuous in the environment, and thus to succeed as skilled hunters. Such processes resemble meditative self-discipline so strongly that they too must have contributed to the 'invention' of meditation.

Other experiences of primal human beings, too, may have contributed to the discovery of ecstasy itself, as an altered state of consciousness, as well as of the disciplines which would induce it with control. Just as the hunter approaching game must rid his mind of anxious thoughts, becoming as if 'not there' in the environment, so the primal warrior also had to practise the same skills when stalking the enemy. The contemporary descendants of these tactics include the 'martial arts' of Far Eastern extraction, all of which eventually depend on achieving a meditative ecstasy, the emptying of the mind of its self-conscious, action-crippling anxieties. On the other side of the coin, the physical act of making love could well have contributed, since in the abandon of orgasm, human beings become ecstatic, temporarily standing outside themselves in the bliss of sexual consummation. Trauma provided another common source of ecstatic states. Apparently, the most common response to traumatic physical accident and disease comes when individuals, unable any longer to bear their pain or perceived danger, lapse into ecstasy or an 'out of the body' experience. In contemporary times, Moody (in *Life After Life*) reports many cases of 'clinical death' after which patients report having experienced ecstatic states in response to the trauma of impending death. Surely, our ancestors experienced such reactions to severe health challenges as well, thus providing another access to the reality of ecstasy; for those who survived, the possibility of returning to such states, even the desirability of doing so must have been attractive, leading to the development of meditative means for doing so.

From this kind of soft, speculative evidence, we now turn to more concrete observations of contemporary peoples who still live at the level of primal, arachaic peoples. The !Kung San of the Kalahari desert in Africa exist today as men of the Stone Age. Researchers have studied them extensively (see *Kalahari Hunter-Gatherers*, a collection of articles edited by Richard B. Lee and Irven De Vore, Cambridge, Mass.: Harvard University Press, 1976), noting that once or twice each week members of this group deliberately enter into states of ecstasy as a means of maintaining the health and well-being of its members (see in Lee and De Vore the article by Richard Katz, 'Education for Transcendence: !Kia-Healing with the Kalahari !Kung', pp. 282–301). Not only do they use deliberately induced ecstasies for healing, but they understand how to educate younger members of the group to achieve such transcendent ecstatic states of consciousness. Clearly, this Stone Age practice of ecstasy indicates that human groups understood and controlled ecstasy far back in time, and confirms that proto-meditative practices existed long before we have the first evidence for such in written, historical records. In fact, Katz's evidence shows that about half the older adult males and one-third of the females learn to achieve *!kia* (ecstasy) – percentage-wise, this is considerably more than in any civilized community, past or present! This alone should cause us to become more thoughtful about meditation.

Who Invented Meditation?

Participants induce the *!kia* ecstasy for healing others during dances which last from dusk to dawn. Everyone attends the dance, wherein women sit round a fire, singing songs and rhythmically clapping their hands while men dance round them, gradually entering into ecstasy. What they describe resembles closely the *kuṇdalini* experience of Indian yoga, as well as the experiences of mystics, both Western and Eastern. Describing the power or energy which is activated by the dancing as *n/um*, they describe the onset of ecstasy as being produced when this power, which ordinarily resides in the pit of the stomach, rises up the spine to the base of the skull. One participant recalled:

You dance, dance, dance, dance. The n/um lifts you in your belly and lifts you in your back, and then you start to shiver. N/um makes you tremble: it's hot. Your eyes are open but you don't look around; you hold your eyes still and look straight ahead. But when you get into !kia, you're looking around because you see everything because you see what's troubling everybody ... Rapid shallow breathing, that's what draws n/um up ... then n/um enters every part of your body, right to the tip of your feet and even your hair.

(Lee and De Vore, p. 286)

This ecstatic state, as one !Kung reported, 'makes your thoughts nothing in your head', indicating transcendence of ordinary modes of consciousness. Katz describes it as a state of transcendence, when the 'individual experiences himself as existing beyond his ordinary level of existence'. He continues:

... a !Kung practices extraordinary activities during !Kia. He performs cures, handles and walks on fire, claims x-ray vision, and at times says he sees over great distances. He does not even attempt such activities in his ordinary state.

(Lee and De Vore, p. 287)

From this example, we can see that primal peoples used various means to induce ecstatic states, including sensory deprivation (the session occurs at night), repetitive sound and

29

movement, and deep breathing. All of these have similarly been used in meditative traditions to induce ecstatic states. For example, Sufis have danced, twirling in circles, or used deep breathing and head-jerking.

Most interestingly, the !Kung use their meditative ecstasy to heal, while many later meditation systems drop the healing possibilities to focus more on the ecstasy's quality of transcendence. At this primal level of human development, then, meditation's ecstasy aided the enhancement of human well-being in a very specific psychosomatic way. Furthermore, the !Kung sufficiently understand it to be able to re-enter the ecstasy deliberately and repeatedly, and they instruct the young in attaining the transcendence, thus passing it on to following generations. This is not an isolated example, but rather the general rule in developed primal hunting and gathering cultures. Anthropologists call such cultures 'shamanistic', after their term for the culture's principal ecstatic healer, the shaman. Among the Kalahari, though all males attempt to become *n/um* masters, or shamans, not all succeed, but some excel, becoming highly respected as healers and as teachers of ecstasy. All individuals who reach ecstatic states go through what anthropologists call an initiatory experience in which they 'die' to a former self-understanding, which does not include ecstatic consciousness, to be 'reborn' into another identity, which does include ecstasy, assuming a new '!*kia*-identity'. In one account of such a transformation, an old *n/um* master told Katz:

In !kia your heart stops, you're dead, your thoughts are nothing, you breathe with difficulty. You see things, n/um things: you see ghosts killing people, you smell burning, rotten flesh; then you heal, you pull sickness out. You heal, heal, heal, heal ... then you live. Then your eyeballs clear and then you see people clearly.

(Lee and De Vore, p. 291)

Such initiatory experiences so strikingly resemble later meditative experiences that they too must be considered a primary source of meditative disciplines. They deliberately led to powerful experiences of self-transformation which individuals sought to achieve the general goal of 'power' – power to be more skilled hunters, power to know through psychic avenues, power to heal and respond to the challenges which beset our primal ancestors in the struggles to survive in hostile and mysterious environments. Such initiatory experiences often came as a result of trauma – severe illnesses, traumatic injuries or poisonings – but also could come in dreams, or unbidden, the result of unknown causes. Persons who experienced these catapultings of consciousness into ecstasy become different, possessing transformed psyches and powers, often adopting the specialized roles of leaders and healers in their groups. Black Elk, the Oglala Sioux shaman, gave an excellent account of his initiatory transformation to Neihardt (see *Black Elk Speaks*, Chapter 3). At the age of nine, he heard voices calling him, and was suddenly struck by a severe illness, during which he experienced ecstatic visions wherein he made contact with the spiritual forces which taught him and gave him his holy power. After his experience other shamans could see 'a power like a light all through his body', and he began to learn to use his new powers, as when he was hunting with his injured father (Chapter 5).

Though Black Elk's initiatory ecstasy came unbidden, it was exceptional. In many more cases, young persons in shamanistic cultures were directed to induce them deliberately, to make contact with the transcendent and to gain the power they would need as adults. The techniques which primal peoples elaborated to induce such experiences later came to be adopted by meditation traditions, which sought to achieve the same goal, the experience of transcendence through ecstasy. Lame Deer, who died only a few years ago in the US state of South Dakota, provides an excellent, more contemporary example of such techniques which induced ecstasy, again from our own indigenous American shamanistic culture. At the age of sixteen, he went on his first vision quest (*hanblechia*, 'vision-seeking'), which involved, apart from his cultural programming, going into his first sweat bath, after which he felt purified and that his brain had become 'empty'. Then he climbed with the old man Chest, his shaman-advisor, to the top of his family's vision quest hill, where he went down into his vision pit, a hole dug in the earth just large enough for him to crawl into. There he meditated for four days and four nights, without food or water, eventually experiencing a powerful ecstasy. In the pit, he felt cut off from everything of the outside world, even his own body. 'It made me listen to the voices within me,' he remembered (John Fire Lame Deer and Richard Erdoes, *Lame Deer Seeker of Visions*, New York: Simon and Schuster, 1972, p. 14). Eventually, he experienced the sought-for transformation, going through fear and dying to his infantile identity, to be reborn into adulthood's ecstatic standpoint. He experienced ecstatic flight into the sky, seeing from high above the earth, and was instructed by the bird spirits, who told him he was 'sacrificing' himself to become a shaman (p. 15).

Lame Deer experienced what hundreds of shamans and later mystics similarly report from such experiences of meditative ecstasy induced through such disciplines of sensory deprivation, fasting, and seeking for a vision-through-prayer and culturally founded expectation. He felt asleep but was wide awake (that is, was visionary); he lost his sense of time and his old self; he experienced visions, from which he learned (as in the vision of his great-grandfather, who gave him his new, initiatory name Lame Deer), and he experienced his transcendent identity, what others call the self or soul; and he achieved his initiatory contact with the source of divine power, as he recounted to Erdoes:

We Sioux believe that there is something within us that controls us, something like a second person almost. We call it *nagi*, what other people might call soul, spirit or essence. One can't see it, feel it or taste it, but that time on the hill – and only that once – I knew it was there inside of me. Then I felt the power surge through me like a flood. I cannot describe it, but it filled all of me. Now I knew for sure that I would become a *wicasa wakan*, a medicine man. Again I wept, this time with happiness.

(Lame Deer, p. 16)

Who Invented Meditation?

Shamanistic cultures place the highest value on such experiences of ecstatic self-transformation. Even though they may occur at very early ages (Black Elk at nine, Lame Deer at sixteen), they provide the individual with an unforgettable contact with the 'divine' and its 'power', thus initiating them into adulthood. Without such contact, the person is considered incomplete, being unable to draw from the ultimate sources of power for well-being.

We no longer 'initiate' young people in this manner, substituting instead innocuous rites of passage (such as first communion, bar and bat mitzvahs, etc.) or relying on the family, the schools, the churches and the temples to mature our children. But something lacks in what these institutions teach – an unforgettable experience of ecstasy – a lack which has existed for millennia. Somewhere between the time of shamanistic hunter-gatherer cultures and the great world civilizations based on agrarian surpluses which allowed cities and individuals to specialize their societal roles, the institution of initiation became so watered down that we no longer systematically attempt to bring everyone into ecstatic modes of experience. The unusual individuals who did become ecstatic, like the Buddha or St Teresa of Avila, did so fairly late in life, as a result of considerable withdrawal from society and lengthy mental cultivation and meditation. One remnant of the archaic past survived in our own civilization until Christianity put an end to it at the Greek initiation centre of Eleusis, where pilgrims went, once in a lifetime, to have their eyes opened to the ecstatic reality of the mysteries of life and death. Without such an initiatory glimpse into the other (ecstatic) side of reality, the Greeks considered that a person remained a living corpse, alive physically, but still unborn, hence dead, to ecstatically experienced reality. In one transforming night, and probably due to the effect of an LSD-like substance (see Wasson *et al.*, *The Road to Eleusis*, New York: Harcourt Brace Jovanovich, 1978), initiates went through the ecstasy which awakened them permanently to the transcendent. Such initiations conferred the rebirth Jesus Christ spoke of in talking with Nicodemus (John 3) when he said that a person had to be born both from the womb ('of water') and of the spirit before seeing the kingdom of God.

Unfortunately, though, we do not bring people to these experiences, either through the compelling, inescapable form of initiation as practised at Eleusis, or through one required of all youth, as in the shamanic vision quest, where to fail to become ecstatic meant social ridicule. As a result, our psyches remain unbalanced, able to experience only through rational or quasi-rational aesthetic and religious modes. Archaic peoples considered such individuals to be incomplete, power-less, since they lacked ecstatic participation in the underlying sources of our very life, what they called the 'divine' or the 'realm of spirit power'. They made young people, while their psyche remained fluid, go through trying initiations because the young had not yet developed the rigid psychological organization imposed upon young adults who increasingly have to adapt to what Freud called the 'reality principle'. As Lame Deer's experience clearly demonstrates, shaman-istic peoples understood very well the mechanisms which could bring on such radically transforming expansions of consciousness.

This desire to initiate the young into ecstatic states, under-stood as being absolutely essential for the well-being of both the person and the human group, must have been one of the major fountainheads of meditation. Over and over again, as I study the earliest records of meditation in historical records, I find how our early civilizations adopted shamanic tech-niques of inducing ecstasy. Since ecstatic experience was so highly valued, it naturally was adaptive, in an evolutionary sense, to elaborate means for inducing it, as we saw in the example of the Kalahari healing dance. This process con-tinued, eventually resulting in the much more sophisticated techniques exemplified in Lame Deer's initiation. All this led to meditation as we have it in the classical civilizations, and what we could have again today.

Finally, the recent work of ethnobotanists, such as Richard

Evans Schultes of the Harvard Botanical Museum, shows us that psychoactive plants must have been another pathway of access to the discovery and inducing of ecstatic states by our primal ancestors. Archaic peoples possessed incredibly sophisticated knowledge of the flora and fauna of their environment, discovering edible, medicinal and psychoactive plants to use as specifics for their goal of survival. Interestingly, when they discovered psychoactives they did not discard them as useless but carefully gathered them, treating them as sacred powers which gave access to the ecstatic realms of spirit and power, using them as ritual sacraments conducive to well-being. Ethnobotanists have discovered the use of such plants among almost all primal peoples. So widespread is their presence in human cultures that they must be considered as one of the sources of meditation. Again, evidence from the earliest historical records shows that the use of such plants was borrowed from prior shamanistic cultures by early developing civilizations, as seen in the *soma/haoma* complex among Indo-Aryan and Indo-Iranian peoples, and in the great interest early Taoists in China had in certain plants supposed to have psychoactive properties, to say nothing of the mysteries at Eleusis in Greek times.

Some indication of how these plants may have been used in shamanistic cultures which left no record comes from the remarkable memoir of Manuel Cordova-Rios in F. Bruce Lamb's book *Wizard of the Upper Amazon* (Boston: Houghton Mifflin Company, 1971). The value of this memoir derives from its account of native Amazonian peoples who essentially existed in pre-Columbian culture, uninfluenced by any contact with the outside world, when the Peruvian Manuel Cordova-Rios spent seven years as a prisoner of the Huni Kui tribe. He had been working in the Upper Amazon as a young rubber-gatherer around the turn of the century when his camp was raided by hostile native peoples; all but he were killed. The boy was captured and brought to a village deep in the jungle, to be put through a remarkable set of transformations at the direction of the old chief, who knew he was soon to die and needed the young captive to replace him. From the point at the beginning when the boy was an unsophisticated alien in the jungle, the chief, in specifically conceived and carefully executed night-time meditative vision sessions, initiated the boy into the vast tribal lore and knowledge he would need to direct the tribe, developing especially his meditative psychic powers which he could use for the tribe's survival. These vision sessions were aided by the use of a *'nixi honi xuma'*, or vision-producing extract of two psychoactive plants, *Banisteriopsis caapi*, containing the alkaloids harmine and harmaline, and *Psychotria viridis*, containing N, N-dimethyltryptamine. By the time of the chief's death, the boy had become a man, fully equipped with exquisite knowledge of the jungle and psychic powers which allowed him easily to take over the potentially hostile tribespeople as their new leader.

This amazing story shows that so-called primitive people knew how to use psychoactives for specific meditative goals, as initiators into psychic reality and control, and how the old chief prepared his young initiate with intestinal purges, herbal baths and special diets, and then in psychoactive-aided vision sessions taught him to deepen his awareness of the environment and other people. Clearly, the old chief knew how to bring a young adult through a series of astonishingly sophisticated transformations, leading him to achieving a highly developed maturity of mind and knowledge, including the psychic powers which the chief used to aid his people. In the first teaching session, the boy experienced nervous system changes, confusion of sense perception and chaotic visions, along with a loss of sense of time and a growing fluidity of his mental awareness (after the session he could understand his captors' language to a much greater extent; see Lamb pp. 23–8). Subsequent vision sessions led to the creation of a new being, reborn out of the destruction of the old immature personality of the boy. In the second session (pp. 33ff.), he experienced 'knowledge completely divorced from my physical being', that is, ecstatic knowledge, and again, a sense of timelessness. In following sessions the chief led the boy through a series of 'incredible sessions' in which he transmitted, telepathically, 'the accumulated tribal knowledge' of plants and animals and principles of jungle survival, this being the boy's 'apprenticeship' (pp. 86ff.).

Lamb's book shows that primal peoples used psychoactives to gain access to ecstatic states during which was made possible significant learning as well as knowledge transfer. The meditative features of the vision sessions strongly resemble later meditation practice. First, their underlying structure of initiatory self-transformation also characterizes later meditation traditions. Secondly, the reduction of sensory domination of mind in favour of other mental developments is meditative; the sessions were held at night, and accompanied by ritualized purifications with smoke (like incense in later contexts), powerful, mind-altering chants, even quiet sitting in protected jungle clearings away from the village. Thirdly, the psychoactives produced ecstatic states, which later meditative traditions sought similarly to induce through non-psychoactively aided means. So psychoactives also figure prominently in the development of meditation and human access to meditative states.

Shamans are the immediate ancestors of the meditation and spiritual masters we hear of in early literature. Moses demonstrated shamanic powers repeatedly, including going up to the mountain for knowledge, seeing visions (e.g. the burning bush) and apparently transforming inanimate objects into animate ones. In ancient India, the sages of the Upaniṣads and early Buddhism took the soma ecstasy of the prior Vedic age (see Chapter 3) as their goal, attaining it not through soma, but through meditative yoga practice. Ancient Taoist contemplatives, such as Lao Tzu and Chuang Tzu, as well as diviners and alchemists, all borrowed heavily from earlier shamans adopting their archaic ways by transforming their somewhat distrusted but obviously useful skills, lore and techniques.

The figure of the shaman thus looms large on the prehistory of meditation. Note what shamans and shamanesses used their induced ecstatic states for: first, to further the physical well-being of the group, to detect game distant from their camp, to predict weather changes, and psychically to monitor the psychological tensions and conflicts of the group's individual members; secondly, to heal physical injuries and ailments, diseases and psychosomatic disturbances, as well as to divine the sources of misfortunes afflicting the group's survival in the physical environment; and thirdly, to act as psychopomp, guiding the souls of diseased individuals to their proper place in the other world. This last function spills over into the mysterious realm of the shaman's perception of the 'invisible' world of the 'other side', since it affects nothing present in the sensory experience of others. All of these goals have been served by meditation, in more recent times, still surviving today in the activities of psychic healers and 'trance mediums' who bring us psychic information and power from the invisible spirit realms.

So, to the question 'who invented meditation?', we must answer 'our human ancestors'. Like all other human abilities and knowledge acquired through evolutionary development, meditation developed gradually, as the mental equipment which evolved very early in hominids began to experience situations which vastly increased the mental horizons. Then, as these groups became more and more like ourselves today, specialists, called shamans, arose, who increasingly gained the ability to induce controlled ecstatic mental states, discovering and mapping the diverse powers of the mind itself. By the time of the gradual replacement of hunter-gatherer cultures by early agrarian-based civilizations, a process which began about ten thousand years ago, shamans had all the techniques of meditative induction of ecstasy and self-transformation fully elaborated, whence they were adopted by the new leaders of humankind's fates in the increasingly complex civilizations that developed in the Nile, in the Tigris and Euphrates, in the Indus and the great Chinese river valleys, and later in the region around the Mediterranean sea, in South-east Asia, and in the Americas. We pick up the story in the next chapter, using evidence available to us only after the development of recorded literature from the early civil-izations, especially of India and China, when meditative disciplines and techniques came more and more to the fore as the principal techniques for the initiation into and repeated induction of ecstasy by priests, prophets, sages, and holy individuals who sought to alter the sensory domination of consciousness.

Ox-Taming 2   *Sighting the Tracks, Finding the Ox's Traces*

In this second picture, the boy finds the first traces of the vanished ox, and begins his journey homeward. He sees them on down the road; they draw him onward, full of resolve. He no longer looks backward, but he shades his eyes, for seeing is difficult. A new direction guides his striving, leading him on to a distant yet all-important goal. There is still far to go, but the journey has begun which will change the boy.

What, in this picture, do the faint tracks on the dusty trail represent? If the ox is *karma*, the bundle of consequences of one's past actions, all that lies submerged, iceberg-like, in the psyche, the traces must somehow betray that *karma* and its nature. The ox may have vanished, and temporarily be out of control, but it still, to the observant, leaves tracks, the very means to apprehend it. Left in this state, we have little hold on the ox which in truth controls those who do not tame it, however much they might imagine themselves in charge.

Experimental psychologists show how this mechanism of *karma*, or consequentiality, works. Rats, when deprived of food in their early development, become hoarders in later life, even when they have abundant food. That is their ox-nature. Being only animal, they do not possess conscious mechanisms of will and intention, so they can never change. What drives them is a complex of deeply set past inappropriate motivations which leads them, later in time, to act in unrealistic or unadapted ways. So in this series, the ox symbolizes that part of us which causes us to act inappropriately or 'immaturely' in a situation.

This ox-nature forms very early in our lives. Freud thought that the source or experience prototype of all our anxieties and mental conflicts came from the primal separation situation, when we began to experience our mother as being separate from ourselves. Born in a bliss-filled unity of mother and child which did not distinguish the two, soon we begin to recognize an other, then others, and with a sense of separation frustration arises, as when the other throws one into the insecurity of unsatisfied need. For the first years of life, we are unable to direct our own lives, so things happen to us in the process of growing that imprint adaptive patterns indelibly on our developing psyche. We adapt to situations in

40

ways which seem appropriate and 'right' to our infantile perceptions. Crying obtains us certain of our desires, so we learn to cry, or pout. Fighting and yelling gain others, so we settle on these means as ways to our ends. Things happen to us – we are hurt, unloved, become frustrated or angry – experiences that we do not like, or want, which cause us, in the innocence of childhood, to encode the injury (as *karma*) in the form of blocks in our psyche's functioning. These unresolved blocks and immature ways of adaptation, which are inappropriate to our adult responsibilities, remain influencing us, though submerged below the threshold of our adult consciousness, like the masses of ice below the tip (the conscious part) of our iceberg-like awareness. These are all the ox.

The ox and the boy are apt images for the process of meditative self-transformation. The ox is our animal-like, out-of-control selves, which act not like mature humans but like animals. Animals without thinking seek their ends; in particular, large, powerful animals are useless to their owners unless they are trained or subjected to discipline to harness their power. In a way, our instinctual or primitive infantile fantasies are animal-like, and to 'correct' this nature we need to go through a process, sometime in life, of maturing into our potential, fully conscious humanity.

The problem, psychologists and therapists know, comes when we try to come into touch with these primal complexes to clear them out, submerged deep in the psyche as they are. We 'forget' or repress what is painful, and would be too embarrassed to realize, at every point, that the reasons for our actions do not stem from the conscious motivations we attribute to them but from these deep infantile fantasies and unresolved conflicts and anxieties. Until these are resolved everyone, in this sense, is neurotic, though some are more obviously so. We can identify the extreme cases because of their grossly inappropriate forms of behaviour but not realize that, in the same way, much of our behaviour is similarly based in outmoded infantile adaptive patterns. They worked once, but in the context of adult action and motivation they are, like the ox, inappropriate or uncontrolled from a mature, adult perspective.

This picture shows the boy making the first step to identifying these submerged contents of the psyche. How does one do it? Not by approaching them head-on, directly, because the psyche has built elaborate defences (such as self-deception) to conceal them. The best way is to identify them by their 'traces'. Just as one follows a runaway ox by its footprints, so too we can identify these submerged complexes and anxieties by understanding their effects in our conscious behaviour. I try to observe myself being 'animal-like'; this often comes out when I am in a situation of stress or pressure, or when I am angry, anxious, fearful or apathetic, or somehow unhappy or disturbed. Then I begin to see the traces of ox I have to tame within me. Other avenues may also lead to this animal within. Our dreams show it to us, repeatedly, if we would but remember them. Other people, especially those close to us, if only they would be courageous and perceptive, can show us our inner animal, reflecting it in their comments and actions towards us, mirroring to us our unrealized selves. The people I have loved, and spent much time with, seeing how I behave, have helped me to discover my ox over and over again. Their help promoted my growth, along with experiences, just growing older, and other experiences in which I saw myself, as the world, mirror-like, showed me to myself. Those bent on discovering the traces observe themselves, especially in stereotyped and anxious behaviour patterns, because these indicate deeply instilled, 'archaic' sources of motivation and action choices which need dissolving. In dreams we see the ox in a thousand transformations, past, present and possible futures. The boy does not want to remain at the mercy of these inappropriate, prototypal archaic sources, for, like the rats' need for hoarding, these derive from infant, not mature, consciousness.

Albert Camus recognized his ox and said, 'I make rules to correct my behaviour'. He was speaking of writing, but his observation applies to acquiring any skill or making any creation, even that of a mature mind. At this point, the only way for the boy to change is to live for the time with a set of guiding rules, the primary of which says: 'Observe thyself'. This cannot leave him open to the charge of narcissism, for, as Confucius observed, it means relentless self-examination, day after day. One observes behaviour to be able to evaluate it and try to eliminate its inadequacies. The boy traces the prints, for clues to the unruly ox hidden within.

3

The First Records of Meditation in World Civilizations

The invention of settled agriculture, which began in western Asia around ten thousand years ago, eventually put an end to most hunting and gathering cultures, terminating a vast epoch of human history. Few people realize that of the estimated eighty billion people who have lived on the earth, only four per cent have lived in industrial societies like our own, and a mere six per cent have lived in agrarian civilizations. The rest, a full ninety per cent, lived as hunters and gatherers in primal horticultural or shamanistic cultures! Or, put another way, for the two million years that men have lived on earth, ninety-nine per cent of the time was spent as hunters and gatherers. With the domestication of plants and animals, a revolution transformed our life as far-reaching in its effects as the much later Industrial Revolution. Gradually people learned how to produce and accumulate agricultural surpluses, freeing more and more individuals from the daily necessity of putting time and effort into mere physical survival. Villages, towns and eventually cities arose; specialized functions arose too, as different persons became traders, artisans, scribes, politicians, tax collectors, soldiers, poets, priests, princes, and policemen.

One of the earliest developments, the need to record information, that came as a result of these changes brought the gradual evolution of systems of writing. Eventually, this led to the preservation of the first records of meditation. Shamans left no records of their meditation, since their culture depended entirely on oral communication, but their direct descendants, as soon as writing came to be used for such purposes, left some remarkable early records of their meditation practice.

Take ancient China as an example. Of the earliest literatures we have from China, one, the first, recorded archaic divinatory practices. Then, at a somewhat later time, the Emperor supposedly collected the lyrics of popular songs from around his domain so as to be aware of the thoughts and feelings of his subjects (see Arthur Waley, *The Book of Songs*), and later another literature sought to record the impressive sayings of the sage Confucius and his group of followers (again, see another Waley translation, *The Analects of Confucius*). Nothing in any of these extensive though specialized literatures says anything about meditation. Probably, their authors had little or nothing to do with it. On the other hand, the Taoist literature attributed first to Lao Tzu (Master Lao) and Chuang Tzu (Master Chuang) explicitly describes meditation practices. From this literature, we can be sure that meditation existed in ancient China in a systematized, conscious form at least as early as 300 BC, and by implication for some time, even centuries before these first records.

A passage collected in the aphorisms attributed to Chuang Tzu is to my mind the most beautiful and revealing description of this basic form of this early Chinese meditation. It describes how Tzu-ch'i of South Wall entered into an ecstatic state of mind through clearly meditative techniques so as to speculate about the mysteries of life itself with his companion Yen Ch'eng Tzu-yu:

Tzu-ch'i of South Wall sat leaning on his armrest, staring up at the sky and breathing – vacant and far away, as though he'd lost his companion. Yen Ch'eng Tzu-yu, who was standing by his side in attendance, said, 'What is this: Can you really make the body like a withered tree and the mind like dead ashes? The man leaning on the armrest now is not the one who leaned on it before!'

Tzu-ch'i said, 'You do well to ask the question, Yen. Now I have lost myself.'

(Watson, p. 31)

This passage shows Tzu-ch'i achieving through meditative means an ecstatic state in which he can still converse with his attendant. It contains many indications of the achieved ecstasy: he is 'vacant and far away, as though he'd lost his companion', showing that he 'stands outside or beside himself or his ordinary awareness'. In the last line of the first paragraph Yen says that even he is aware that Tzu-ch'i is different, indicating that the ecstatic transformation is apparent, and Tzu-ch'i confirms this by saying, 'Now I have lost myself'. This does not mean he is confused, but rather that he has transcended his normal worldly personality to be conscious through another level of his psyche. Yen also describes this in symbolic terms as making 'the body like a withered tree', which indicates the common feature of ecstasy that it makes the body immobile and as if lifeless, and as making 'the mind like dead ashes', pointing to its ecstatic transcendence of its ordinary functioning.

How does Tzu-ch'i induce the ecstasy? By the meditative discipline of body, mind and breath, as the first sentence indicates. First, he calms the body by taking a comfortable position to relax it completely; in China, this meant 'leaning on his armrest'. Then, rather than allowing his senses and their objects or his usual inner thoughts to dominate his consciousness, he was 'staring up at the sky', intentionally emptying consciousness of its ordinary content. And thirdly, he was 'breathing'. Now we know already that he must be breathing, since he is alive, so this must mean that he is breathing in some extraordinary, specially meditative fashion. In fact, meditators know that deep breathing very efficiently causes alterations of consciousness to occur. Tzu-ch'i's practice shows a well-thought-out, systematic approach to deliberately inducing a state of enhanced, ecstatic consciousness, the goal of meditative activity. Surely, this passage deserves to be included in the hall of fame of meditative literature!

If you look at the subsequent paragraphs of Watson's translation of this passage, you will see that Tzu-ch'i uses his ecstasy to speculate about the nature of the life process, speaking of the forces which result in the creation of the phenomena of the natural world around us. Thus, he used meditative ecstasy to achieve philosophical insight! Interestingly, Chuang Tzu's direct counterpart in our own philosophical tradition, Socrates, was also an ecstatic, although apparently he did not deliberately induce his ecstasies through meditative means. In fact, from the scanty evidence available (see W. K. C. Guthrie, *Socrates*, Cambridge: Cambridge University Press, 1971, pp. 84–5) we must conclude that Socrates experienced ecstasies unbidden (that is, they occurred naturally or by what theistically inclined mystics call 'grace'). Plato's *Symposium* even noted one incident which happened as Socrates was going to a dinner party, when he stopped and asked his companion to go on ahead of him. When he did not arrive a servant was sent to find him. He was standing on a nearby porch completely wrapped in ecstatic withdrawal, only to arrive mid-way through dinner. Aristodemus commented that this was his usual way of 'going apart and standing still wherever he happens to be' (Guthrie, p. 85). On another occasion, while on the Potidaean campaign, Socrates stood still from early morning, for a full twenty-four hours, until the next sunrise. Other soldiers stayed near him, to see when he would arise from his ecstatic state, which he did, departing after offering a prayer to the sun.

What are we to make of these reports? From other materials in Socrates' biography, I think we can conclude that, from a very early time in his life, Socrates possessed the ability to enter into ecstasy. Perhaps all of us are born with this ability, but most soon lose it in the hodge-podge of confusing experiences which allow the sensory domination of consciousness to take over our acquaintance with or access to these inner states. Both of Socrates' earliest biographers, Xenophon and Plato, refer to a related feature of his extraordinary psyche, what he himself called his *daimonion* (Guthrie, pp. 82–4), his 'divine sign', or 'spiritual guide', or 'inner oracular sign'. In Plato's *Apology*, Socrates says:

> I experience a certain divine or daemonic something, which in fact Meletus has caricatured in the indictment. It began in childhood and has been with me ever since, a kind of voice, which whenever I hear it always turns me back from something I was going to do, but never urges me to act.

> *(Apology* 31c-d, Guthrie, p. 82)

Since Socrates says he experienced this in childhood, I think that somehow he had ecstatic access to his deeper psyche, which meditators also seek and which Lame Deer experienced in his initiatory ecstasy. This allowed Socrates to listen to his 'inner voice' or deeper self, which protected him from misfortune by advising him not to do things which the deeper psyche knew would bring ill consequences. The ordinary mind, caught as it is in desires and sensory input, usually does not possess such deep insight, and leads us into 'temptation'. Ecstasy gives 'power' in part by allowing access to this deeper, more all-knowing aspect of the psyche, which advises us in its own interest on how better to make our way through life's confusing challenges.

I imagine that Socrates' excellence as a philosopher and his profound impact upon our entire civilization derived from his natural ecstatic abilities. In much the same way, Gilgamesh, Moses, Plato, Christ and Muhammad used ecstasy to tap the deeper reaches of their psyches and to allow their profound insights to shape human destinies. What is interesting, when comparing ecstatics from the early civilizations of the West with those of the East, is that we see much less systematic cultivation of ecstasy, and very little teaching of the techniques of ecstasy to others in the West. Much of the later Western meditative cultivation of ecstasy may derive indirectly from influences coming from the East, originating probably in India, though these are extremely difficult to trace, given the paucity of historical evidence (see Jean W. Sedlar, *India and the Greek World*, Totowa: Rowman and Littlefield, 1980).

Turning, then, to the earliest recorded literature of ancient northern India, the *Ṛg Veda* (composed *c.* 1500–1000 BC), we find occasional mention, apart from the soma-ecstasy cult, of individuals who consciously practised techniques for achieving meditative ecstasy. Perhaps some members of the orthodox soma cult split away, founding unorthodox groups of renegade ecstatics, the distant ancestors of the Upaniṣadic sages and early Buddhist and Jaina sects. A most remarkable poem, datable back to at least 1000 BC, describes one such ecstatic, called the *keśin* ('long-hair'), or *muni* ('silent, inspired or ecstatic person, enthusiast'). Note especially that in the third verse the long-hair speaks autobiographically, reporting for himself and his fellow ecstatics that they have ascended, in ecstasy, to the skies:

> The long-hair carries fire, philter, heaven and earth,
> The long-hair has heavenly light to see all,
> The long-hair says, 'It's light!'

> The ecstatics dress in the wind, or clothe themselves
>   in soiled-yellow robe,
> They follow the course of the wind, when the gods
>   entered them.

> 'Ecstatic with the practice of our silence,
> We ascend to the winds –
> Our bodies alone, ye, O mortals, see!'

> He flies into the atmosphere, looking down on everything
>   below,
> The ecstatic is a friend to each god, prepared to do
>   pious service.

> A steed of the wind, friend of the wind-god, even is
>   the ecstatic impelled by the gods.
> He abides by both oceans, on the east and on the west.

> Wandering on the paths of the heavenly lads and lassies,
>   as well as those of wild beasts,
> The long-hair knows (others') desires, he is a friend
>   sweet and exhilarating.

The wind-god churned it, Kunaṃnamā crushed it,
When the long-hair drank from the philter cup,
  along with Rudra (the storm-god).

(*Ṛg Veda* 10.136)

Neither this poem nor any other evidence from the *Ṛg Veda* (about a thousand hymns in all) mentions the systematic use of formalized meditative disciplines to induce ecstasy, such as those later used by Tzu-ch'i. However, the long-haired ecstatic does induce the state by drinking a 'philter', or potion, presumably extracted from a plant source, as soma was. The word *soma* is not used in the poem; but another, *viṣam*, is, which later came to mean poison but here should not be understood in this sense, though some translators still make that mistake. Staal (in *Exploring Mysticism*) thinks that since this other word figures in the poem, the extract is other than soma (see pp. 197ff.). However, it could still be soma, called by another name, perhaps because these ecstatics were considered renegades by soma ritualists, who took soma only in the context of the orthodox ritual. Or, perhaps it was, as Staal suggests, another psychoactive known to the early Vedic peoples. Since Rudra is mentioned as drinking it too, and Rudra gave much form to the later Śiva conception, it could have been datura, as Śiva wears a flower of this highly deranging and toxic ecstaticant plant in his headdress during later classical times (*Datura alba*, white thornapple, akin to the jimson weed used in the Americas).

Whatever the identity of this *viṣam*, it clearly was used to induce ecstatic states, as shamans did in prior times. As in the case of soma, as I will argue shortly, such archaic experiences with psychoactive ecstaticants may have provided the impetus for the development of alternative means for inducing ecstasy, and thus a major push for systematizing meditatively induced ecstasies. Also, psychoactively induced ecstatic experience probably helped to develop a sense of the possible full range of ecstatic modes of consciousness, adding additional motivation for developing alternative means for inducing ecstasies not dependent on psychoactives. This poem alone mentions among these ecstatic powers ecstatic flight (not literal flight, but perception by psychic means from a distance, far beyond the capabilities of the senses), knowing what is in the minds of others, ecstatic knowing based on so-called 'out of body' experience, and ability to move among the forests frequented by dangerous wild beasts. Also, the poem mentions the experience of light, so commonly described by both shamans and mystics. All of these 'powers' figure prominently in later meditative yoga literatures of the Indian tradition.

We are hard put to interpret these passages describing experiences which we have been taught to attribute to the realms of pure fantasy. Since scientific rationalism denies reality to anything which is not physical, and thus in principle at least observable through the senses, we have been led to reduce such reports of ecstatics to mere imaginative fictions. Here, in a passage from the Chuang Tzu collection, we see another of these ancient ecstatic 'wonder-workers' described in terms equally suspicious, to our contemporary ways of understanding:

He said that there is a Holy Man living on faraway Ku-she Mountain, with skin like ice or snow, and gentle and shy like a young girl. He doesn't eat the five grains, but sucks the wind, drinks the dew, climbs up on the clouds and mist, rides a flying dragon, and wanders beyond the four seas. By concentrating his spirit, he can protect creatures from sickness and plague and make the harvest plentiful ... There is nothing that can harm this man. Though flood waters pile up to the sky, he will not drown. Though a great drought melts metal and stone and scorches the earth and hills, he will not be burned.

(Watson, pp. 27–8)

Indeed, such an account of an ancient ecstatic's experience tests to the limits our abilities to interpret the often symbolic, sometimes hyperbolic style in which these descriptions are couched. Many times I have delighted with students in trying to 'figure out' this passage. To start with, this Holy Man has

51

'skin like ice or snow', probably referring to his reduced levels of metabolism often recognized in bodies which have become ecstatic; being 'gentle and shy like a young girl' seems to be Taoist language for the receptivity or perceptiveness characteristic of meditatively sensitized persons. Not eating the five grains? – he fasts as part of his meditative discipline (or does this mean he turns the five senses inwards, in a sensory experience fast?); 'sucks the wind' probably indicates another meditative discipline, that of breath control. That he 'drinks the dew' may refer darkly to something concerning the physiology of ecstasy, as meditators and mystics often refer to extraordinary physiological experiences as the Kalahari *n/um* masters do. Such experiences usually immediately precede ecstatic breakthroughs: later Indian tradition considered these indications of the rising of the *kuṇḍalinī*. Surely, the next items refer to the onset of ecstatic flight – climbing on to the clouds and mist, riding the dragon and 'wandering' beyond the four seas (i.e. having no bodily limitation). To 'wander' is the Taoist code word for becoming ecstatic. The subsequent 'powers' list what the Holy Man can do with his ecstatic access to the deep psyche. Just as Socrates could be protected by his inner voice, and the long-hair could not be hurt among wild beasts, so too the Taoist sage could survive physical harm and help others, shaman-like, to combat sickness and plague and worldly misfortunes.

Perhaps some of these interpretations strain your ways of looking at the world and human abilities within it. But remember, we deal here with archaic materials and human potentialities which may have been thrown out, like the baby with the bathwater, when scientific rationalism discarded the whole mass of medieval superstition which had accrued to the occult and mystical traditions of the Western world since the time of Socrates and even before. Or do you agree with some who consider that as long as there are fools in the world there will be occult phenomena? As Staal argues in *Exploring Mysticism*, the only reasonable course, at this point, is to consider these questions still open and properly addressed by our own best investigative principles, using 'a combination of reason and an open mind' (p. 199); and this surely includes trying to meditate to the point where some of these psychic phenomena traditionally associated with meditation could come into play in our own experience.

Another early testimony concerning the archaic background of meditation in India comes from the soma hymns of the *Ṛg Veda*. Over 120 hymns, fully a tenth of the sacred *Veda*, describe its soma cult. Recently, several concerted efforts have brought us closer to knowing the identity of the original plant source of this substance considered divine by the Vedic priests. The word itself means 'extract', indicating that it came from some plant source through a process of extraction minutely described in the hymns of the *Ṛg Veda*. Unfortunately, its identity was kept secret by the priests and probably around 700 BC its use was discontinued, substitutes taking its place. R. Gordon Wasson published the first contemporary attempt to identify the plant in 1968 (in *Soma Divine Mushroom of Immortality*, Harcourt Brace Jovanovich), shocking Orientalists with the idea that soma extract came from the red-capped *Amanita muscaria* mushroom. The hypothesis elicited considerable praise and acceptance, and some strong criticism, until recently, when a scholar from Berkeley, Dr David Flattery, approached the problem again, this time from Indo-Iranian sources. The extract was also used by Indo-Iranians, who called it *haoma*. Flattery concluded, on extremely carefully gathered and considered evidence, that the plant source was a desert weed, *Peganum harmala*, still common in Iran; but the matter remains unsettled today, though I favour Flattery's hypothesis since his evidence is more convincing.

Despite these problems, we have no trouble, using the *Ṛg Veda* sources, in concluding that the psychoactive soma initiated early north Indian religious ritualists into the unforgettable experience of ecstasy. In a famous verse, the priests recorded this paean to their extract:

We have drunk soma, we have become immortal;
We have reached the light, we have found Gods.
What harm can now come to us,
What mortal malice, O Immortal Soma?

(*Ṛg Veda* 8.48.3)

Here again, as in the long-hair poem and countless accounts of shamanic and mystic ecstasy, the experiences of light and the interpretation of having transcended the ordinary mortal realm clearly characterize the soma experience. The importance of such experience I think came in that it showed Vedic Indo-Ayran spiritual leaders a realm of human experience distinct from the ordinary. In such ecstasy, they composed hymns of praise to their Gods and performed rituals designed to secure the protection and bounty of life's divine creative forces. Later seekers though they had no soma sought to achieve similar and additional goals through meditation, which replaced the psychoactive substance.

Since we are attempting to learn what possibilities lie in ecstatic experience, I will review the other verses in this one soma hymn (*Ṛg Veda* 8.48) to see what the Vedic priests thought of their ecstasy. In the first verse, the poet says that he has wisely partaken of the soma which stirs good thoughts and banishes cares, and in the second invokes soma to cause his people to thrive. The fourth asks soma to give long life (as does the seventh) and to be good to the heart (spiritual sense), as a father to his son, and in the fifth verse, he calls soma 'freedom-giving' and protector from accident and disease. Then, the poet sings:

As friction kindles fire, light me!
Illumine us, make us more prosperous!
Since then, in our ecstasy, O Soma,
I consider myself wealthy, enter us for well-being!

(verse 6)

Subsequent verses ask soma to further their well-being and to not abandon them to their foes (8), to be gracious to them when entering their 'every limb' (9). Several verses show a worshipful attitude towards soma, once it has been drunk (12, 13), while others (10, 11, 14) seem to address soma to ward off frightening experiences brought on by the psychoactive; in verse 10, the poet thinks of drinking it with good company, in verse 11 he says the powers of darkness have been dispelled, with verse 14 asking that neither sleep nor idle talk overpower the soma communicants. The final verse calls soma a universal giver of strength and one who finds the light for humankind.

As a part of my book, *Poetry and Speculation of the Ṛg Veda* (Los Angeles: University of California Press, 1980), I translated several hymns not about soma but about the comradehoods of priests who took it together to perform rituals and to debate over speculative issues in the Indo-Aryan equivalent of the Greek symposium. As in Plato's account of this descendant of shamanic contests of wit, participants drank and then speculated on spiritual matters of common interest. One poem (*Ṛg Veda* 10.71) reports that only some succeeded in achieving the level of visionary awareness but others became intoxicated into immobility and abandoned their comrades. This might give us some hint as to why this worshipped substance disappeared so completely from use in India (except in the form of non-psychoactive susbstitutes) right before the time of the great early flowering of meditation and the movements that meditation produced, seen in the Upaniṣads and early Buddhism which transformed the Indian spiritual scene. In effect, soma worked for a while, but had elements which impeded rather than furthered its goals. Eventually, the soma experience had revealed all it could to its devotees; they had received that plant's initiation into its special ecstatic state, so they no longer needed it. Here lies one of the major sources of the development of meditation. The whole context of the ritual use of soma itself was proto-meditative, involving chants, ritual actions, and other highly disciplined forms of action. Surely, it would have been easy to discover how these actions themselves, without the soma, could also induce the desired ecstasy. This accords with a more sophisticated view of the nature of psychoactives put forth by Dr Andrew Weil some time ago in his book *The Natural Mind* (Boston: Houghton Mifflin, 1972), in which he argues that the psychoactive is only an active placebo (p. 96). He explains this as:

a substance whose apparent effects on the mind are actually placebo effects in response to minimal physiological action ... all psychoactive drugs are really active placebos since the psychic effects arise from consciousness, elicited by set and setting, in response to physiological cues.

In short, the *Ṛg Veda* soma cult could well have matured its participants to the point where they realized the placebo effect of their sacred soma and dropped it, avoiding both dependence on it and its negative features. Soma may have been 'lost' intentionally, being replaced indeed by meditative means to induce the ecstasy. Surely, it was not the soma which was valued, but the ecstasy. Historically, we need no longer be puzzled by its loss, and the issue of its true plant identity remains but a tantalizing historical mystery. The ecstasy holds the real importance of soma, not the placebo. In considering this cult, we have come upon another source of meditation – the ritualized use of ecstasy. Vedic priests thought their ritual actually propelled the creative forces of the universe, so they operated it like a machine, with precision and discipline, in ecstatic states which allowed them to identify totally with its imitation of the cosmic machine. Chanting, precise action, and ecstasy, with its concomitant physiological experiences, gave birth to much of the later development of meditation in the Sanskrit tradition of India.

The soma cult, then, indelibly impressed upon the Sanskrit tradition a sense of the possibilities of ecstatic experience. Let us review these, first by quoting another rare, very early (before 1000 BC) autobiographical account of ecstasy, from a poem in the *Ṛg Veda* composed by one of the comrades of the speculative comradehoods:

Far beyond soar my ears, far beyond my eyes,
Far away to this light which is set in my heart!
Far beyond wanders my mind, its spirit [goes] to remote distances.
What really shall I say? What indeed shall I even think?

(*Ṛg Veda* 6.9.6)

Here the poet enters ecstasy, which causes his senses ecstatically to depart from their physical limitations; he experiences spiritual light in his heart; his mind and spirit depart in psychic transcendence. Wonder falls upon him. Remember, this man is about to enter into the symposium contest where he will be tested by other ecstatics to determine whether he has successfully achieved the enhanced consciousness needed for proper participation in the ritual. So the first use he will put the ecstasy to involves a contest of quick wit, where he will attempt to respond to questions posed to him. Thus, just as in the case of Tzu-ch'i and the symposiasts of Greek times, ecstasy was used to understand and to experience reality from its special point of view. When later, mystics claim to understand everything in their ecstasies, they follow in this very tradition.

So ecstasy introduces persons to deeper levels of understanding. Further, from the soma hymns, we can also conclude that it acquaints them with transcendent levels of their existence, levels which seem not mortal, but somehow immortal. Ecstasy confers mortal protections and benefits, too. From the report of the Holy Man of Ku-she Mountain, it confers psychic powers which permit personal survival of disasters and which can protect others from misfortune. These sound very much like the shamanic powers of the 'medicine man'. Further, the soma hymn shows ecstasy stimulates good thoughts and spiritual realizations, relieves anxiety, and protects from disease and accident.

Many centuries separate these archaic accounts of ecstasies from the descriptions of systematized meditative disciplines we find in early literatures, such as the ecstasy induced by Tzu-chi's leaning on his armrest, staring up at the sky, and breathing. That we find descriptions of ecstasy long before we have accounts of systematized meditation forms indicates that the experience of ecstasy came first, followed by the development of more and more sophisticated techniques for re-achieving this highly valued, much desired state of awareness. Though passages describe ecstatic states dating from earlier than 1000 BC, the first reports of meditative disciplines leading to them group around 300 BC, in both India and China. Somehow, civilizations in the western part of Asia did not systematize techniques for the attainment of ecstasy as did those of south and east Asia, and it was especially in India, perhaps because of the powerful influence of the soma cult, that the exploration of meditation underwent the most vigorous development (see Chapters 4 and 5).

Still, some very early passages from the first Taoist texts show such developments in China. A few in Chuang Tzu describe meditative self-transformations as proceeding through stages (usually three) to states of ecstasy (see Watson, pp. 47–7 and 78–9, for two). Another, cast in symbolic terms, goes:

Yen Hui said, 'I'm improving!'
Confucius said, 'What do you mean by that?'
'I've forgotten benevolence and righteousness!'
'That's good. But you still haven't got it.'
Another day, the two met again and Yen Hui said, 'I'm improving!'
'What do you mean by that?'
'I've forgotten rites and music!'
'That's good. But you still haven't got it.'
Another day, the two met again and Yen Hui said, 'I'm improving!'
'What do you mean by that?'
'I can sit down and forget everything!'
Confucius looked very startled and said, 'What do you mean, sit down and forget everything?'
Yen Hui said, 'I smash up my limbs and body, drive out perception and intellect, cast off form, do away with understanding, and make myself identical with the Great Thoroughfare. This is what I mean by sitting down and forgetting everything.'

(Watson, pp. 86–7)

To me, this passage clearly indicates that by 300 BC the Taoists practised meditative self-transformation in a conscious and systematic fashion. It describes Yen Hui going through a three-staged transformation in a process of 'forgetting', first conventional morality (with which the Taoists did not agree), then conventional religious practice, and finally 'everything' (conventional, I suppose). His goal? Mystical transcendence, which he describes in the last, highly metaphorical paragraph. First, he transcends body (not literally smashing body and limbs, but temporarily rendering them inactive, as Tzu-ch'i did by taking a comfortable position), then by stilling his ordinary mental functioning (perception, intellect and understanding), hence becoming ecstatic (casting off form) and uniting mystically with the Tao, the 'Great Thoroughfare'. In this case, we have concrete indication that meditation is being applied to achieving a new goal – not shamanic ecstasy but mystical union with the whole.

A passage, also using a skill metaphor to describe meditation, describes fasting as a means of transformation. I wonder whether this means fasting just from food, or also from sensory experience? Woodworker Ch'ing produced marvellous wood products, so the Marquis of Lu asked how he did it.

Ch'ing replied, 'I am only a craftsman – how would I have any art? There is one thing, however. When I am going to make a bell stand, I never let it wear out my energy. I always fast in order to still my mind. When I have fasted for three days, I no longer have any thought of congratulations or rewards, of titles or stipends. When I have fasted for five days, I no longer have any thought of praise or blame, of skill or clumsiness. And when I have fasted for seven days, I am so still that I forget I have four limbs and a form and body. By that time, the ruler and his court no longer exist for me. My skill is concentrated and all outside distractions fade.

(Watson, p. 127)

He then goes to the mountain to select his wood, and proceeds to carve. Just as in the case of the ancient Indo-

Aryan charioteer, Ch'ing's 'yoga' disciplines the body and mind for the purpose of some specific action, requiring both his utmost skill and his finest concentration. Shamans and mystics have long known that fasting from food (and sometimes even from water) produces dramatic alterations of consciousness. When one fasts, one confronts one's habitual nature, interrupting the normal flow in favour of some extraordinary form of being. Chuang Tzu elsewhere speaks of two kinds of fasting, distinguishing the conventional fasting which involved abstaining from wine and strong foods in preparation for a sacrifice from the 'fasting of the mind' (pp. 53–4). This passage apparently speaks of this second, enhanced kind of fasting which 'stills the mind', probably involving a physical fast of some kind, but more importantly, the meditative fasting from sensory distractedness which affects the deeper sources of anxiety and 'self-consciousness'.

Another indication that by this time Chinese meditators had become quite sophisticated in their development of meditative techniques comes from what we know of their meditative breathing techniques. In one passage, Chuang Tzu betrays a finely developed conception of the centrality of breath in health and well-being as well as in meditative discipline:

All things that have consciousness depend upon breath. But if they do not get their fill of breath, it is not the fault of Heaven. Heaven opens up the passages and supplies them day and night without stop. But man on the contrary blocks up the holes. The cavity of the body is a many-storied vault; the mind has its Heavenly wanderings. But if the chambers are not large and roomy, then the wives and sisters will fall to quarreling. If the mind does not have its Heavenly wanderings, then the six apertures of sensation will defeat each other.

(Watson, p. 138)

This passage says, in symbolic terms, that physical and mental health depend on breath, while contemporary medicine probably would admit only the first. Just as the body's many-storied vault to be healthy needs to be filled with sufficient breath (irrigating the lungs with oxygen through deep breathing so the wives and sisters [the organs?] do not defeat each others' functioning), the mind also must have its 'Heavenly wanderings', that is, its ecstatic states. Otherwise, the senses will be out of control, not understood from the perspective of the awareness gained through meditative ecstasy. No wonder Taoist meditation elaborated many special meditative breathing techniques. Frankly, I believe that many of our ills, mental and physical, stem from 'blocking up the holes' (the breath passages), our habit of constricted, shallow or nervous breathing (not to speak of smoking, which destroys the air people 'breathe' along with the lungs which supposedly absorb it). When we learn of the skills of life, who teaches us to deep breathe? Our fault stems not from being unable to cure illness but from our steadfast refusal to prevent it in the first place! A friend once told me that, after doctors had removed one lung and part of the other, he recovered after reading and practising what Yogi Ramacharaka recommends in his little book, *The Hindu-Yogi Science of Breath* (London: L. N. Fowler & Co., 1960).

Chuang Tzu's comment that if 'the mind does not have its Heavenly wanderings' the senses will be at odds with each other, producing mental 'dis-ease', leads me to reflect on the clear value that he places on meditatively induced ecstatic experiences. He puts this elsewhere (p. 48) in the marvellous image of the swamp pheasant:

The swamp pheasant has to walk ten paces for one peck and a hundred paces for one drink, but it doesn't want to be kept in a cage. Though you treat it like a king, its spirit won't be content.

Chuang Tzu means that to nourish merely the physical being does not lead to complete satisfaction. The swamp pheasant must wander to be happy, just as we need to 'wander' (ecstatically) to satisfy nature, as much as we need to eat to maintain the physical. How little today do we value such meditative wandering, and how little to do we find complete satisfaction, even in the earth's most affluent civilization.

There seems little time left to maintain consumption at such a massively wasteful level. Perhaps a partial solution to our problems of resource shortages and environmental destruction lies not in the realm of the physical but in discovering alternative satisfactions in the mental realms of experience, such as discovered through meditation. We seek constantly for 'freedom', placing great value on this ideal without realizing that freedom cannot only be from physical want but must also be for spiritual development and the happiness which traditions around the world identify with ecstatic experience.

This to me is what early Taoist meditation and meditatively based strategies of living are all about. Reading Chuang Tzu and Lao Tzu leads me to understand their commitment to the unification of the psyche, not letting one side or the other (the *yang* or the *yin*, the left or the right hemisphere) dominate consciousness to the exclusion of the other. Since the left, sensory, rational mind is most likely to dominate the right, extra-sensory, perceptive mind, meditative achievement of ecstasy provides the necessary counteractive. In Waley's masterful translation of Lao Tzu's Chapter XII (see *The Way and Its Power, A Study of the Tao Te Ching and its Place in Chinese Thought*, New York: Grove Press, 1958, p. 156), we see Lao's stand:

> The five colours confuse the eye,
> The five sounds dull the ear,
> The five tastes spoil the palate.
> Excess of hunting and chasing
> Makes minds go mad.
> Products that are hard to get
> Impede their owner's movements.
> Therefore the Sage
> Considers the belly not the eye.
> Truly, 'he rejects that but takes this'.

The last two lines state Lao Tzu's affirmation of the inner

experience over the outer, as a counteractive to the domination by the outer of the inner. The sage pays attention to the inner (the belly, which the Chinese thought to be the locus of the 'inner sense'), rather than the eye, which leads outward through the sense of sight; he rejects that (the world outside, as Waley's footnote says) but takes this (the psyche's realms within). Excess of 'hunting and chasing', striving and entering into conflicts with the world, others, and oneself, leads to disturbed, anxious minds. Both Taoists recommend a strategy of adaptation to these challenges which is based on seeing them through the alternative (and altered) viewpoint of ecstasy. Chuang Tzu puts the dilemma nicely in the image of the archer:

When you're betting for tiles in an archery contest, you shoot with skill. When you're betting for fancy belt buckles, you worry about your aim. And when you're betting for real gold, you're a nervous wreck. Your skill is the same in all three cases – but because one prize means more to you than another, you let outside considerations weigh on your mind. He who looks too hard at the outside gets clumsy on the inside.

(Watson, p. 122)

Here, Chuang Tzu focuses on the crucial problem of anxiety, which arises, he says, because of the values we place upon external things, thus crippling us within. If, on the other hand, one starts off from a meditative inner cultivation, such external worries will not afflict one's skills and abilities.

Lao Tzu's classic, the *Tao Te Ching*, repeatedly returns to this theme of having a strategy of action in the world which comes from inner meditative cultivation. He favours ecstatic awareness ('Without leaving his door/He knows everything under heaven. Without looking out of his window/He knows all the ways of heaven', Waley, p. 200, Chapter XLVII) and a self-transformative discipline clearly meditative in character:

> Block the passages,
> Shut the doors,
> Let all sharpness be blunted,

> All tangles untied,
> All glare tempered.
> All dust smoothed.
>
> (Waley, p. 210, Chapter LVI)

Dust, as Waley notes, symbolizes the 'noise and fuss of daily life'; to block the passages and shut the doors means to exercise sensory control. A similar passage spells out the implications of such meditative discipline:

> 'Block the passages, shut the doors,
> And till the end your strength shall not fail.
> Open up the passages, increase your doings,
> And till your last day no help shall come to you.'
> As good sight means seeing what is very small
> So strength means holding on to what is weak.
> He who having used the outer-light can return to the inner-light
> Is thereby preserved from all harm.
> This is called resorting to the always-so.
>
> (Waley, p. 206, Chapter LII)

To use the outer-light means to perceive creation and learn of its source, the Tao; to return to the inner-light means to participate in one's inner spirit which partakes of this source. When in harmony with it and thus with the ecstatic knowledge it allows, then one's way will be safe through creation's outer forms and challenges.

Westerners can well benefit from Lao Tzu's meditative strategy in these days when goods of all kinds are scarce. Lao Tzu's meditation taught him to be careful about possessions and contentment:

> No lure is greater than to possess what others want,
> No disaster greater than not to be content with what one has,
> No presage of evil greater than that men should be wanting
> to get more.
> Truly: 'He who has once known the contentment that comes
> simply through being content, will never again be
> otherwise than contented'.
>
> (Waley, p. 199, Chapter XLVI)

These are strong words in the light of the present crises, both physical and spiritual, which our entire earth now faces. Lao Tzu, and meditation, present a counter-challenge. Lao asks, 'Fame or one's own self, which matters to one most? One's own self or things bought, which should count most? In the getting or the losing, which is worse?' (Waley, p. 197, Chapter XLIV). Chuang Tzu reminds us, from over two millennia ago, that there are two modes of understanding: that reached through the senses, and that attained through meditative ecstasy. Naturally, meditative ecstasy is little understood by our ordinary understanding, so he leads into recommending meditation with a series of enigmas:

'It is easy to keep from walking; the hard thing is to walk without touching the ground. It is easy to cheat when you work for men, but hard to cheat when you work for Heaven (i.e. the Tao, the way things go by cosmic law). You have heard of flying with wings, but you have never heard of flying without wings. You have heard of knowledge that knows, but you have never heard of the knowledge that does not know.'

Each enigma contrasts the outer way with the inner. Then, Chuang Tzu invites one to enter through meditation the inner reality:

'Look into that closed room, the empty chamber where brightness is born! Fortune and blessing gather where there is stillness. But if you do not keep still – this is what is called sitting but racing around.'

(Watson, p. 54)

What a wonderful invitation! The 'closed room', the 'empty chamber' designate the innerness which we cover with our busy, rational, worrying, scheming minds. Underneath all these, brightness – the familiar ecstatic light image returns here again – is born, and therein, in the stillness of the perceptive mind (right hemisphere), fortune and blessing gather. The opposite, to sit (in meditation) but to not still the mind – this changes nothing, and the racing around continues. The archaic meditation tradition speaks, it seems, with one human voice, despite its age, whether shamanic or from early civilizations, despite its culture, place or purpose.

Meditation, it says, leads to well-being, physical, mental and spiritual; it frees one from disease, misfortune, early death, anxiety and poverty of spirit.

In the following two chapters, we will see what meditation masters from Indian civilization did to develop this human treasure of meditative self-transformation.

Ox-Taming 3 *Glimpsing the Ox*

In this third episode of the ox-taming series, the boy perhaps hears the ox, then just barely glimpses it as it disappears again, around the next bend. The wily and elusive beast has managed to slip away from the pursuing boy. The occasion's momentous import is that, however inadequately, the boy directly identifies the ox. Though it disappears again, here the tamer enters into a new relation of greater knowing of the self which the ox stands for, as symbol of *karma*. He has traced the ox long enough to reconstruct a glimpse of it from the faint tracks it leaves day by day.

The traditional commentaries liken the seeing of the ox to the first taste of meditative quiet, which, once identified, must be developed and deepened. They say the boy has entered the gate, in the sense that he has seen what is inside it (meditative quiet). In the same manner for my interpretation, the glimpsing of the ox gives the boy the first glance into the deeper structures or forms of immature consciousness. Reconstructing from observing one's behaviour a set of patterns (the ox), one makes the important step towards resolving the dilemmas which arise out of them. The mental level of intrapsychic conflict and anxiety comes into conscious perspective. The sources of conflict and complex lie bare in a difficult, sometimes stormy moment of awareness. In such mindfulness, consciousness (the boy) faces its deeper motivations, desires, immature fantasies and adaptive patterns, the ways which succeeded before. Since they worked then, the conflicted mind (ox) sends directions to act which, as one ages, become increasingly inappropriate. The new element is that the boy has finally glimpsed this ox.

The patent fact remains that the ox does not yet work for the boy. It exists independently of the boy, defying him, still able to plunge his fragile mental economy into neurotic anxiety, fear or hatred, depression, apathy or loneliness in a world which should be his home. Untamed, the ox runs wild, carrying or leading the boy unwittingly on its uncontrolled path. The ox does not help the boy grow in maturity, but expresses the uncorrected features of immaturity, however subtle and adult in form. Underlying fight-flight responses, the a-rational motivational inheritance from archaic time and childhood make this ox's way in the world the source of dis-ease, or imbalance (Sanskrit *duḥkha*, elaborately analysed in Indic spiritual thought). The ox has great animal power, but untamed; the power runs counter to the boy's best interests. Maturation is the process wherein one deliberately and consciously examines one's action, its sources and consequences, with the intention of making them more responsible and in the future to be guilt free. Yet motivation seethes with complexity and depth. How can one inspect the deep sources of one's actions? One observes behaviour, the words one uses, the dreams which come at night, the habitual and off-guard impulses, the mirrors of others' reactions, all to follow the traces of the inner selves which have become a part of one's *karma* accumulation. 'Mindfulness' meditation, as taught in Burmese and Thai (Theravāda) Buddhist traditions, locates the central meditative endeavour in just such self-observation (*smṛti*, Pali *sati*, 'mindfulness'). Self-knowledge means to know also the self that is more difficult to observe, less the subject of experience, and thus not to be like ignorant Euthydemus. Asked by Socrates whether he had followed the Delphic injunction to 'know thyself', Euthydemus responded, 'no', continuing, 'you see, that was one thing I thought I did know. I could hardly have known anything else if I hadn't even been acquainted with myself' (Xenophon, *Memoirs of Socrates*, iv. 2, Penguin translation, p. 190). Socrates and the ox-tamer knew better.

This crucial moment pits the boy against the fleeing ox. In psychological terms, the challenge involves whether we can keep the ox in sight, persevering, not backing down from the confrontation. Self-deception mitigates against the boy's success, for we all protect ourselves from realizing too much about the unconscious sources of our motivations, since they are so deeply coloured with negative affect which requires that they be repressed, or 'forgotten'. Yet, to keep them from consciousness, one must in some sense know them, otherwise the strategy of forgetting (self-deception) would be ineffective, as they would well up into consciousness over and over again. We 'forget' the painful and the immature, even though the ox never, unless tamed, lets us forget anything.

At this point, the boy may need guidance and help to free himself from the immature or animal nature to achieve a multiform but unitary, consciously integrated mind. Beyond a certain point, even with meditation, the path becomes extremely difficult to follow. Buddhists practise 'mindfulness' (*smṛti*) meditations for years, seeking to reconstruct the ox from its traces; but strait is the gate and narrow the path. This is why in Zen meditation, you regularly see the *rōshi*, your meditation master-therapist, who checks on your progress in identifying and transcending the ox. The ox nature is fraught with affect, which avoids yet terrifies the conscious mind (the boy), so he must strive drawing upon all his courage.

Our contemporary culture rarely provides systematic help at this point, and, admittedly, meditation without the traditional meditation master is partially unable to open access to this deep level of the conflicted mind (see Carrington, *Freedom in Meditation*, pp. 270–5). Sometimes someone else very close to us can help, as a mate or a lover with whom one shares much time, and thus who has a good opportunity to observe our subtle behaviour; or a close friend at times can do it, a counsellor, advisor or a therapist. These people take what we do and say, see it from another perspective, then reflect it back to us, so that we can begin to reconstruct the ox, thereby to realize the confrontations in which we must begin to make changes at this deepest level. Also, unexpected consequences of our actions, or severe trials like chronic illness, can reveal us to ourselves, making the ox real, after years of its evasive tactics. Then, and only then, can a person do something about it.

The alternative always remains to neglect the task of reconstructing the ox from its traces. Then, sometime, during a crisis, in radically changed circumstances, under great stress, during trauma or in an uncontrollable personal crisis (an accident, a 'bad trip', etc.), the barriers break and the ox runs over persons, leaving them vulnerable, dependent as a babe, desolate. Or one can survive, year after year, keeping all this just below the surface, striving for a happiness that will be forever denied, whatever 'success' one might achieve in the world's terms. Thus one postpones the confrontation to the last moment, when one must, as all Shakespeare's golden lads and girls, 'come to dust', when death brings all the postponed, avoided confrontations with separation to the moment of final necessity. In death, the untamed ox will be there, mockingly triumphant, ready still to run away, some believe with the greatest prize of all, one's own immortality.

I think there is considerable opposition to these psychological ideas in contemporary thought. Critics claim that such deep changes are either impossible or undesirable. B. F. Skinner's behaviourism and secular pessimisms claim that the individual will always fall under the sway of conditioning, unable to reverse the influence of prior experience or current conditions. Others, prophets of consumerism, the cults of experience, or even just the merchants of TV and liquor, seek to drown the insistent inner cries of the spirit, our innately human swamp pheasant nature, in turn glorifying the ox nature. The immaturity of individuals turns up again in our immaturity as a civilization and as 'a people' (inhabitants of the 'West'), with greed motivating apparently altruistic actions at home (in business, government, even religion) and abroad (international business conglomerates, wars and economic exploitation of third-world resources and peoples). Which Euroamericans, travelling abroad, have escaped the reflection of our collective ox in the taunts, insults and jeers of our supposed hosts? At interpersonal levels at home, the ox returns, too, hauntingly, as women and minorities strive for their right to be treated as human beings rather than as objects of sexual aggression, greed and hostility. The opposition to change, whether theoretical in our conception about the possibility of confronting and taming the ox, or practically, as when sexists, bigots and those greedy for wealth and power continue avoiding their ox, does not bode well for our collective or individual futures. Civilizations, none of which have been able to throw off their immaturity, all also 'come to dust'. Somewhere along the line, civilization may mature collectively, opening the way for the first time to a truly human future. Though nothing holds the entire answer, perhaps meditation can help to break up the log jam sufficiently to allow us to proceed towards more adequate solutions to these all too human dilemmas.

The next picture shows how the boy takes action.

4

Early Meditation's Psychology and Metaphysics

Each world civilization distinguishes itself from others by the special features of human potentiality it develops. Each civilization exemplifies, indeed, the usual universal elements of humanness, but develops its own, unique forms. Western civilization promoted, from African-Egyptian, Semitic, Indo-European and Arabic sources its certainty that God is one, and that physical laws, by their unity, allow for humankind to shape his creation to their ends; contemporary scientific rationalism ironically resulted, creating the first fully secular world view of any civilization out of the 'death' of God. In China and Mesopotamia, divination developed from universal shamanistic roots to such an extent that all other civilizations must be considered underdeveloped when it comes to the ways of divinatory knowledge. Indian civilization 'invented' several cornerstones of world civilization, including grammar, psychology and the notion of emptiness. Emptiness probably came from its profound acquaintance with meditative ecstasy, grammar from its fascination with the verses deriving from the ecstatic inspirations of soma-cult priests, and psychology and its underlying metaphysics again from the early experiences of ecstatic states.

In this and the following chapter I will survey some of the ideas which India developed about meditation during the highly creative period between around 200 BC to 200 AD. A remarkable florescence of meditation occurred in those centuries, the likes of which has never again been seen on earth. I should emphasize that neither here nor elsewhere in this book am I trying to describe or teach the techniques of meditation. This is better done in a class by a meditation teacher; alternatively, if you wish to read about such techniques, many books on the subject flood our bookstores. Instead, I am surveying what people have thought about meditation, how it originated and developed in world civilizations, and what we know about it today. Also, this is a short account of a vast subject, so many times I will send you, in references, to other books whose contents I do not even try to summarize. In the case of Indian meditation, for example, the most reliable and complete work is undoubtedly Mircea Eliade's *Yoga, Immortality and Freedom* (Princeton: Princeton University Press, 1969). Of all the available books on Indian meditation, this book reliably reports the ideas from India's many and diverse meditation literatures, placing them firmly in the perspective of Western analysis, and thus making it an excellent introduction. A complement to Eliade is Jean Varenne's *Yoga and the Hindu Tradition* (Chicago: University of Chicago Press, 1976), which also presents a scholar's review of the Indic meditation tradition.

The Indo-Aryan experience of soma-ecstasies led by 500 BC to a revolutionary development of psychologies of bondage and release. The immortality experienced in the soma cult prompted north Indians who felt unsatisfied by the increasingly outmoded ritualism of the Vedas to look towards other means of gaining true happiness and mental broadening of the horizons of consciousness. Old Vedic cultists sought much as the early Greeks for long life on earth, within a simple, Indo-European metaphysics which assumed that 'seeing is believing' (something which survives today in scientific rationalism). So the world, metaphysically, was considered real, worthwhile, and the arena in which one found one's ultimate satisfactions, prolific cows and fertile women, the favours of the gods, and a happy afterlife in the realm of the gods. Somewhere between these ideals represented in the *Ṛg Veda* and the time of the growing ascetic renunciant movements of the eighth to the sixth centuries

BC these basic assumptions radically changed. The world, in this revised metaphysics, was thought to be 'only a little bit real' (a contradiction in terms to Aristotelian logic), and not able to lead to ultimate satisfaction, since it was always changing (Plato may have borrowed this kind of metaphysics from India). By becoming attached to or dependent on transient things, we gain, so the argument went, only transitory happiness. Furthermore, attachments to transitory things become frustrated when the things change or disappear; we suffer 'dis-ease' (Sanskrit *duḥkha*, usually translated as 'suffering'). Added to this came another idea – that of continued reincarnation – so that by 500 BC many spiritually sensitive north Indians became convinced that the only way to gain true and lasting happiness was somehow to achieve transcendence of the world altogether.

They had the prior experience of the soma ecstasy as a potential model for the ideal state. The prince Siddhārtha, by becoming the 'Buddha' (that is, awakened to ecstasy) dramatized the ideal for all generations to follow by renouncing his princely inheritance of all that the world could offer (a parallel myth for the Hindu tradition can be found in the story of Nachiketas in the *Kaṭha Upaniṣad*, composed about the same time). After leaving the palace, he followed a course of meditative self-discipline until he reached the desired state of ecstatic transcendence under the Tree of Enlightenment (a fig tree). But the Buddha had no corner on the market. Many other groups shared in the great vogue for meditation-achieved ecstatic transcendence including the sages of the Upaniṣads (both Buddhists and Upaniṣadics included women among the ranks of their ecstatics) and the ascetics of the Jaina way, followers of Mahāvīra. In this sense, meditation was the means of realizing whatever ideal vision one held able to release one from bondage to the woes of transient world experiences. What I think happened was that the myth of the Buddha polarized the various parties to the ecstatic spiritual tradition in northern India after the 'historical' Buddha died in 483 BC. Before and during his lifetime a few men and women from all classes and walks of life were similarly renouncing secular life, or the highly ritualized religious life of the Vedic Aryan priestly orthodoxy, thus to seek an alternative spirituality. They made up what might be termed the ancient Indian spiritual underground. From among them the Buddha gathered a considerable following by the time he died, leaving a strong order to spread his teaching through India within a century or two. As a response to this, around the teachings of the more orthodox Upaniṣadic sages, a second major party, which we now call the Hindu religion, formed to counteract the Buddhist challenge which consciously took an anti-Vedic stance. Radical rightists (such as Vedic ritualists) and radical leftists (the highly ascetic Jaina, fatalists, world espousing materialists, and so forth) completed the spiritual spectrum, each preaching a different ideal state, but the majority using meditation in some form or another to achieve the goal (ritualists and materialists excepted.)

To begin reviewing some of the basic ideas these various parties held about meditation, here follows a passage from the *Kaṭha Upaniṣad* (composed *c.* 400–300 BC) on meditation's psychology.

> When the five [sense] knowledges become calmed,
> Along with the surface mind [*manas*]
> And the deep mind [*buddhi*] wavers not,
> That, say the wise, is the deepest state [of consciousness].
>
> That state they claim is [realized through] meditation [yoga],
> Being the steady-holding [*dhāraṇā*] of the powers of sense
>   and action [*indriyas*];
> Then one becomes undistracted:
> Indeed, meditation [yoga] is the beginning and the end!
>
> (*Kaṭha Upaniṣad* 6.10 and 11)

This passage understands meditation as being the disciplining of the various constituent parts of our consciousness. Meditation controls or holds steady the five senses or, more inclusively, the ten powers of sense and action (the *indriyas*, consisting of the five powers of sense experience: seeing, hearing, smelling, tasting and touching; plus the five powers of action: speech, handling, walking, eliminating and sexual activity). This in turn allows the surface mind (*manas*), which usually takes messages from and sends directions back to the senses and powers of action, to reverse its orientation during the meditation, no longer being directed distractedly to the hubble-bubble of the external world. This allows three things to happen.

First, it calms the mind, as when a wind dies down allowing rough water to become calm and sediment to settle again to the bottom. In this calm mind, then, secondly, other, inner features can become objects of attention for the surface mind, such as how one feels, what one is anxious about, or how nice the temporary withdrawal from the sensory domination of mental contents can be. Meditators experience all of these. And thirdly, meditation can lead 'to the deepest state', when the powers of sense and action temporarily cease their action and the various levels of mind, surface (*manas*) and deep (*buddhi*) no longer can be drawn for the duration of the meditative state into the sensory-motor flux. Is this 'deepest state' ecstasy? I hope you have already realized that I am not using this term loosely, in the meaning of 'extremely happy'. Rather, ecstasy means etymologically, 'outside (*ek-*) one's (ordinary) place (*stasis*)', thus passing by one's ordinary self (sensory-motor activity, and the consciousness it engenders). In this sense, the state which the Upaniṣad describes as resulting from the steady-holding of the sensory-motor powers does qualify as ecstasy. Naturally, as Chuang Tzu warned (see my Dedication page), if the mind which undertakes temporary sensory-motor curtailment does not also calm itself, no ecstasy results, but that is taken for granted.

The passage describes meditation, the means to this 'undistracted state', as the 'beginning and the end'. In this phrase, it places ultimate value on meditation. But how could meditation be so all-encompassing in its value? The answer, I think, lies in the ecstatic experience to which it provides access. Repeatedly, in shamanistic and mystical sources, the idea surfaces that in ecstasy one temporarily stands outside one's ordinary self to learn. New perceptions, new experiences, new, more holistic ways of understanding occur; one feels somehow released from the overbearing burden of the ordinary self's concerns, anxieties, woes and habits, allowing other ways of feeling and seeing to develop. Lame Deer had such an experience in his vision pit, as did the Buddha under his fig tree. Lame Deer's vision became the basis for his power, his ability to help and heal, while the Buddha's visions that full moon night led to the enunciation of saving wisdom, the Buddhist *dharma*, or teaching. Notice that meditation leads temporarily to such a state of enhanced perception and learning, but does not continue for ever. As any psychological state, it is temporary, but when consciousness reverts to its 'normal' levels the experience can have so transformed the individual, either all of a sudden or over a period of repeated ecstasies, that significant, sometimes profound changes occur. The Upaniṣad claims as Lame Deer did of his 'vision seeking' that using meditation can produce those sorts of changes which put one into contact with ultimate value and meaning in one's life. Lame Deer thought himself blessed by a once-in-a-lifetime experience of the *nagi*, or the spirit-essence of his being, and became flooded with its power; the Buddha 'saw everything', achieving release, he thought, from the bondage which would keep him after that lifetime from reincarnating any more into a transient, frustrating life-experience on worldly planes of existence.

Because somehow north Indian metaphysics came up with the world description they had around 500 BC, involving its strongly pessimistic feelings about the physical world and reincarnation into it along with its optimism that one could escape from these, spiritual leaders sought extensively into the human psyche for the reasons for frustration (*duḥkha*, 'dis-ease') and for the mechanisms of bondage to transient things and experiences. They elaborated a psychology which anticipated our contemporary science (as they did with grammar) by two thousand years. The whole notion of consequentiality (*karma*) in the development of personality which Freud brought to our collective attention constituted a cornerstone of that psychology. It understood fully approach-avoidance intrapsychic conflicts, it fathomed the ill-effects of libidinal drive, aggressive drive, and neurotic self-deception, the desire, hatred, anger, and ignorance in the centre of the Buddhist wheel-of-life image, and it identified clearly the binding features of psychological stereotype, what Freud called 'chains' in his remark that 'analysis sets the neurotic free from the chains of his sexuality'. (For a lucid analysis of the parallels between psychoanalysis and Eastern mysticism, see Herbert Fingarette's *The Self In Transformation*, especially Chapters 3–7.)

Indian psychology, both Hindu and Buddhist, clearly described bondage to immature and dependency adaptations in formulations of 'causal chains'. We have all seen small children fighting over some trivial thing upon which they feel their entire happiness depends, or who go into fits of despair when deprived of some coveted object. By not maturing out of such mechanisms of adjustment to the physical world, Indian psychology said, adults bind themselves to the transient world's necessary frustrations. As the *Bhagavad Gītā* says, it all begins with the undisciplined, impetuous powers of sense and action (Chapter 2, vs. 60), explaining,

> When a person dwells on sense objects,
> Attachment to them arises.
> From that attachment desire is produced;
> And from desire, anger upwells.
>
> From anger, intense confusion results,
> From confusion comes loss of self-possession [*smṛti*],
> From loss of self-possession, the deep mind fails,
> And from its failure, one dies.
>
> (*Bhagavad Gītā*, Chapter 2, 62–3)

Unfortunately, most translators spoil the inner logical progression of this 'causal chain' by using the word 'memory' for *smṛti*, which, as Buddhist meditative literature shows, really means self-observance, or self-awareness. The idea is that, like immature children, adults seek all their satisfactions in external objects, which produces attachment or habituation

to them; then, when that attachment needs additional satisfaction, it feeds a desire, which when frustrated, results in
anger (the frustration-aggression hypothesis of current
psychology), with the result that one's mental states become
unbalanced, one's self-possession fails to control intrapsychic
conflict and anxiety. Then the deep mind's ability fails
completely to advise us (as Socrates' inner voice did) on
proper courses to take to lead to more appropriate forms of
action and more lasting satisfactions, and this eventuates in
self-destructive forms of behaviour. Examples abound all
around us in cigarette, alcohol and drug addictions. For
example, the deep mind knows that smoking leads to pre-
mature death, but can do little to advise the habituated mind
on the true state of affairs with respect to the self-deception
that the habit is innocuous.

The *Gītā*'s prescription to counteract such states which
challenge the viability and even survival of the self involves
controlling the sensory-motor and mental apparatus through
meditative self-discipline. Note that the following verse
recommends not withdrawal from the world, but moving
through it with controlled sensory-motor responses:

> But the person who goes through the world
> With sensory-motor responses under self-control,
> And free from desire and aversion [approach-avoidance],
> That person achieves inner tranquility.
> In that tranquility, the person transcends
> All dis-ease [*duhkha*] ...
>
> (*Bhagavad Gītā* 2.64, 65 ab)

This text's definitions of 'yoga' or 'meditation' repeatedly
stress that it results in skilful action in the world. One passage
reads, 'Yoga [results in] proficiency in actions' (2.50 d).
Although the classic's hero, Arjuna, eventually must experience ecstatic vision to complete Kṛṣṇa's teaching (*Gītā*, Ch.
11), the purpose of the instruction is to enable Arjuna to transcend his dilemma – his reluctance to fight the civil war which
his class duty required him to wage against former friends,
teachers and even his relatives – so that immediately after

Kṛṣṇa's teaching he returns to the battlefield to pursue with full commitment and skill the bloody, eighteen-day battle against his enemies, those aligned with evil.

Another passage from the *Kaṭha Upaniṣad* spells out the psychology of meditative self-discipline, adding a metaphysical dimension to the archaic *Ṛg Veda* image of the *yogin*-charioteer by comparing the chariot owner to the *ātman*, a person's inner, spiritual essence. This *ātman* metaphysically, by its essential nature, that is, transcends all phenomenal change. It dwells in every human being, so that, in this sense, everyone is already transcendent by essential nature, hence free from all the limiting conditions of the transient, disturbing world of form and change. What then leads to freedom is not somehow becoming free, but realizing that one is already free; and this realization occurs most reliably in meditative ecstasy. The verses clearly sketch out this meditative psychology and metaphysics:

> The essential Self [*ātman*] is the chariot owner, understand,
> The body only the chariot;
> The deep mind [*buddhi*] see as the charioteer,
> And the surface mind [*manas*] as the reins.
>
> The powers of sense and action are the horses, they say,
> And the sense objects the fields where they travel.
> Those who know say: the body, powers of sense and action,
> And the surface mind are the experience mechanism.
>
> Indeed, who is not mentally aware,
> Whose surface mind is forever undisciplined [lacking meditation]
> That person's powers of sense and action will be out of control,
> – Like mean horses uncontrolled by a charioteer.
>
> But whoever becomes aware,
> With surface mind always disciplined [by meditation]
> That person's powers of sense and action will be under control,
> – Like good horses, under the charioteer's control.
>
> (*Kaṭha Upaniṣad* 3.3–6)

As in old Indo-Aryan times, the most important individual

is the chariot owner, metaphysically, the inner self, or *ātman*, which ecstatics and shamans repeatedly experience. Lame Deer called it *nagi*, something within, not perceivable by the senses, the source of personal power. Though Lame Deer's description does not adopt metaphysical concepts to describe it, he obviously experienced the same 'something' which has led people in every culture to postulate an invisible spiritual essence which somehow constitutes part of our identity. The experience, and the postulate, occurs in the most archaic Stone Age cultures we know today, so it must be a primary human intuition. The Dugam Dani (see Karl Heider, *The Dugam Dani, A Papuan Culture in the Highlands of West New Guinea*, Chicago: Aldine Publishing Company, 1970) call this element of human reality the *edai-egen*, soul, seat of the personality of spirit, considering that it inhabits the solar plexus at birth and registers the spiritual ups and downs of an individual throughout life. We can presume that many of the earliest burial forms of our primal ancestors (flexing of legs to chest, breaking of skull, etc.) assumed something invisible which survived death, implying that this conception may be one of the first religious ideas held by human beings. By the time of this early period of Indian civilization, the doctrine had advanced beyond the primal and shamanistic conceptions to become fully metaphysical. The *ātman*, according to Hindu thought, transcends by essence all existence; it never dies, never changes, never suffers. Thus, it provides the guarantee of salvation from phenomenal flux and the 'necessity' of reincarnation.

This soul essence is the owner of the chariot, the body, which exists for it alone, along with the rest of the psycho-physical mechanism. The *buddhi*, or deep mind, is likened to the charioteer, which indicates the primary importance Indian psychology gives to it. This mental function can make decisions and direct one through the world, as the charioteer does the chariot. The *manas*, or surface mind, the mind which pays attention to the inputs from the senses and motor functions, like the reins of the chariot, mediates between consciousness and the powers of sense and action, the horses. The picture presents mental functions metaphorically, but with sense. As the last verses say, when a person allows the deep and surface minds to be undisciplined through meditative practice, the horses – our powers of sense and action – run away with us, being out of the charioteer's control. While if one practises meditation, and becomes perceptive of oneself, the *buddhi* can make, as Socrates' inner-voice did, the proper decisions, and these would be properly relayed through the reins to the powers which we then could use with skill and efficiency in the world.

To spell out fully the implications of this introspective psychology, a diagram identifying the constituents of the mental process would look like this:

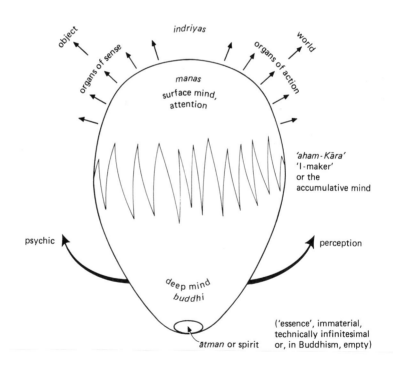

By virtue of our sensory-motor experience of the object world, which first comes to us as infants, we gradually 'adapt' to reality by learning how to perceive and act through the *indriyas*, the powers, or horses. The *manas*, or surface mind, like the surface of a deep pond or ocean, becomes involved in the action of the *indriyas*, 'agitated' by their reports and by the consequences of their actions. A sense of individuality develops as more and more sensory and motor experiences accumulate in the memory portion of consciousness (both conscious and unconscious), which I have called the 'accumulative mind', and which Sanskrit psychologists designated as the '*aham-kāra*', literally the 'I-maker'. Our sense of identity gradually builds around the experiences we accumulate on the constantly recording memory, which steadily gathers input (positive, negative and neutral, the yoga texts tell) forming a definite personality. In the meditatively unpractised individual, this process of the sensory-motor domination of consciousness is never interrupted, but continues until death. Such consciousness rarely stands outside itself in ecstasy, never glimpsing its spiritual dimension (the *ātman*, or spirit). Its deepest level of mind often remains 'unrealized', though it, with the accumulative mind, results in spontaneous productions, as in our nightly dreams, as well as psychically mediated 'intuitions' or 'hunches' which direct us, as do the *indriyas*, but through their own psychic perceptions and actions.

It is the accumulative mind's *karma* or 'making' that mindfulness and meditation seek to begin to undo, thus freeing the *manas* to look deeper within, to the stiller, more sure foundations of consciousness. The accumulative mind produces an 'I' over a period of experience (which Indians considered to extend over many lives, but Freud thought began at birth). This 'I', when untamed, like the ox, runs away from deeper consciousness experiences, since it is motivated by the 'complexes' it has formed at superficial levels in adapting to its experience world. Often, such complexes are set deep into the accumulative mind very early in life, long before self-observation and adult awareness can

:operly evaluate experience and resist infantile adaptation patterns. Once an early attempted adaptation is successful, its very success, no matter how infantile, becomes recorded as a pattern in the accumulative mind, the first (often in the most traumatic circumstances) being models for later adaptations. Positively rewarded forms, whether adequate or not, become fixed in consciousness as habitual or stereotyped patterns, producing the anomaly of infantile actions (however disguised or covered up) undertaken by adults to adapt to adult situations. The inappropriateness of such actions derives from their infantile origins; they might have been appropriate then, or at least successful (in the presence of adults), but are no longer so beyond their time of origination. Much 'adult' behaviour may be analysed in such a manner as unworked-out infantile patterns. Furthermore, this accumulative mind has a deep heritage, whether via a series of past life experiences, or some inherited pattern of adaptive mechanisms which as a whole has ensured our survival as the life-form *Homo sapiens*. One can imagine that at the dawn of human consciousness, the *indriyas*, our sensory-motor responses to the object world, were dominated by that world, since bare survival depended on adapting, namely either by killing or fighting others for supremacy or by consistently and successfully fleeing from death. Such patterns receive some reinforcement in both infantile and adult experience, despite our 'evolution' out of that kind of situation.

In fact, to return to my speculative history of meditative consciousness, when we first domesticated fire, our first real opportunity for breaking out of such fight-flight or kill-or-be-killed survival forms must have occurred. Sitting around a blazing fire for warmth and security probably provided the *manas* its first opportunity to transcend its primal survival response in a consciousness qualitatively different from both the dilemmas, fight-flight, kill or be killed. Because, while seated before the security-providing fire, the *indriyas* could loosen their grip on the object world (which consisted of giant, twenty-foot-wing-spanned birds and a great diversity of fearsome beasts). This liberated the *manas*, or attention, so that it could turn inward to deeper levels of consciousness. These very experiences were our first steps in the evolution of spiritual consciousness, or awareness not based on the overpowering motive of self-preservation. In such situations the primal, savage 'I-maker' could be temporarily transcended, and intimations of the qualitatively different ecstatic consciousness could begin. Similarly, in our own personal 'evolution', by meditatively altering the *indriya-manas* domination of awareness, the accumulative mind can be attended to, in a therapeutic sense, with the consequence of enhancing awareness of the buddhic or psychic level of consciousness, as well as deeper, spiritual potentialities of consciousness, since these, by definition, are outside fight-flight or other infantile and immature adaptive patterns.

Let me point out how my use of the term 'ecstasy' as a cover-all word designating meditative states fits into this model. Ecstasy results when one transcends both the fight-flight, kill-or-be-killed and the infantile adaptive patterns of the accumulative mind, releasing consciousness into an apparently 'unlimited' realm (at least an expanded consciousness by comparison to adaptive, instrumental consciousness), beyond the demands which such self-preoccupied or anxious forms of consciousness require to be met in all perceptions or actions. Ecstatic experiences are 'different', instructive and 'fun' (to put things mildly) because they lift awareness outside these instrumental constraints which must always serve the perceiver's needs, transmuting consciousness into a consummatory mode, where experiences have value for themselves alone, not as means to some particular goal or to serve some need or dependency. Thus, ecstasy entails not withdrawal, either from consciousness or from the senses, but a transformation of the basis of both of these, so that awareness can be of and for itself alone ('self-knowledge' in one of its senses). It thus can be conversant with love, empathy and compassion and all the possible 'I-Thou' relations experience brings to us, even a 'purified' sensory experience, as sought, for example, by Zen Buddhist meditators and nature mystics. This two-sidedness of ecstasy indicates its introvertive and extrovertive forms. Ecstasy surely includes many different modes; it is a multi-form, rather than a uni-form, experience of consciousness, but it includes moments of self-transcendence (of the 'I-maker' and accumulated karmic self) whose learning derives precisely from such momentary liberation from adaptive modes of self-preoccupation, moments when consciousness absorbs itself in its own depths, and moments when consciousness looses itself in the newly discovered Other, whether person, plant, starry sky or thing. Meditation produces such states by temporarily releasing consciousness from constraints 'to learn', thus even reflecting back on the constraints and hopefully aiding in the process of transforming them. We all know the model of the happy person who seems not to have an excessive care in the world, even in the toughest situations.

Meditation effects these changes by turning the attention inward during special self-introspective therapeutic interludes, preferably undertaken in a regular daily manner. By temporarily withdrawing from the ordinary flow of becoming, one can take stock of one's being, unpreoccupied by external demands and entanglements. Indian psychology distrusted the untrained, apparently 'natural' state of the impetuous senses and powers of action, which seem to do their appointed task in the world, seeking satisfactions and acting in the interest of the self. On the other hand, however, it trusted the deep mind, which I consider to be the 'psychic' mind, in touch as it is with reality not through the senses, but through its own ways of intuitive understanding (in scientific terms, the right brain). This deep mind knows in ways which seem so amazing to us that we, and our left-brain modes of thought, have discounted its ability to guide and serve us. Meditation can open up access paths to this deeper level of awareness; then, like Socrates, we can use its superior ability to know the world and help to direct the 'experience mechanism' of surface mind, the body and its powers. What Indian meditation proposed, as we see in the biography of the Buddha, is that we undertake through meditation to come into greater contact with this deep mind, leading to 'skill in living'. The horses, our powers of sense and action, indeed have great power, but not in an unharnessed, untamed state. (For more on these meditatively accessed powers, see Chapter 8.)

The Buddhists used the same basic psychology, but expressed it even more completely, especially in their realizations of the wheel-of-life image and their emphasis on *karma* and its law of dependent co-arising (see Robinson and Johnson, *The Buddhist Religion*, Chapter 1, for a complete account of these). Remember that Buddhism and Hinduism were not distinct religions, but two sides of the same Indian spiritual tradition. The Buddhists, on the one hand, had more interest in the individual's salvation through meditative self-transformation, while the Hindus, on the other, emphasized the individual's salvation through social class duty and action in the world of family and state. Both accepted the same world view, and both affirmed the eventual goal of human spiritual striving to be meditative transcendence of the limiting conditions of recurrent rebirth into unsatisfying realms of existence. Buddhists developed meditation in the early centuries far more than did the more orthodox groups which fed the growth of Hinduism, and later systems, including Patañjali's *Yoga Sūtras* (see next chapter), drew heavily on Buddhist sources. This followed naturally from the career of Siddhārtha himself. Born a prince, hence educated in the old orthodox ritualism which later became identified as 'Hinduism', he left his home, inheritance and apparent material happiness for the alternative course of meditative self-transformation at the age of twenty-nine. After six years of meditating and practising ascetic self-discipline, he experienced a meditative breakthrough to ecstasy on a full moon night under a fig tree. In the ecstasy, he saw all his former births, the mechanism of *karma*, or action consequentiality, and how to transcend these, founding the Buddhist elaboration of Indian psychology. Buddhist psychology thus directly stems from Buddhist meditation, since Siddhārtha became 'Buddha' through meditation, and in meditation he 'understood' what had formerly made him turn away from attachment to the physical world and thus to free himself from it. (He also died while meditating, in the same state as that in which he experienced his enlightening visions.)

Fundamentally, Buddhist psychology posits three mechanisms which cause 'dis-ease'. These are ignorance (of the basic features of transient reality and of the self); desire, which results from the ignorance; and hatred, which arises from the desire. These feed into the stream of one's 'dis-ease', becoming further consequences which need to be resolved both as problems in themselves and as motivations for future *karma*-formations. *Karma* means the sum total of one's past actions and their consequences. The Buddhist path of self-discipline seeks to eliminate these three motivating factors so as to eliminate future *karma* creation, thus to stop producing *karma* by cutting it off at the roots. Then the being, no longer attached by *karma* to gaining satisfaction through the physical world, no longer needs to be reborn into it, as the lesson of spirit has been learned.

Most Westerners have a hard time identifying the truth of this Buddhist picture of life, since they do not believe that escape from reincarnation in repeated physical existences is the highest goal, or even a meaningful one. The picture may be re-drawn in another way. Thus 'rebirth' would occur each time we wake to face another day; 'dis-ease' means the frustrations we experience; '*karma*' means the reasons for these frustrations as well as their consequences. So how does meditation fit in? Meditation allows one to intervene in the continuing creation of the chains of *karma*, first by therapeutically withdrawing, every day, from one's involvement in their process of creation; secondly, by allowing one to confront one's motivations, deep in self-examination; and thirdly, by helping one to change these deep structures which lead to *karma*'s chains being forged. Siddhārtha, according to the myth, had no therapist to help him dig to the deepest levels of his being, to the sources of ignorance, desire and hatred. I have often wondered why he had to meditate for six years before the ecstasy he achieved transformed him. One reason may be his age: he was much older than Lame Deer (who after all, at sixteen spent only four days in the process of achieving ecstasy, but many years in working out the *karma* of his infantile nature). After twenty-nine years of self-indulgent palace life, Siddhārtha's *karma* deeply coloured his being with infantile fantasies and deep, underlying psychic conflict and anxiety, needing considerable time to be confronted and worked out. Perhaps ecstasy is much easier to reach when one is young, before the adult organization of mind, produced by the challenges of the 'reality principle', has effected its consequence of hardening the mind's youthful flexibility. Lame Deer's earlier ecstasy did not save him from *karma*, but just gave him a source of confidence and power to which he could always return, in his battle with the horses and the fascinated surface mind.

A passage on meditation from a fairly early Buddhist text (*Milindapanha* 139–40) summarizes all that it does in the Buddhist view, extending from its worldly benefits, through personal benefits, its virtues, its ability to root out karmic motivations and *karma*, to the attainment of ecstasy, wisdom and release from rebirth:

Meditation preserves him who meditates, it gives him long life, and endows him with power, it cleanses him from faults, it removes from him any bad reputation giving him a good name, it destroys discontent in him filling him with content, it releases him from all fear endowing him with confidence, it removes sloth far from him filling him with zeal, it takes away lust and ill-will and dullness, it puts an end to pride, it breaks down all doubt, it makes his heart to be at peace, it softens his mind, it makes him glad, it makes him grave, it gains him much advantage, it makes him worthy of reverence, it fills him with joy, it fills him with delight, it shows him the transitory nature of all compounded things, it puts an end to rebirth, it obtains for him all the benefits of renunciation.

(T. W. Rhys Davids, *The Questions of King Milinda,*
New York: Dover, 1963, p. 197)

This remarkable list traces meditative self-transformation through every level of development, from the first changes in one's life which it brings to the last, self-shaking releases from bondage. Many of these consequences of meditation involve goals set by Buddhist doctrine, which do not belong intrinsically to meditation, but are what Buddhists use it for. The most interesting features to me, in the entire list, are that meditation, it claims, can remove *karma*-producing motivations, lust (desire), ill-will (hatred) and dullness (ignorance) or rather can be used to do such; that it 'puts an end to pride', or lessens the hold on the mental awareness of excessively anxious self-preoccupation; that it makes the heart peaceful (literally 'one-pointed'), free from immature karmic habits; and, most interesting of all, that it 'softens the mind' (Pali *'mānasaṃ snehayati'*, literally 'lubricates, makes pliable, softens'). Why, indeed, would one want to soften the mind? Well, to make it amenable to changes one considers desirable. Through self-awareness, we can become aware of the sources of our deepest conflicts and anxieties; then, using meditative techniques, we can soften their matrix, allowing new structures to form which are more in consonance with our mature ideals and intentions. These features seem much more relevant to my conception of meditation than the doctrinal goals of becoming aware of the 'transitory nature of all compounded things' and abolishing rebirth.

I hope this provides some idea of the psychology and metaphysics developed by early north Indian thought to found and support the practice of meditative ecstasy. The field of Buddhist meditation – just the textual and secondary literature dealing with it – is admittedly large and beyond the scope of this book. We shall learn more about the psychology of meditation in Chapter 7, and particularly from Patricia Carrington's book, *Freedom in Meditation*. Suffice it to say that, on the basis of the ideas briefly sketched here, Indian meditators developed the most systematic, elaborate systems of meditation known to any civilization, which is one of the reasons that most meditation teachers in the West today trace their roots back to either Hindu or Buddhist systems. The Chinese also produced sophisticated meditation systems, but, apart from Sino-Japanese forms of Buddhist meditation, have as yet failed to export these primarily esoteric, Taoist meditation practices to us. From Indian sources we hear of all kinds of 'yoga'. Essentially, meditation has no goal intrinsic to it. When you buy a car, it has no single destination, but you need to steer and operate it. By the same token, meditation is a means to reach whatever ends or goals you select for it. Indians used meditation to enhance action (*karma-yoga*), devotion (*bhakti-yoga*), physical self-discipline (*hatha-yoga*), ritual self-transcendence (*tantra-yoga*), spiritual self-realization (*rāja-yoga*), and so on. The psychology underlying all these uses of meditation basically focuses on the harnessing of the surface mind and the sensory-motor powers, which if left in their infantile state defeat the deep mind's ability to guide us through life and to help us achieve our deepest desires and finest goals.

I learned two important features of meditation from this early material on its psychology and metaphysics. First, that through meditation one can become aware of and begin to counteract the heritage of one's earliest years of experiencing the world, one's *karma*. Without confronting and reducing the powerful negative affect associated with events in our early years, and going beyond the infantile ways we achieved security and the satisfaction of our desires in childhood, we remain throughout our adult years mere children. Though physically adult, in personality and motivation we remain in the mental world of our infantile fantasies and gratification forms. We emphasize many kinds of maturation in growing up – physical, intellectual, social – but rarely consider the processes of achieving psychological maturity and personality maturation. Why should we consider meditation so irrelevant to learning, even in primary and secondary schools? Surely, the secularized, puritanical, Protestant tenor of our institutions today rejects such forms of self-introspection because it identifies them with the pride of self-intoxication and withdrawal from the realm of work and social responsibility. The result, all too often, brings 'successful' individuals to a point in life when nothing seems meaningful, and self-reliance fails. Or our new generations, cut loose from early twentieth-century morality, drift in limbo, recklessly vandalizing schools, adopting bizarre behaviour, defying authority, turning to crime and social deviance, destroying themselves, 'trying' everything, on the model of their parents, to 'feel better' or to 'forget', playing out the old approach-avoidance conflict inherent in the infantile psyche.

The second important feature of this early meditational psychology comes in its emphasis on ecstasy as a crucial experience in achieving maturity. In primitive and shamanistic cultures, institutionalized initiations brought individuals inescapably through an unforgettable ecstatic experience, usually before the age of sixteen and, furthermore, used ecstasy systematically to maintain the well-being of the group. After the advent of civilizations, ecstasy was no longer learned in regular initiatory experiences, but had to be sought, by those who felt the deep need to do so, in later life, often at the expense of secular and social ends. Though some seem natural ecstatics (like Socrates), others laboured for it extensively. Siddhārtha started at the age of twenty-nine and achieved Buddhahood only at thirty-six; Muhammad became ecstatic only around forty and Confucius, in one famous passage, described the entire course of self-transformation as requiring an ideal time of seventy years (see *Analects* Book 2, 4). Why is ecstasy so important to maturation? I think because it acquaints one with a basic, underlying two-sidedness of experience, counteracting the one-dimensionality which we ordinarily assume exhausts all the possibilities of reality and experience. Ecstatics place ultimate value on what they learn from this extraordinary experience. Whether one agrees or disagrees with what they learn, it seems vital that every human being should somehow experience it, and allow whatever new experiences it brings to provide the yeast of change which will direct that person to enhanced life and maturity. Unfortunately, we achieve ecstasy these days in the worst of ways: as by-products of accidents and near-death experiences, through hallucinogenic 'trips', through borderline cult experiences directed sometimes by near psychopathic personalities, or through such uncontrollable media as alcohol and drug abuse, UFO and snake-handling cults or rock and roll concerts, to name but a few of the many ways by which this deepest of human experiences can sometimes be produced.

One can see why these ways 'work', but shrinks from their consequences. They do produce ecstasy, but little can be learned from it without some kind of awareness, and some kind of expectation of significant results. Our culture steadfastly refuses to develop safe, institutionalized means for reaching ecstatic states. Certainly the churches have shirked their responsibility, caving in under pressures from a secularized scientific rationalism to support its blatantly profit-motivated industrialism. The schools consider ecstasy anathema, as they too seek to provide industry and service occupations with docile, immature workers and unthinking consumers habituated to self-indulgence. The entertainment media, once exclusively (in the hands of shamans and shamanesses) devoted to the ecstatic service of human well-being, rarely venture forth into realms beyond the surface forms of colour and sound, though much classical music (as Bach's) was composed to lead to ecstatic perception. People go to nature for rest and relaxation, but bring along the entire complement of paraphernalia, from kitchen cooking styles to television sets and mattressed beds, to their overcrowded camping grounds which mimic the cities from which they sought to escape. Many seek to travel, and thus to find alternative experience, but insulate themselves in luxury hotels and with luxurious entertainments, surely designed merely to perpetuate the boredom that set them to travelling in the first place.

In all this plethora of activity made possible by our growing cultural prosperity, I am surprised that meditation has not attracted more people to its door. Surely, one reason involves our prejudices that see it as an alien import, suitable for cultist freaks, hippies and monastics, but hardly acceptable to middle-class concerns or suited to the interests of the urban populations of our great cities. But meditation hardly can be called alien, if we would but look to our own cultural roots. As with other spiritual forms of culture, it merely has been deluged by contemporary scientific secular culture with its handmaidens of industrialism and consumerism driven by greed. Our most 'advanced' civilization on earth exhibits all the characteristics of self-indulgent infantilism, just as was argued by Jesus Christ, the Buddha, Confucius, and Socrates in their times. Have humans made progress in the last two thousand years, in terms of collective personality maturation?

Ox-Taming 4   *Catching the Ox To Turn It Round*

The ox is finally caught, but hardly tamed. The boy holds on, struggling to pull the bucking head round, trying to reverse its direction. The mean ox here begins to be changed, but clearly shows its fierce, powerfully obstinate, impetuous nature. It puts up a terrible struggle against the boy's firm determination, as can be expected, but now it is firmly grasped by the lead rope. The boy catches the ox to turn it round, to transform its nature, making ally of enemy. The great instrument of civilized humanity is domestication. In our survival in the physical realm, domesticated animals and plants released sufficient energy to build the cities and create the accumulated written knowledge and sciences of civilizations. On the spiritual side, a similar domestication would be the taming of the stubborn and mean inner ox.

The traditional commentary notes here that the ox nature must be subdued with unbending heart, subjecting it to severe discipline. Transforming the unruly self requires direct, sustained effort. This stage symbolizes the taking of new action to reverse prior modes of development and old outmoded motivational patterns. Having accepted responsibility, the ox-tamer must follow through with suitable actions which counteract prior forms, and bring new elements into the creation of the future. Something must break into the prior forged chains of karmic bondage or habitual self-preoccupation. One must at this point bring new motivations and insights into the knowledge one has of oneself, so as to make responsibility effective in bringing about more maturity. Religious ethical systems propose such changes, hoping to further spiritual maturity in strategies such as loving rather than hating. One must have new intentions to reverse the runaway ox. These arrest and begin to reverse its direction and nature.

That the ox resists with its intrinsic power shows how resistant to change are its features – the preoccupations, habits, needs and immature modes of adaptation it has evolved through time and experience. It is a victory in itself just to identify these, a victory celebrated in the previous scene. Now, at this stage, one must do something about it. These confrontations involve stormy times for the persona. One struggles to re-order one's personality, eliminating *karma*-producing motivations, facing the consequences – and bearing the full brunt – of unresolved conflicts from the past and of the painful immaturity of the being one has come to defend and protect from change.

If you as a gardener have ever contended with weeds, or moles, snails or other predators, or with too much or too little water, you know something of the struggle involved in such personality 'gardening'. The fruit grows very slowly. First the tender plants (new ways of acting) must survive every kind of danger, and many perish; then, as they mature, so do the weeds, which apparently have a far greater ability to survive. Then, just as the fruit ripens, moles, field animals and birds must be fended off. Finally, after months of back-breaking labour, perhaps there will be fruit enough to harvest, or perhaps another season will have to come to bring renewed struggle and greater experience and knowledge to bear on the work.

In the eight limbs or stages of yoga originated by Patañjali (see next chapter), the first, second and fourth, that is three of the first four preparatory stages, have names using noun derivatives (*yama*) of the Sanskrit verb √*yam*, which means 'to tame', especially applied to the breaking in of horses. By this action the charioteer is able to bring them, as much as it was formerly against their 'natural' will, to accept the harness and thus to put their power to use in pulling the chariot owner's vehicle. In this sense, in meditation one must be the trainer of one's own wild animal nature, made up largely of immature sensory-motor and surface mind expressions of our personality. Our animal instincts and infantile inclinations and desires, the sum total of our past actions, must be taken in hand, first turned round, and then led (as in the next picture) to become more amenable in following directions more in harmony with our maturing outlook on life and its goals. For as children, we have little ability to change, modify or often even understand what happens to us. Worse, during those very years, what happens to us deeply impresses itself on our tender psyches, even from the moment of conception in the womb. Still we must accept responsibility for the things which happened then, admitting that they have become a part of the deep structure of our nature, and then, like the ox at the end of the boy's tether, we must begin to turn their inappropriate, impetuous ways round. In the next picture, the boy will put the ox on the path of his new intentionality, thus leaving behind for ever the outmoded immaturity, on to which so many blindly hold until the final critical moment of death which no child ever can understand.

5

Stopping Mind's Waves with
Patañjali's Yoga Aphorisms

Around 200 AD, Patañjali, an otherwise unknown Sanskrit author, composed his aphorisms to create the *Yoga Canon*, or the *Yoga Sūtra*. Some centuries before, another writer, Pāṇini, had composed a similar collection of *sūtras*, or aphorisms, on grammar, and several centuries later the *sūtra* collection best known in the West, the *Kāma Sūtra*, was written. In each case, the author summarized in a highly systematic fashion the essence of the existing knowledge on each subject, making a statement of its basic features so they could be taught more easily to the next generation; the *sūtra* collection became the fountainhead for all future teaching of the subject, and many later works about it. Pāṇini's grammatical *sūtras* literally founded the Sanskrit language as it was to be for two millennia, and as it still is today. The *Kāma Sūtra* stated the normative doctrines about the pursuit of love, one of the orthodox Hindu goals of life, and many with the leisure to do so followed its outline to the amorous art. Similarly, Patañjali drew from the vast experience and literature which had grown up in India for nearly a thousand years, condensed it into a printed text which extends no further than sixteen pages, and thus set for centuries to follow, the 'science of yoga'.

Sanskrit *sūtra* writers took their task of systematizing a vast store of knowledge very seriously. Their style condensed knowledge into short *sūtras* designed to be memorized by students and then elaborated in commentaries, oral and written, by the great yoga masters. Each *sūtra* consisted of as few syllables as possible, so to enhance their mnemonic function. Thus, when reading *sūtras* translated into English, you should always have a commentary to accompany the text. Unfortunately, the available translations today do not have objective commentaries, usually having been translated by an author who has a sectarian stance to support; thus the translation is as much an interpretation, its commentary designed to support the translator's particular interpretation. One popular (and the most available) translation of Patañjali's *Yoga Sūtras*, called *How to Know God* (Mentor Books), betrays its slant in the title alone. The entire text devotes only six aphorisms to God as one among the many alternative meditative objects (I.23–8), but the title of this translation proclaims this to be the sole subject of the work. Actually, yogic meditation can be used to know anything, so to call a translation of Patañjali's work the way to know God does not fairly represent its original. Although it too has an interpretative bias, I prefer, from among the translations available, I. K. Taimni's *The Science of Yoga* (Wheaton, Ill.: Theosophical Publishing House, 1961), because the commentary, though taking a theosophical slant throughout, is fairly detailed and complete, and the translation relatively free from error. If you decide to read Patañjali's *sūtras*, I think you should also try reading a classical Indian commentary, translated years ago by Harvard philosophy professor James Haughton Woods, called *The Yoga-System of Patañjali* (now reprinted by Delhi's Motilal Banarsidass) which includes the works of the two best known Sanskrit commentators.

If you were to study yoga in ancient India, your master would first ask you to memorize these *sūtras*. When you have done so, he would have chosen in his lectures to expound at great length on various of the verses, as he saw fit. Then, as you practised yoga, your own experience would have rounded out your understanding of these, the aphorisms that were intended to guide you into the world, fascinating but at the outset strange, of meditative experience. What a grand way, indeed, of learning, combining guidance, by word and letter, and empirical, experiential feedback. What can we learn from Patañjali? In a sense, this work began the scientific study of meditation, and thus deserves as much attention and respect, to cite a parallel case, as does Freud's in contemporary therapeutic psychology. Surely, it stated for the many Indian yogic traditions the key ideas available at the summarizing point of the development of meditation in Indian civilization. By that token it presents to us an overview, or map, of potential meditative realities and ways of understanding these, the first of its kind, and the only one yet attempted. Perhaps in fifty years, someone from either West or East will write a new 'Yoga Sūtra' encompassing the knowledge and experience we are now just beginning to accumulate, but until then Patañjali's work stands out head and shoulders above anything else on the subject.

I call Patañjali's *sūtras* the 'first scientific literature' on meditation, not in the sense that we use the term 'science', but in the ancient Indian sense to denote a systematic account, precise and in summary form, of a body of accumulated knowledge. From our point of view, we may consider some of the things Patañjali records to be culturally biased opinion and interpretation about meditation, and not as 'objective' as we would like it to be. We should remember that from his point of view, this was as close as he could come to the truth about yoga, and so merits our closest attention. I will translate and comment on some of the high points of his work, and invite you to read it in complete form on your own.

In the text as we have it today, Patañjali divided his work into four chapters; the fourth seems to be a later addition, dealing with abstruse philosophical matters, so I will not comment on it. Then, apparently, the first chapter is self-contained, to which was joined Chapters 2 and 3, which obviously belong together. The first chapter is on *samādhi*, which I translate as 'ecstasy', though etymologically it means more literally 'to bring or put together completely'. This refers to the action of meditation in uniting all the mental and sensory-motor functions of consciousness into a single ecstatic awareness, the goal of meditation. As is proper, in the first *sūtras*, Patañjali provides an overall definition of yoga:

I.1: Now the instruction on yoga.

I.2: Yoga is the (temporary) stoppage (*nirodha*) of the waves (*vṛtti*) of the mind (*citta*).

What a beautiful definition; in Sanskrit, it consists of only nine syllables! Meditation means the arresting or calming (the word is related to *nirvāṇa*, the Buddhist word for stopping becoming) of the mind's waves, that is, of the mind's ordinary contents, which Patañjali lists as the ways of correct sensory and rational knowing, error, fantasy, dream and memory. When these five disappear, albeit temporarily, from consciousness, through meditative arrest the resultant state is ecstasy. In the absence of the ordinary waves, anything else that occurs is allowed to occupy consciousness including, I would say, experiences of extra-sensory perception, profound feeling and intuition, and psychokinetic (i.e. non-motor) activity at a distance; these and the more objectless meditative states characterized by non-discursivity, a powerful, overwhelming quiet, and light. Ecstasy is the state which results from stopping the usual five types of waves.

In the current climate of thought, claims that our minds could shift gears from 'wave' or thought-filled consciousness to 'non-wave' thoughtless consciousness does not strike many as being either viable or laudable. We associate thought with the only way to think or know, leaving behind other possible modes of awareness. Yet many people use these other modes in conjunction with their thought processes, as scientists and mathematicians do, when they appeal to intuition to discover truths, or when artists seek reality in the creative process; and everyone uses non-thought modes of awareness to some extent, in conjunction with thought, as when for example we recognize a person's face but cannot remember the person's name (see Carl Sagan's lucid discussion in Chapter 7 of *The Dragons of Eden*). Patañjali says that meditation proposes to maximize temporarily in *samādhi* this alternative functioning of consciousness. He continues (I.12–16) by saying that the stoppage of the mind's ordinary waves comes from repeated practice of meditation and from an attitude of not grasping on to objects through the sensory-motor powers.

The next section of this first chapter focuses on the means of attaining the stoppage of mind's waves, or *samādhi*. Basically, some have it by birth (I.19), and I have met a few such people who seem to have resisted the processes which cause us to lose the primal calm of our innocent consciousness. But for the majority, the rest of us, Patañjali recommends either a very Buddhist-sounding quintuple technique or devotion to the divine:

I.20 Stoppage for others comes from confidence (in teacher and technique), (exerting) strength, (by practising) mindfulness (*smṛti*), meditation and (cultivating) ecstatic insight (*prajñā*).

I.23 Or it results from devotional meditation on the Divine.

I.29 From these comes consciousness focused within, and elimination of obstacles (to meditative ecstasy).

Buddhist meditation masters and I think Patañjali himself used the means of the first verse while Hinduism (as in the *Gītā*) favoured the theistic meditation recommended in the second; both resulted in a consciousness turned away from the sensory-motor domination of the surface mind, temporarily immersed in meditative ecstasy. The practice of taking a meditative object on which to focus consciousness (I.32) results in the elimination of obstacles to the new mode of ecstatic consciousness, a 'purifying or calming of mind' (I.33) which Patañjali says can be achieved in any number of ways (which he lists from I.33 to I.39).

Finally, he distinguishes several grades or types of *samādhi*, and concludes with a description of the fruits of this meditative practice, including the following:

I.47 On attaining proficiency in (the highest form of) ecstasy, inner spiritual calm arises.

I.48 In that state, ecstatic insight (*prajñā*) yields truth.

The classical commentator (see Woods, p. 93) says this in the phrase, 'inner spiritual calm arises':

When this clearness arises in the super-reflective balanced-state, then the yogin gains the internal undisturbed calm, (that is to say) the vision by the flash of insight which does not pass successively through the serial order (of the usual process of experience) and which has as its intended-object the thing as it really is. And in this sense it has been said, 'As the man who has climbed the crag sees those upon the plain below, so the man of insight who had risen to the undisturbed calm of insight, himself escaped from pain, beholds all creatures in their pain.'

The person in meditative ecstasy or *samādhi* passes by the ordinary self (and its cares), seeing everything from another point of view, temporarily withdrawn from the animal-like struggle of the sensory-motor mechanism efforts to survive. From that selfless perspective, no 'dis-ease' ('pain' in the commentator's passage) afflicts one's knowing, for it transcends or passes by, for the duration of the ecstasy, the limited, narrow viewpoint of the survival oriented self, thus providing non-mediated 'immediate' knowledge of the objects it cognizes 'as they really are.' Mystics claim such an ability to know something, as they say, by becoming one with it, that is, not in the usual form of perceiver/act of perception/perceived. This latter pertains to sensory-type experiences, while ecstatic knowing, being freed from the limited senses, knows without the mediation of such a mechanism and the motivational distortions that modify its perception of truth. The Sanskrit term for truth, which Patañjali deliberately used in his verse 48, is '*ṛta*', an archaic word from the *Ṛg*

Veda for the underlying powerful order which produces all phenomena. The meditator, he thus claims, can come into contact with the source of reality, knowing it 'as it really is', without perceptual or motivational distortion. This indeed claims much for the ability of meditative ecstasy to know, something we Westerners have been remarkably unwilling to admit, convinced as we are of the superiority, or the unique ability of scientific, sensory means of achieving reliable information about reality.

Until recently, I have always considered such claims to special 'truth' to be some kind of religious appeal to doctrinal superiority, distrustful because different religions claimed the same absoluteness for radically different doctrines. I have softened my view now, after having to accept convincing descriptions of alternative ways of knowing. Scientific rationalism proposes one means of knowing reality; it assumes that knowing through the senses acquaints us with the shape of reality as it is, but short-sightedly denies that any other access can be had to how reality is. Divination, however, considers itself to be in touch with reality as well, not through the senses, but rather through procedures which science would consider random (and hence meaningless). Psychics have demonstrated another means of knowing reality. Edgar Cayce, the most fully documented developed psychic of this century, knew specifics at great distances while in deep trance, which Patañjali would call *samādhi*. He could spot a medicine hidden on a back shelf hundreds of miles away which had been completely forgotten even by the pharmacist. In *samādhi* he successfully diagnosed illnesses of all kinds and led thousands of people back to health when doctors relying on empirical, sensory means had thrown up their hands in failure, or had made incorrect diagnoses. These kinds of alternative approaches to knowing reality make me reconsider our cultural presupposition that we can reliably know reality only through the senses (the Indo-European heritage that 'seeing is believing'), as scientific rationalism claims. We should experiment with Patañjali's *samādhi*-state, to see whether as I now suspect there is something more than religious absolutism in his claim that ecstasy gives direct, immediate access to truth with a capital T.

I find it interesting that Patañjali should claim that 'truth' can come from an entirely non-sensory, inner (hence 'spiritual') calm. That, too, contradicts our usual procedures for arriving at reliable conclusions about the world, since I rarely see people sitting down to enter into a calm inner state to understand something better. More likely, they fidget nervously, trying to 'figure things out' (the commercial metaphor betrays anxiety), or, even worse, feud and fight without trying to calm anything – mind, breath, or body – obstinately, regardlessly, considering themselves right. But finally our very survival depends on correct information about the reality of challenging or problematic situations, making the espousal of multiple approaches to solutions much more appealing than unidimensional ones such as the absolutisms of either science or religion. Meditation, doctrinally neutral but non-sensory, hence truly an alternative way to knowing by sensory means, should gain more attention as we try to become more sophisticated in our appreciation of the human mind and its role in our adjusting to reality.

Patañjali devotes his entire second chapter to meditation's psychology and the first five stages of the progression to *samādhi*. The third chapter elaborates the last three rungs of the ladder to *samādhi*, then turns to discuss what happens in that state. To a large extent, these two chapters treat psychological features of the meditative experience, thus providing information of great value to anyone interested in meditation today. In his second chapter Patañjali begins with a psychological analysis of the 'afflictions' (*kleśa*) of mind which keep it from ecstasy. These, he says all derive from ignorance, our fundamental error in thinking that we can find completely satisfying experiences based only on transient material things (2.4 and 5). Out of this ignorance come self-preoccupation (2.6), approach and avoidance conflicts

(2.7 and 8) and excessive or neurotic attachment to life (2.9). In verse 11, Patañjali says that these afflictions can be cleared out of one's psyche through meditation (*dhyāna*), but that, if they are not, they will continue to result in the burdens of *karma* (2.12). Actions result in consequences either pleasurable or afflicting (2.13), depending on the nature of their intention; but in truth, Patañjali says (2.15), those who see with insight conclude that experience dependent on material satisfaction alone always fails to satisfy. This results from both the inherent changeability of the physical world and the fluctuations of the mind which depends on the physical to achieve happiness, as well as from residual karmic influences from prior actions (2.15; pages of commentary follow this verse). But, Patañjali counters, 'Future dis-ease is avoidable' (2.16; betraying the optimism of Indian psychology). The cause of 'dis-ease' (2.17) derives from the 'conjunction' or interaction of the more naturally calm depths of the psyche, through the surface mind and the sensory motor apparatus, with the inherently instable, changing, material world, whose paradoxical purpose it is to make the deep mind realize that it can be happy without seeking beyond itself for satisfaction (2.18). The problem, in Patañjali's analysis, derives from the deep mind's embroilment and entanglement in sensory experience through habituated (ox-like) surface mind and sensory-motor functionings. This eventuates in the false notion that the mind is capable of being a possessor of possessions (2.23), which is utter ignorance, the one being immaterial (spirit), the other material (matter).

It would take considerable space to do justice to, let alone evaluate, Patañjali's psychology, along with the metaphysics of matter/spirit distinctions which it assumes. I am in my own mind unsure just how to evaluate the metaphysics involved; as I grow older, it looks more and more attractive, though I was taught in college to be suspicious of such dualities, and still cling to the evolutionary notion, that mind is an evolute of nature, so that it cannot be metaphysically other than matter, but somehow is continuous with it. I think that Patañjali's psychology does properly focus on how mind becomes excessively attached to, hence dependent on, instable physical conditions for its happiness, and that his optimistic vision of *karma* and its unravelling should be taken to heart. It seems obvious that mind does become entangled in experience of material things, particularly during our early years. The idea that possessing *x*, *y*, or *z* can lead to deep, personal happiness, whether a thing, or a person, or some intangible like fame or honour, must result in instable happiness experiences at best, since things, persons and intangibles change with regularity so predictable that only fools think them eternal. We all experience the frustration which arises from our dashed expectations of enduring happiness, but no one looks around to find another source of the kind of happiness we apparently instinctually seek, the kind which somehow lasts and survives the world's incessant changing. Patañjali, as also Chuang Tzu, Lame Deer and many mystics, say that such happiness lies within 'that closed room' (the deep mind) which one reaches through meditation and the changes it brings in one's psyche.

The remainder of this second chapter, appropriately called the Chapter on the Means of Realization (*sādhana*), Patañjali devotes to the first five of the eight 'limbs' or 'rungs' of the ladder of yoga practice which culminates in *samādhi*. Patañjali's greatest claim to fame involves his formulation of this ordered series of stages whereby meditation produces ecstasy. Theoretically, one must master each stage before going on to the next. The first five prepare the way for the cultivation of inner ecstasy, the subject of the last three which come at the head of Chapter 3. In Sanskrit, these first five are: *yama*; *niyama*; *āsana*; *prāṇāyāma*; and *pratyāhāra*.

Both the first two limbs use noun derivatives of the verb √*yam*, which means 'to restrain' or 'to discipline'; one might translate *yama* as 'the restraints', and *niyama* 'the disciplines'. In both cases, they seek to 'correct one's nature' (recalling Camus' statement, 'I make rules to correct my nature') in preparation for meditative experience. A friend once explained to me that, in meditation, we enter into some very sensitive, very powerful states, so if we have not cleared negative personality features out of our nature, they can emerge in these states to be acted upon with disastrous consequences for self and other. So, under the *yama* category (2.30), Patañjali recommends the cultivation of non-violence, truthfulness, abstention from stealing and sexual misconduct (or continence, however you interpret this), and not coveting possessions. The *niyama* category (2.32) includes self-purification, achieving contentment, self-discipline, study (especially of meditation) and setting up the Divine (or spirit) as primary. The commentaries spell out what these meant in ancient Indian morality, which may differ from your own, but they make the point clearly enough. These steps prepare the psyche as ploughing prepares a field for planting; without them, however one interprets them to fit the context of one's own sense of right and wrong, the practice which follows could produce unwanted outcomes.

The third limb, *āsana*, describes meditative seating posture, which Patañjali defines simply as any position which is steady and pleasing (2.46) and which results from a relaxing of physical effort and a similar balancing of mind (2.47). In later days, the *haṭha*-yoga system elaborated many *āsanas*, commonly taught in the West today, but Patañjali mentions none of this. Presumably, the meditation master would have taught his favourite way of achieving a steady, relaxed, pleasant (i.e. no painful or negative feedback), mentally comfortable position, which in India probably would have meant sitting somehow with one's legs crossed. Since this involves tendons stretched since birth for Indians, but not for Westerners, I think that Patañjali never meant us to do the same! Since Tzu-ch'i of South Wall adopted his culturally conditioned way for relaxing (sat, leaning on his armrest) to enter ecstasy, quite different from Patañjali's, I conclude this to be a matter of a civilization's conventions, so we should feel free to do as our culture does, namely to sit in a chair or with a backrest to meditate. However one sits for meditation, one need not wrench one's legs into any awkward position, but find some way of sitting which will eliminate any awareness of sitting, as such awareness produces only more mind waves. Then Patañjali says (2.48) the dualities (pain/pleasure, hot/cold, etc.), the occasions for approach-avoidance conflicts, will not afflict the meditator. Unfortunately, Zen teachers insist on their (to us culturally awkward) lotus seating posture to help break the ox, which I prefer insight to accomplish.

As body in meditation is the first to be calmed, breath comes second, followed by the all-important mind. Thus, Patañjali next (2.49) recommends that one should practise breath control, *prāṇāyāma* (*prāṇa*, breath, *āyāma*, control). The classical commentary on the verses dealing with this breath control is quite short, indicating that, again, the master's direct, oral teaching contains the instructions on how to carry this out. Such controlled breathing, he says, results (2.52) in rendering powerless the *karma* which covers the deep mind, and prepares the mind for meditative concentration (2.53). Almost everyone who teaches meditation instructs in a favourite form of breathing, especially to counteract our usual highly constrained, shallow, nervous breathing forms. By taking deep breaths, and by inhaling and exhaling in controlled, regular ways, one can induce consciousness changes essential to the next developments in meditative discipline.

The last two *sūtras* (2.54 and 55) of this second chapter Patañjali devotes to *pratyāhāra*, or the withdrawing of the sensory-motor powers from their objects in the world. Once one has sat down to meditate, and initiated deep breathing, one must cut the last line of sensory-motor distraction by withdrawing these powers, albeit temporarily, from their familiar world. Mind in this action reverses its orientation, merging back into itself rather than looking outward on to the panorama of sensory experience. From this comes the control necessary for the discipline, coming in the last three stages, of the inner functions of consciousness.

Patañjali identified the subject of his third chapter as the results or attainments (*vibhūti*) achieved through meditation, thinking they were but twofold. The first attainments to arise out of ecstasy he clearly identified as what we would call psychic powers or purely psychic experiences (since no sensory-motor activity is involved whatsoever), something which scientifically-minded and literal-leaning observers and interpreters have blithely dismissed as yogic 'fantasy'. It behoves us to suspend such valuations and listen to what Patañjali and other meditators tell us of their experiences, regardless of how we may later evaluate their ability to discern what we think to be real (the term 'reality' being, in the context of cross-cultural comparison, merely the honor-ific designation of what individual cultures have defined as their 'real'). Secondly, Patañjali considered the ultimate attainment made possible through meditation to be utter transcendence of the realm of existence, for psychic powers merely led one into the subtle forms of matter, while meditative ecstasy, he thought, could allow escape from the material altogether. This, naturally, is the goal which the Indian world view posited as the highest attainable by any person, the realization that deep within the mind one can make contact with that which transcends both matter and mind (itself only a subtle form of matter).

Patañjali claims that these two types of meditative attain-ment come from mastery of the last three limbs of meditative practice, which as a unit he calls concentration (*samyama*). They consist of *dhāraṇā*, fixation of the mind on the medita-tive object (3.1), *dhyāna*, keeping the mind on the meditative object (3.2) and *samādhi*, the ecstasy which results from these two activities (3.3). The prior stages have all prepared for this crucial set of three. The body quieted, the breath regulated, and the senses controlled, creates an innerness of conscious-ness which then can (not to speak lightly of a difficult activity) be focused on the meditative object. Buddhists (and Patañjali, in 3.11) define *samādhi* as 'one-pointedness of mind', which reveals the primary means of achieving ecstasy.

The mind, once withdrawn from its ordinary sensory experience and attending to sensory and motor activity functions, wells up with all kinds of inner contents, worries, stray thoughts, recurrences of attention to sensory input (sounds, smells, etc.) or even flights of imagination or fantasy; or, as many know, it descends into sleep. To counteract all these forms of distraction, meditators take an object to fix the mind upon (*dhāraṇā*), and then extend that fixing over time (*dhyāna*), until a remarkable transformation of consciousness occurs, when it becomes ecstatic (*samādhi*). A great diversity of objects exists to be used, and meditators have ingeniously invented a whole inventory of meditative objects, some visual (pictures, diagrams, imagined scenes), some having to do with bodily processes (such as counting the breaths, or feeling the breath at the nostril) and so forth.

Patañjali's definition of *samādhi* shows he thought it to be a state of non-mediated, psychic identification with the meditative object, consciousness being emptied of its usual forms or waves:

3.3. *Samādhi* is just this (*dhāraṇā* and *dhyāna*), when only the thing (meditative object) radiates (in consciousness), which is as it were devoid of its usual content.

To this, the classical commentator can only add (Woods, pp. 204–5):

When the contemplation only shines forth (in consciousness) in the form of the Object-to-be-contemplated and (so) is, as it were, empty of itself, in so far as it becomes identical with the presented idea as such, then, by fusing (itself) with the nature of the Object-to-be-contemplated, it is said to be *samādhi*.

What should we make of this definition? Surely, we would know more by experiencing the state, but from the definition alone, I again come upon the idea expressed so often by mystics that ecstasy brings one to experience things (or, in the process of reaching the ecstasy to experience the chosen meditative object) in a way where consciousness fuses with

111

them, becomes one with their reality. In sensory perception, or motor activity, we exist and think of ourselves as subject of the perception or action, and what we see or hold as the object. Not so in ecstasy. Rather, the subject and object no longer necessarily remain distinct in all respects. This must be why psychics consider ecstatic consciousness to be independent of the limitations of space and time, since the experience, not being mediated by sensory-motor functions, cognizes in a different mode, free to merge deeply with a contemplated object, or experience, or reality, whether distant or near, in the past, or in the present (and some say, even in the future), eyes open or closed. But now, frankly, we have gone beyond my own experience, and I must ask you, as I ask myself, to try to experience it for ourselves.

However we interpret Patañjali's definition of *samādhi* it remains nevertheless a very real human experience, possible for us all to achieve. This no one can deny. Further, it is not the end in itself, but a means to which one may join any number of possible ends. Meditation as a means to our ends constitutes a largely unknown land to Westerners, so we should remain open to all its possibilities lest we prematurely close the doors to its revelations before we even give ourselves a chance to experience them. In our own cultural past, not to mention oriental spiritual traditions, generations of mystics have affirmed ecstasy and earnestly sought for ways of knowing their highest object (be it God or Nature) not through the mediating senses but in the immediate participation in it, like knowing by feeling. What Patañjali's definition urges us to do is to experiment with non-sensory means of knowing and non-motor ways of acting, and to investigate the possibilities of achieving states of inner contentment not dependent, as most of our pleasures are these days, on the abundance of things and diversions we have been able to create from the raw materials nature provides. To neglect these possibilities in this the most remarkable age of human discovery, when we have history hanging in the nuclear balance, seems as foolish and wasteful as any act could be.

Well then, to what ends did Patañjali think his *samādhi* could be put? Strangely enough, he described only two, though I think many others can be suggested (see Chapter 8). Even more strangely, he devoted the longest portion, a full thirty-five *sūtras* of this third chapter, to an exhaustive listing of the psychic powers, or *siddhis*. The majority of Indian religious texts, especially those of the Buddhists, contain many warnings about these powers, since after all they, like sensory-motor skills, can quite well bind a person to the material world, not conducing to transcendence of it. Patañjali himself, after listing them all, does not make such a warning, but says only that one can renounce these *siddhis* to attain total transcendence (*kaivalya*) of the world. However, this goal and warnings against meditative psychic powers stem from the peculiar valuations on the world which the Indian world view made, and need not turn our attention away from Patañjali's fascinating map of the psychic powers which derive from *samādhi*. By 'psychic' in this context I mean non-sensory, non-motor abilities to know and to act, which apparently operate by subtle physical mechanisms (such as those described by quantum physics) which we little understand today. Also, we should realize that this list of powers pertained to the mental horizons and concerns of Indians two thousand years ago, while we may want to describe different ways of using *samādhi's* psychic powers.

What, then, did Patañjali give as the potentials of the human psyche in ecstatic states? I list them, with little explanation, for often even the commentaries give little help in interpreting what they mean: knowledge of the past and the future; understanding of the sounds of all beings; knowledge of previous incarnations; knowledge of the mind of another; ability to become invisible to the eye (inaudible to the ear, and so forth, for the other senses); knowledge of impending death; development of the strength of one's feelings (of friendliness, compassion, and joy); attainment of animal (i.e. superhuman) strengths; knowledge of the infinitesimal, the hidden and the distant (i.e. beyond the reach of the senses); knowledge of the cosmos and the configurations of the stars and their movements; knowledge of the body's anatomy; the ability to suspend hunger and thirst; to achieve absolute stability; to see perfected beings (in the subtle realm); to understand all creation by psychic intuition; the ability to understand the mind and (its distinction from) Spirit, and, from this, psychic sensory knowledge (at a distance); the ability of mind to enter another's body (to possess it); the capability of rising up (the commentator says at death) and of escaping water, mud, thorns, etc.; achievement of psychic (or gastric?) blazing; supernatural hearing; flight through the ether; uncovering of the deep psyche; control over the five material elements, resulting in ability to become infinitesimal; to levitate; to become massive; to extend one's reach over great distances; to go unrestrained through matter; to master all physical objects, to rule over them and be able to direct them; to have a perfect body and not allow the powers of material elements to obstruct its functions; control of the sense and motor powers, and, from that, psychic speed unmediated by any instrument, and control of the source (of matter's creation); and, finally, omnipotence (3.16–50).

Now that is quite a catalogue of psychic powers. The first temptation to resist in interpreting them involves the notion that any of these 'physically' occur; because they do not, at least as we usually think of sensory-motor physical reality. Rather, these pertain to the psyche's knowing and doing; the body, in ecstasy, remains as if lifeless, sometimes for quite long periods of time. Since we acquaint ourselves so little with the psyche which acts and knows independently of the senses and powers of action, no wonder we experience great difficulty imagining what indeed Patañjali describes in his list, and how it could possibly be anything but fantasy. We have little to fall back upon, in terms of experiences attested by others of our civilization, that would illumine Patañjali's summary report of at least a thousand years of Indian meditatively induced psychic experience. This does not diminish it one bit, but only points to the poverty of our own experience and development. Still, what can one say to a determined sceptic about the possibility of such 'powers' being anything but self-deluded fantasy? I can well imagine someone saying, 'Listen. You know, those people in ancient times had really very little physical power and control over their world, such as we have today, so, to compensate, they fantasized them; but their reports are pure bunkum.'

Well, I wonder. We may have to change our ideas to accommodate this psychic modality, so that it may be included in the mind's inherent set of possibilities. Perhaps two parallel realms of reality exist side by side (as Indic ontological speculation went), the gross physical realm, known by our senses and acted upon in and through our motor powers; then, corresponding to it, a subtle realm, known to the psychic powers of perception and action as another underlying or materially invisible reality dimension which scientists have not yet discovered and described (lacking proper instruments). If materialists do not want to admit materiality to an unperceivable subtle reality, the problem of accounting for the psychic could be resolved epistemologically by postulating that we know the same reality from two points of view or states of mind, one sensory, which perceives the gross physical features of things, the other psychic, a form of consciousness with very different characteristics which, being unmediated by any ordinary sensory-motor apparatus, has a much less limited reach and ability. All this may sound occultish, which it has been, but here I propose serious emendations to our usual descriptions of consciousness. Either of these avenues would admit psychic perceptions and activities into the range of possibilities attributed to consciousness, at least so that we may gather evidence supposedly documenting the phenomena for adequate analysis. Furthermore, as an implication of this more precise delimitation of the map allowing for both types of knowledge and action, it follows that to comment from the point of view of the sensory-motor perspective on the impossibility of the psychic seems inappropriate, just as it would be for a contemporary ecstatic to deny the reality of fossil fuel, land, sea, and air transportation, electricity, nuclear energy and reaching the moon. Meditators seem quite willing to admit that we fly in aeroplanes so sceptics should similarly open themselves to the case for psychic powers, albeit to something their myopic science has denied out of hand.

I myself have believed the full gamut of alternative positions on the psychic powers, from that of a complete sceptic to an enthusiastic embracer of their possibility. As an undergraduate student, I was steeped in scepticism by my philosophy professors, while as a graduate student I began to read accounts, in Buddhist texts, of the psychic powers. I grilled my teachers for their interpretations, which involved ways of 'psychologizing' the powers, interpreting them as purely psychological experiences without any evidence or ability to know or act with a validity we could confirm by sensory-motor inspection of the world. But then I graduated again, this time from graduate studies, and kept finding the accounts of psychic powers in the records of civilizations other than our own. I steadfastly avoided reports of occultists in our own day, as occultism here is not the issue.

Lately, after reading biographies of Edgar Cayce, like Joseph Millard's *Edgar Cayce*, some of my scepticism has drained away (notice that I am older now, too); I am quite willing to admit the possibility of these powers, because Cayce, though quite ordinary, had access to them in deep ecstasy, to know of and act in the realms of subtle physical reality. He convincingly used them to know the future, to describe the present far distant from himself, to read letters not yet received, to predict wheat futures and horse race outcomes (he did this only once, as it made him sick), to communicate with the dead, and to diagnose the sick and lead them, often through procedures deemed ridiculous by our established doctors, to health and well-being.

Look again at Patañjali's list of the *siddhis*. Cayce used

many of them in his work of helping others, including psychic knowledge of the past and future (he made predictions about the Wall Street crash of 1929 and the Second World War, and could tell people about their past without ever having met them); he conveyed information about many people's past incarnations (including his own); he was able to know what others were thinking (even in his waking state, as his assistants experienced many times); he was able psychically to travel anywhere in the world and to know at a distance specific details (hence was invisible); he knew when he was to die; he had ability to influence his own body psychically (like the power of suspending hunger and thirst); he could see perfected beings on other planes of existence; he understood by psychic intuition; and so on and so forth. This indicates to me that if one remarkable individual reliably had these powers, apparently from birth (Patañjali admitted this possibility), then, first, we should give them much greater credence, and, secondly, we should feel free (not foolish) to try to develop them, as Cayce said everyone could do. The greatest limitation to the human psyche, to be sure, is disbelief in its potentialities; this limitation keeps us in bondage far more than any chains or any prison could. Our own incredulity, not their impossibility, blocks us from realizing the possibilities of these psychic powers.

The second end to which Patañjali thought ecstasy could be put required going one step beyond the aforementioned psychic powers. The result of this disinterestedness he termed *kaivalya*, 'uniqueness', 'aloneness', which describes the 'oneness' of one's metaphysical unity with Spirit. In the metaphysics which Patañjali espoused, everything is either matter (*prakṛti*), even the subtlest forms of the deep mind, or Spirit (*puruṣa*), that which by its essence utterly transcends and is absolutely distinct from matter. *Kaivalya* occurs when the mind purifies itself to such an extent that though still subtle matter, it approximates and thus can know Spirit, having divested itself of all hindrances to Spiritual awareness and any attachment to materiality (3.51 and 56). I think

Chuang Tzu similarly identified this experience (see Watson, p. 79, ' . . . he could see his own aloneness . . . ') of being pure Spirit, of realizing that, in Spirit, a person can go completely beyond the material world. For Patañjali, and for that matter, much of Indian metaphysics and Plato in the Western tradition, ignorance results from failing to distinguish between our material and spiritual natures, thinking that somehow the material has spiritual features or content, while in reality they must be distinct. When, in ecstasy, a person realizes that non-contingent, non-material identity or freedom can only be in the spiritual, a sudden realization occurs which frees one from all delusion, that one is pauper, poet, policeman, prince, priest, or president; or that a lump of sod or a nugget of gold are in any way of greater or lesser value.

Patañjali clearly considers that the experience of absolute transcendence of matter is the supreme goal to which meditation can be put. Meditative ecstasy somehow can go so far beyond our ordinary experience that it conveys the impression that some radically other state of being has been reached, one so utterly distinct from our usual modes of existing as to require a whole new way of describing (or not describing) it. In part from these sorts of experiences comes everything, from accounts of other worlds to metaphysics, which founds its philosophical discipline on the notion that the surface reality our senses know does not exhaust the real, but conceals its underlying features. Similarly, our usual experiences, even our experiences of psychic powers, so enmesh themselves in matter that they too exist merely on the surface of things. Somehow this experience of transcendence indelibly imprints itself on the consciousness of human beings, wherever they have lived. Lame Deer experienced that mystery, call it Soul or Self or Spirit, during his initiatory vision, as did the ancient soma cult priests, who thought it their portion of immortality, and as did Chuang Tzu, who identified his 'aloneness' as allowing him to 'do away with past and present' and to 'enter where there is no life and no death' (Watson, p. 79). Even Stone Age peoples shared this intuition, prompting them to lavish great care over the dead, preparing them innocently for life after death by providing them with grave goods, food and clothing for the world beyond and performing special funeral rites to release and guide the ghost or spirit of the dead to that world, the residence of the ancestors.

I find great difficulty in deciding how to interpret transcendence during our age in which, as Jung wrote in one of his last letters, the human psyche still exists in its adolescence. He wrote, 'The human mind, still an adolescent boy, will sacrifice everything for a new gadget but will carefully refrain from a look into himself (*C. G. Jung, Letters,* edited by Gerhard Adler, Princeton: Princeton University Press, 1975, Vol. 2, p. 609). I struggle with this in myself, wondering whether I have fallen victim to the facile immaturity of scientific rationalism which proclaims that all will be well for the human family as soon as we provide each of its children with sufficient material satisfactions to quell their restless, increasing needs. Do conceptions of spiritual transcendence merely express consciousness's reluctance to contemplate its own termination, thus producing the compensatory fantasy of a transcendence which survives death? Metaphysically, *kaivalya* transcends death because Spirit includes no material components, thus cannot change, decay, or die. However we evaluate the metaphysics of transcendence, the experience, it seems to me, remains real, and a valid goal for our efforts to expand consciousness to include all its possible modes.

Since so many persons have sought the transcendence experienced in ecstatic states regardless of their differing philosophical interpretations of it, I think it best to interpret the experience rather than bother over its vexing metaphysics. What difference would it make, in my life, to have such experience, meditatively achieved as Patañjali recommends? Taimni (*The Science of Yoga*, p. 373) gives this interpretation which accords with the Indian tradition:

[A person] may remain within the realm of *Prakṛti* [matter] and yet be in full realization of his Eternal nature. From this *Sūtra* it is clear that *Kaivalya* does not necessarily mean the separation of *Puruṣa* [Spirit] and *Prakṛti*. If the *Sattva* [the light component of matter] has been purified to the necessary extent the *Puruṣa* can function through *Prakṛti* in full realization of his Real nature, and always [be] free. Thus, it is the realization of his *Svarūpa* [essential nature] in the fullest degree which is the characteristic and indispensable condition of *Kaivalya* and not the separation from *Prakṛti*. The 'isolation' of *Kaivalya* is thus subjective and not necessarily objective. The vehicles that have been built up and perfected by him in the realm of *Prakṛti* can then be used by him for any kind of work without egoism and without any illusions. Such are the perfected men of humanity, the Adepts of Yoga who are the masters of this Sacred Science and who guide humanity in its progress towards perfection.

In the last sentence, Taimni's theosophical interpretation comes out clearly, but he does provide a sense which I consider to be more in accord with meditative meanings. He claims that when the material mind is purified, the *sattva*, or light component of matter, pervades consciousness allowing the *puruṣa* – the spiritual point of view or essence – to experience through *prakṛti* – the material mind – but without attachment. *Kaivalya* as a state of consciousness must indicate some kind of spiritual realization which allows one to observe and experience phenomena in the world from a point of view or perspective other than that adopted since archaic childhood. This new orientation expresses features of maturity, a loving acceptance of others, empathy, responsibility and a sense of self-presence or autonomy. Both Taimni and I are resisting the cave in the Himālayas interpretation of yoga and meditation. Perhaps indeed *kaivalya* meant for Patañjali the total withdrawal (which Eliade calls 'enstasy', to indicate the Hindu predilection for innerness) from the material world into a psychological essence for long hours. Some yoga texts report such inner-withdrawn type ecstasies, but that is just what some Indic meditators used yoga to produce. All peak experiences bear the imprint of their culture, however individual the experience is in each case. For our day, I agree with Taimni that the reason for meditatively calming the mind (the ox) is to make it better fit for mature (spiritual) experience and action in the world. Such a person uses 'the vehicles that have been built up and perfected by him in the realm of *Prakṛti*', a process which I have been tracing in the ox-taming series, so that these 'can then be used by him for any kind of work without egoism and without any illusions'. These ideas approximate a description of spiritual maturity. The maturity recognizes the other and responds responsibly, while the spiritual provides inner direction and the proper sense of things. *Kaivalya* to me means the experience of innerness I reach in meditation which though not being deliberately cultivated at all times never deserts consciousness, becoming a kind of 'spirit' which directs and gives insight to life.

Ecstasies, and the deeply inner states pointed to in such terms as *kaivalya*, transform one's understanding of self and world and provide the model for becoming non-dependent (i.e. 'alone', autonomous) on materiality for one's sense of wisdom and well-being. Maturity shifts the focus from things to values like inner calm and freedom from inquietude. *Kaivalya*-type experiences identify or make known another source of happiness, insubstantial yet just as real, a spirit rather than a thing which gives pleasure. As persons mature spiritually, they acquire a new hierarchy of values not excluding time and energy allotted to activities quite unlike those of wholly unspiritual secularized individuals. One becomes more loving and accepting of others, enjoying oneself and them beyond the needs and forms created by our immaturity. Though all meditators, yogis in the Himālayas or Zen folk in Euroamerica's urban sprawl, must remain in the world, those who mature experience the world's necessary ups and downs in a much more satisfying, adaptive manner. Because matter and conditions always change, our experience of that material world prompts us to be tied to its undulations, thinking some experiences 'good' (the 'ups') and others 'bad' (the 'downs'). This is a necessary consequence of attachment to and dependency on material sources of pleasure, since those sources always change. The ecstatic who experiences *kaivalya* suddenly has an alternative point of view from which to evaluate attachment. The state allows a certain distance from which to handle everything delicately, so that in any situation one has a sense of an inner balance or centre of awareness enabling one to steer through the external fluctuations without crippling anxiety or disappointment.

I do not know how Patañjali would respond to my commentary on his *kaivalya* goal; and again here, experience would be more instructive than additional words. We do need to understand the ancient sources both accurately in comparison to their language and context (historical, cultural) and against some experience of our own, if they are to become vivid and alive. The meditative maturity of the ox-tamer derives from the changes induced in the ox. No longer do animal habits and needs run away from the boy, once the taming intervenes. The alternative viewpoint of the *kaivalya* experience provides the perspective; then, in the downs, the opportunity for gathering and building strength calls, and during the ups, the opportunity for being thankful, humble and helpful to others arises. Quite apart from the other side-effects and benefits of practising meditation, if it does lead to *kaivalya*-ecstasies, it can serve to develop spirituality. As I look back on Patañjali's aphorisms I feel tremendous admiration for the succinct summary he constructed using the raw materials of the early Indic meditative traditions. The *Sūtras* make Patañjali one of the originators of the meditator's art, and a giant in the human spiritual tradition (though we know nothing of his personal life). Nearly two thousand years ago this person, undoubtedly a meditator, concisely formulated meditation as a human potential. He saw that human consciousness could cultivate *samādhi* to achieve its *siddhis* (powers) and its *kaivalya* (its release from materiality), and whatever other ends these can serve in the name of life. No one in any other civilization came to such a formulation, though many, as the next chapter shows, experienced the states he described, making them 'mystics'.

Ox-Taming 5   *Leading the Ox On the Path*

Now this episode introduces quite new elements into the boy's progress. In a significant reversal the boy leads the ox, not the other way round. This is the proper turning point, in the fifth of ten stages. Now the boy, though he must keep a firm hand on the tether, is thoroughly in command. Behaviour and attitudes have changed considerably, and though the ox can still get 'out of hand', the boy only has to guard against the recurrence of old patterns, and the temporary reversals when repeated effort still fails to keep it within the proper bounds. The tether symbolizes the boy's guarded attitude, as well as his imparting a whole new mode of being to the ox. He leads the ox to the point when it can act as his vehicle or power in the world.

At this stage in self-transformation, one needs to provide one's inherent mental powers and potentialities with strong direction, cultivating the desired new forms of behaviour. The time of counteracting old preoccupations by strong discipline cedes here to a subtler form of discipline which provides the ox new directions, qualitative transformations to bring forth the serving and supporting powers of the ox-animal mind. Leading the ox symbolizes radically reshaping one's personality and motivations through discipline, values and proper choice. In this way, one shapes one's powers to come more into accord with one's adult, responsible consciousness. Here the future's promise gives birth to spiritual aspiration, for the boy holds the ox's lead, and both their futures. Ordinarily, people try to extend infantile gratification and adaptation patterns into their adult world only sooner or later to find them increasingly inappropriate or intolerable, since they import frustration and anxiety into the mental economy.

I experience this phase in the self-transformation process often. After observing an immature pattern of behaviour or reaction, I consciously resolve to alter and change the complex. I have changed many facets of my *karma* systematically in this fashion. For example, at one point in my life I noticed while driving an automobile that I was trying to go too quickly, and once or twice nearly hit a pedestrian or another car. Each time I forced myself to observe how I had led myself into the compromising, irresponsible form of driving. Then, I made resolve to change the behaviour pattern (driving too quickly) and persevered until I became a more skilled, slower driver. I constantly try to import into the stream of my development new maturing and spiritualizing features, trying them out to discover the realms of mental possibility open to my consciousness.

The ox's domestication promises the power it puts at our disposal. Once tamed, the ox can serve the boy. Yet most people consciously and deliberately must tame that ox, not having done so in their early years. In those years, parents, environment, experience and our predispositions made us what we became. We had little control over these factors developing us, becoming diverse persons, the majority of us to some degree or another acquiring mean or unruly ox natures. To become a new person, everyone at some time in life must take tether in hand to confront the ox. Before, in youth, we had developed little of the mind's reflective self-examination and responsibility, but once maturationally we enter adulthood, we have the chance to re-create and tame that prior acquired selfhood to make a spiritually mature alternative.

6

Meditative Mysticism in World Literature

A good university library contains thousands of books and articles on mysticism, but few of these even mention meditation. I am surprised at this, since the mystics of any traditional civilization comprise, more than any other group, its meditators. In part, this omission derives from the habit of mystics to talk not about the meditative experiences which brought on their ecstasies, but about their products, whether it be what they learned, or the poetry which resulted from their ecstatic states, or how they had been transformed by them. The mystic is civilization's shaman; the mystic inherits the shaman's ecstasy, along with the special access it gives to certain aspects of reality. Just as in shamanistic cultures shamans specialize in ecstasy, in civilizations, mystics stand apart as the persons who enter into the special realm of the mind which so often heals and transforms not only themselves, but also those around them.

To realize how universal in human civilizations meditative ecstasy is, we need to focus on the records which mystics have left in world literature. No civilized literature that I know of does not record some mystic's experiences or teachings, though many civilizations, including our own, have shunned or persecuted their mystics unmercifully. Mystics tend to rip through the fabric of conventional forms of action and understanding, putting themselves at odds with their society's established interests which by nature seek to protect ordinary position and prestige against extraordinary inspiration and insight. Mystics make poor soldiers, miserable administrators and followers, and impossible ecclesiastics. Most mystics do not choose to be so, but rather seem to be born with an excess of sensitivity which immediately distinguishes them from their fellow human beings. While most people agree on things, the mystic sees other dimensions of reality, such as burning bushes or a grandmother who died years ago. Consequently, they walk to different drummers, little understood by others. The mystics of a civilization are its spiritual geniuses. Just as in a given population, several out of millions will excel in mathematics or music or language skills, several will have extremely deep feelings, involving intense internal longings or spontaneous visionary experiences which torment them until they come to integrate these into their lives, despite the lack of understanding evinced by all others about them. Like shamans, mystics journey to 'other worlds', see things in the forest which others fail to notice, hear voices which others label fantasy, and respond to longings which others may feel, but which they feel less intensely, and thus do not seek to fulfil.

A mystic, then, begins with a special nature or genetic potentiality which needs to be responded to, or dire consequences, at times including severe illness or insanity, can result. Mystics frequent what William Blake called the 'desolate market', where, deprived of the comforts of the usual human satisfactions, they experience inner calls and experiences which lead them far deeper into the human psyche than most people are ever capable of journeying. When I wonder about how civilized peoples have used meditation, or have been forced, by their mystical natures, unwittingly into it, I see that it is the mystics who have meditated and thus to them we must turn for further information about meditation and the states of experience which it brings.

I will take three mystics to survey what I consider to be the testimony of these, our civilized shamans. One is a near contemporary, Henry David Thoreau. Another, Japan's most famous *haiku* poet, Matsuo Bashō ('Banana Tree') comes from far beyond our cultural boundaries. Finally, Teresa of Avila brings us back to our own religious tradition in the autobiographical account of her 'interior castle' experiences.

Many people today think of Thoreau as a misfit, someone who did not have the courage or strength to 'grow up' and take his proper responsible place in society. He rarely held a steady job, lived with others for most of his life, and read a lot; further, he found himself strongly attracted to Hindu literature, then arriving for the first time from the Orient. Yet, when reading *Walden*, his masterly mythological auto-biography describing his experiment of living in his desolate market on the edge of commonplace society, I begin to wonder. Two recent books have sensitized me to the mysti-cal aspects of *Walden*: Charles R. Anderson's *The Magic Circle of Walden*, and Stanley Cavell's *The Senses of Walden*; both give excellent reading and great insight into Thoreau's classic. I would rather understand Thoreau's experience as deriving from his mystic's temperament, and the experience he tries to convey to readers as those of a person who naturally knew how to meditate and found himself again and again attracted to meditative ecstasy. I shall examine several relevant passages from *Walden* to support my contention that Thoreau was one of the foremost mystic-meditators.

As most Western mystics, Thoreau does not tell us how he meditates, but we know that he deliberately enters into meditative states from what he describes of his activities beside the pond. 'This is a delicious evening,' he writes at the beginning of his chapter on solitude, 'when the whole body is one sense, and imbibes delight through every pore. I go and come with a strange liberty in Nature, a part of herself' (*Walden and Civil Disobedience*, edited by Sherman Paul, Boston: Houghton Mifflin Company, 1957, p. 89). Here Thoreau tells us that his senses all focus on one object, as if being one bodily sense. His meditative object? Nature, her 'delicious evening' which Thoreau feels himself a part of in mystic merging. Is what Thoreau is doing meditation? I think so, since although he has his eyes open, and may be sitting or walking, he has reduced his sensory input to one focus, the delicious evening, centring all his senses on it, to unify his consciousness through this meditative object. He has removed distractions, is unusually alert, and seeks self-transcending ecstasy.

Another passage in which Thoreau describes his Walden Pond meditation practice comes at the beginning of the previous chapter on sounds:

> I did not read books the first summer; I hoed beans. Nay, I often did better than this. There were times when I could not afford to sacrifice the bloom of the present moment to any work, whether of the head or hands. I love a broad margin to my life. Sometimes, in a summer morning, having taken my accustomed bath, I sat in my sunny doorway from sunrise till noon, rapt in revery ...

(Thoreau, *Walden*, p. 77)

Can anyone doubt, reading these words, that Thoreau is meditating? He has separated himself from ordinary concerns and activity, entering the special state of meditative selflessness. In the lines which follow he observes how ecstasy involves an experience of timelessness, and immense learning for the self (using the metaphor of corn growing at night, which my father once told me you can hear and see when the weather is hot):

> ... I sat in my sunny doorway from sunrise till noon, rapt in a revery, amidst the pines and hickories and sumachs, in undisturbed solitude and stillness, while the birds sang around or flitted noiseless through the house, until by the sun falling in at my west window, or the noise of some traveller's wagon on the distant highway, I was reminded of the lapse of time. I grew in those seasons like corn in the night, and they were far better than any work of the hands would have been. They were not time subtracted from my life, but so much over and above my usual allowance. I realized what the Orientals mean by contemplation and the forsaking of works. For the most part, I minded not how the hours went. The day advanced as if to light some work of mine; it was morning, and lo, now it is evening, and nothing memorable is accomplished. Instead of

singing like the birds, I silently smiled at my incessant good fortune.

(*Walden*, pp. 77–8)

Thoreau's exuberant taking of Nature as his meditative object reminds me to remark that what we have seen as the means of meditation – withdrawing the senses from the sensory flow and making the body immobile, for example – should not be taken as its end but merely as its possible means. Indeed, Thoreau at this point in his life, far from needing to withdraw his senses, could allow them to be the avenues of his meditative stillness, for he had unified them with his quiet, deeper psyche, producing his 'incessant good fortune'. The experience of well-being is meditation's goal, whatever its means, along with entering into that quiet transcending of the ordinary self's anxiety (its apathies, fears, angers) such that though nothing 'memorable' be accomplished, it leads to an ineffable felicity prized over all else.

Probably the most important matter concerning meditation about which we can learn from these meditative mystics comes from their description of mystic selflessness. Meditation can be used to lift oneself outside one's 'self', to become a spectator, as Thoreau calls it, of life's flow. This experience of self-transcendence brings both learning and freeing; one learns to be less anxious about self and world, and one frees oneself from bonds which lead, eventually but inexorably, to death in all its forms. Observe how Thoreau describes this ecstatic selflessness:

With thinking we may be beside ourselves in a sane sense. By a conscious effort of the mind we can stand aloof from actions and their consequences; and all things, good and bad, go by us like a torrent.

(*Walden*, p. 93)

To be '*beside ourselves* in a sane sense' is Thoreau's witty way of describing ecstasy. Interestingly, he says this state can be attained 'by a conscious effort of the mind', by which he means by disciplined meditation (see Anderson, *Magic Circle*,

130

p. 91). Although, as we just saw, Thoreau says he enjoyed being a part of nature, he continues his description of meditative selflessness by paradoxically claiming, 'We are not wholly involved in Nature', explaining:

I may be either the drift-wood in the stream, or Indra in the sky looking down on it. I *may* be affected by a theatrical exhibition; on the other hand, I *may not* be affected by an actual event which appears to concern me much more. I only know myself as a human entity; the scene, so to speak, of thoughts and affections; and am sensible of a certain doubleness by which I can stand as remote from myself as from another. However intense my experience, I am conscious of the presence and criticism of a part of me, which, as it were, is not a part of me, but spectator, sharing no experience, but taking note of it; and that is no more I than it is you. When the play, it may be the tragedy, of life is over, the spectator goes his way.

(Walden, p. 93)

Thoreau describes our being as a 'doubleness' either drift-wood in the stream of life or the god who creates that life, looking down upon it from above. This observing, other part, the 'spectator', is the psyche's ecstatic point of view on the physical world, including the body, reached through meditative transformation of awareness.

No wonder then, in his conclusion to *Walden*, Thoreau recommends to his readers that they 'travel farther than all travellers' by exploring themselves, their own 'higher latitudes'; '. . . be a Columbus to whole new continents and worlds within you, opening new channels, not of trade, but of thought' (p. 219). The inner journey, not some globe-trotting odyssey, holds the greatest value for us:

One hastens to Southern Africa to chase the giraffe; but surely that is not the game he would be after. How long, pray, would a man hunt giraffes if he could? Snipes and woodcocks also may afford rare sport; but I trust it would be nobler game to shoot one's self.

(Walden, p. 218)

Thoreau uses the hunting metaphor to describe the 'oxherding' he prescribes, 'shooting one's self', indicating the transcending of one's anxious, animal-like self for an experience of ecstatic spectator consciousness.

Judging by what he wrote at the beginning of his first travel sketch, this must also have been Matsuo Bashō's goal (see Bashō, *The Narrow Road to the Deep North and Other Travel Sketches*, translated by Nobuyuki Yuasa, Baltimore: Penguin, 1966). For, by then, in his fortieth year, he was surely Japan's most famous *haiku* poet, loved by all, supported by his disciples, but a man of frail health who could well have spent the remainder of his days in the secure comfort of the little hermitage which his disciples had provided him in the countryside outskirts of old Tokyo. But Bashō felt deeply the mystic's longing for ecstasy; so, on a fateful day at the beginning of autumn, he wandered forth from his home, much as the Buddha had from his palace, in search of Thoreau's 'nobler game'. In Donald Keene's literal translation, he reported these thoughts at the beginning of his last decade of life which he spent entirely in intermittent travelling:

When I set out on my journey of a thousand leagues, I packed no provisions for the road. I clung to the staff of that pilgrim of old who, it is said, 'entered the realm of no-mind under the moon after midnight.'

> (*Landscapes And Portraits*, Tokyo:
> Kodanasha International Ltd., 1971, p. 96)

By packing no provisions, Bashō meant that he intended to put himself at the mercy of his wandering road's changes, all the better to 'shoot one's self' which becomes anxious over the night's lodging or the next meal, once hunger and loneliness set in. To specify his goal, he quotes from the words of an old Chinese wanderer, who achieved meditative ecstasy or the 'realm of no-(ordinary) mind', through a similar cutting of the habituated self away from its familiar surroundings. As a mystic, Bashō, though successful in the world's terms, found no final satisfaction in the refuge his students provided him, at last surrendering himself to the dangers and difficulties of travelling along the roads and byways of medieval Japan. The road, in his mind, symbolized life itself, the constant changes it brings; it was to be his teacher of transitoriness, the mentor which was to bring him into contact with his spectator-self, for 'sweet are the uses of adversity'.

Life started out well enough for Bashō, who became the study-mate of a prince, with whom he learned the fundamentals of writing poetry and to appreciate beauty. But, when they were both still in their twenties, the prince died, leaving Bashō painfully aware of life's and death's enigmas. For some years he accepted various occupations, throwing himself as the young do into the world of sensation. In his middle thirties, though, he found these held no final satisfaction. At thirty-six, he retired to the Banana Hermitage provided by his disciples, beginning to practise disciplined meditation as a lay disciple with a Zen master named Bucchō. Far from deserting poetry for meditation at this time, Bashō combined the two, using meditation to deepen his psyche's awareness of the world's truth and thus to produce the finer, deeper poetry whose words have stirred the hearts of generations of Japanese. A disciple of Bashō, who was present when his finest *haiku* was composed, shows how he used meditation to further his creativity:

This poem was written by our master on a spring day. He was sitting in his riverside house in Edo [Tokyo], bending his ears to the soft cooing of a pigeon in the quiet rain [thus his meditative object is auditory]. There was a mild wind in the air, and one or two petals of cherry blossom were falling gently to the ground. It was the kind of day you often have in late March – so perfect that you want it to last forever. Now and then in the garden was heard the sound of frogs jumping into the water. Our master was deeply immersed in meditation, but finally he came out with the second half of the poem ...

(Yuasa, *Narrow Road*, p. 32)

Bashō achieved his deep immersion in meditation primarily

by focusing through his auditory sense on the sounds around him; the poem which resulted used the image of the sound of frogs jumping into the old pond to communicate his deep intuition into reality. The point for us to note here is that Bashō meditated to create poetry, and by this creation, through shaping and integrating the materials of experience into the aesthetic object, himself achieved an inner integration of psyche, allowing him to know and to communicate his truth to others. That millions of Japanese know his frog poem by heart attests to its ability to communicate such an apprehension of reality.

When Bashō sought to explain his meditation practice, he wrote:

Go to the pine if you want to learn about the pine, or to the bamboo if you want to learn about the bamboo. And in doing so, you must leave your subjective preoccupation with yourself. Otherwise you impose yourself on the object and do not learn. Your poetry issues of its own accord when you and the object have become one – when you have plunged deep enough into the object to see something like a hidden glimmering there. However well phrased your poetry may be, if your feeling is not natural – if the object and yourself are separate – then your poetry is not true poetry but merely your subjective counterfeit.

(Yuasa, *Narrow Road*, p. 33)

Bashō proposes that meditation involves learning about the meditative object by becoming one with it; otherwise, one remains locked in one's 'subjective preoccupation', which colours every supposed perception of reality with the tint of one's infantile needs and adult anxieties. Bashō used poetry as the vehicle of his self-transformation, for to the extent that he succeeded in writing 'natural' poetry, he had successfully transcended his subjectively preoccupied self and truly participated in the 'real'. A student's commentary on this passage makes these observations:

The Master said: 'Learn about a pine tree from a pine tree, and

134

about a bamboo plant from a bamboo plant.' *What he meant was that a poet should detach the mind from his own personal self* [my italics]. Nevertheless some poets interpret the word 'learn' in their own ways and never really 'learn'. For 'learn' means to enter into the object, perceive its delicate life and feel its feelings, whereupon a poem forms itself. A lucid description of the object is not enough; unless the poem contains feelings which have spontaneously emerged from the object, it will show the object and the poet's self as two separate entities, making it impossible to attain a true poetic sentiment. The poem will be artificial, for it is composed by the poet's personal self.

> (Makoto Ueda, *Matsuo Bashō*, New York: Twayne Publishers, Inc., 1970, pp. 167–8)

Probably the most important achievement possible for us in life is to 'learn' in this, Bashō's, sense. He means not to 'learn' about some such object or phenomenon as mathematics, or a language or business, but to have selfless experiences of the other, other persons, and the world in which we find ourselves living. 'A lucid description of the object is not enough,' the commentator explains; our 'knowledge' must include 'feelings which have spontaneously emerged from the object', not from our fears and angers or anxious self, but from our spectator self's direct participation in the being of the real. Humans all too often project their self-preoccupied consciousness on to others or the world, therefore only experiencing the artificiality, the subjective image of their projection. The righting of this image comes when meditation induces self-transcendence, or when one surrenders to the reality of the aesthetic object, or when, in the accepting, neutral environment created by the therapist, one no longer needs to cling to the self's immaturity.

Throughout the last ten years of his life, Bashō sought for experiences and places which would inspire 'a profound sense of meditation in my heart' so as to forget his fretful feelings (Yuasa, p. 67). Though he returned to his hermitage from travels long and short, he remained until his death without a permanent place to stay, exposing himself at every opportunity to change as well as enjoying the traveller's bounty, the comforts of human companionship. He undertook his wandering journeys at the expense of considerable personal hardship, eventually dying of a traveller's disease while on yet another journey, in his fifty-first year. When I look back on his life, I see that it fits a model familiar in the history of meditative mysticism. Jesus Christ, the Buddha, Muhammad, and many of us, too, grow up without experiencing much ecstasy during adolescence, then after immersing ourselves in the world of adult responsibility and action, come to a time – often around the age of thirty-five or forty – when what we have done is just not enough. Something within this mortal frame, which Bashō calls (p. 71) a 'wind-swept spirit for lack of a better name', never finds peace with itself during those years, as one is 'always wavering between doubts of one kind and another'. Then, some special intervention must occur, wherein one takes responsibility for one's life and begins to build one's self-knowledge on deeper foundations. Then, as Bashō shows, meditation's time has arrived.

In much the same way, St Teresa of Avila found her life's solace in meditative ecstasy. Much like Bashō, early in adult life she experienced the shock of losing someone, her mother, to death. She really did not recover from this loss until, by mystically participating in the reality of her Lord, Jesus Christ, her consciousness achieved wholeness. In the interim, she joined a monastic order, suffered years of physical illness, and struggled with her growing mastery of mystical awareness through prayerful, meditative approaches to the divine. Retrospectively, she described the ideal course of meditative self-transformation in her famous *Interior Castle* (translated by E. Allison Peers, New York: Image Books, 1961) which she addressed to the sisters in her order, instructing them in the stages of meditation as surely as Patañjali did in his eight limbs leading to *samādhi*.

Teresa used the image of an interior castle to describe the stages of approach to ecstasy; just as one could travel through the many rooms of a large castle to reach its centre, so too, in Teresa's image, one travels inward through many rooms, seven sets of 'mansions' in all, to the room where the divine dwells. She composed a marvellous literary masterpiece on the basis of this image, a fitting meditative object itself for her sisters, though today, I find students dismayed by her self-demeaning manner. Teresa did not write this work for us, nor did she write in the liberated twentieth century. She wrote, during the horrible Inquisition, for women of her own time who lived in very narrowly defined limits.

Using the figure of the seven sets of mansions, Teresa describes how, through prayer and meditation (p. 31), the innermost room may be reached. On the outside of the castle is the material world of temptation and bondage to the superficial, recalling Indian meditative psychology. Entering the first three or four mansions involves becoming less and less attached to this external reality. Teresa analyses the initial problem of bondage to externals thus:

... there are souls so infirm and so accustomed to busying themselves with outside affairs that nothing can be done for them, and it seems as though they are incapable of entering within themselves at all. So accustomed have they grown to living all the time with the reptiles and other creatures to be found in the outer court of the castle that they have almost become like them ...

(*Interior Castle*, p. 31)

This describes Teresa's notion of our life of 'exile' from inner spirituality, for which she gives, in medical and biblical metaphor, a very poor prognosis unless people take responsibility for their condition:

Unless they strive to realize their miserable condition and to remedy it, they will be turned into pillars of salt for not looking within themselves, just as Lot's wife was because she looked back.

Like Indian psychology too, she identifies the senses as the primary means of bondage to the external ('How distracted

are the senses ... And the faculties, which are their governors
and butlers and stewards – how blind they are and how
ill-controlled!', p. 35), analysing psychological bondage
much as Indian meditation masters did:

It is as if one were to enter a place flooded by sunlight with his eyes
so full of dust that he could hardly open them. The room itself is
light enough, but he cannot enjoy the light because he is prevented
from doing so by these wild beasts and animals, which force him to
close his eyes to everything but themselves. This seems to me to be
the condition of a soul which, though not in a bad state, is so
completely absorbed in things of the world and so deeply
immersed, as I have said in possessions or honours or business, that,
although as a matter of fact it would like to gaze at the castle and
enjoy its beauty, it is prevented from doing so, and seems quite
unable to free itself from all these impediments. Everyone, however who wishes to enter the second Mansions, will be well
advised, as far as his state of life permits, to try to put aside all
unnecessary affairs and business.

(*Interior Castle*, p. 41)

Many people today object to Teresa's metaphors for the
world outside the interior castle; she calls the 'things of the
world' 'vipers' (p. 48) and 'devils' (p. 49). I think these
dramatic terms are intended to be therapeutic, to cure people
of their habits and attachments by inducing disgust for their
objects. Even to give up the minor but extremely self-
destructive habit of smoking cigarettes, apparently people
have to undertake extreme measures – how much more all
the other attractions that distract the attention from the inner
light? Her metaphor allows a telling observation: 'For, if a
man is bitten by a viper, his whole body is poisoned and
swells up; and so it is in his case, and yet we take no care of
ourselves' (p. 49). As the counteractive to the world's poison,
she recommends cultivation of self knowledge, humility,
detachment, the classic means of regaining the self lost or too
entangled in experience or to the world's ways, all these
promoted through prayer and meditation. At one point, in

the section on the fourth mansions (p. 76), she says (and note the journey metaphor), '... if you would progress a long way on this road and ascend to the Mansions of your desire, the important thing is not to think much, but to love much; do, then, whatever most arouses you to love'. Surely, love constitutes a powerful meditative object, one which indeed can transform consciousness, maturing and deepening it to include the inner reaches of the human psyche.

Teresa's most famous passages describe her ecstasies, the products of her meditative discipline. Already in the section on the fifth mansions, she describes the transformation which occurs in consciousness:

Here we are all asleep, and fast asleep, to the things of the world, and to ourselves (in fact, for the short time that the condition lasts, the soul is without consciousness and has no power to think, even though it may desire to do so). There is no need now for it to devise any method of suspending thought. [How close this sentence is to Patañjali's definition of the goal of meditation!] ... in fact, it has completely died to the world so that it may live more fully in God. This is a delectable death, a snatching of the soul from all the activities which it can perform while it is in the body; a death full of delight, for, in order to come closer to God, the soul appears to have withdrawn so far from the body that I do not know if it has still life enough to be able to breathe.

(*Interior Castle*, pp. 97–8)

Teresa symbolizes becoming ecstatic as a 'delectable death' which recalls the happy sense of dying, withdrawing from immaturity and anxiety to be 'reborn', recognizing the other, spectator self. When the faculties and senses are thus 'dead', she says, 'the soul has never before been so fully awake to the things of God or had such light or such knowledge of His Majesty' (p. 150). Teresa's ecstasy has all the elements of meditative selflessness:

For when he means to enrapture this soul, it loses its power of breathing, with the result that, although its other senses sometimes

139

remain active a little longer, it cannot possibly speak. At other times it loses all its powers at once, and the hands and the body grow so cold that the body seems no longer to have a soul – sometimes it even seems doubtful if there is any breath in the body. This lasts only for a short time ...

(Interior Castle, p. 155)

Such changes in breathing and body metabolism generally accompany those transformations, but not as ends in themselves; rather they occur parallel to the effects which take place in the person's consciousness. Teresa stresses the learning which occurs in the meditative ecstasy, as all ecstatics do. Notice too, in both the following passages from the section on the sixth mansions, how she adopts the metaphor of mystic flight to describe her experience:

Turning now to this sudden transport of the spirit, it may be said to be of such a kind that the soul really seems to have left the body ... He [then] feels as if he has been in another world, very different from this in which we live, and has been shown a fresh light there ... In a single instant he is taught so many things all at once ... This is not an intellectual, but an imaginary vision, which is seen with the eyes of the soul very much more clearly than we can ordinarily see things with the eyes of the body ...

(Interior Castle, p. 160)

And,

Really, I hardly know what I am saying; but it is a fact that, as quickly as a bullet leaves a gun when the trigger is pulled, there begins within the soul a flight (I know no other name to give it) which, though no sound is made, is so clearly a movement that it cannot possibly be due to fancy. When the soul, as far as it can understand, is right outside itself, great things are revealed to it; and, when it returns to itself, it finds that it has reaped very great advantages and it has such contempt for earthly things that, in comparison with those it has seen, they seem like dirt to it.

(Interior Castle, p. 161)

Although obviously not everyone learns the same as Teresa

did in ecstasy, these passages emphasize that mystics use ecstasy to enter their inner stillness, there to learn. Our loss, to my mind, comes from our failure to recognize that meditative states can bring this same learning experience to anyone who accepts the regular discipline required to master the processes leading to ecstasy. In the past, our mystics have included only those so endowed with sensitivities that they could hardly escape their paradoxical fortune. From the perspective we have on meditation and ecstasy today, I think many more of us can gain access to ecstasy, adding its realms to our being. Traditionally, many religious systems, particularly monotheistic ones, have attributed the achieving of ecstasy to a special act of God's grace (this includes polytheistic Hinduism), but the evidence offered in some Buddhist schools, Taoism and Patañjali leads me to believe that one can just as well achieve it through, and as a product of, one's own efforts. One must learn to swim, and no one can learn to swim for you: the creative energies of the divine may be enlisted to help you swim, but you must learn it. So too with ecstasy.

Reflecting on Thoreau, Teresa and Bashō makes me remember a dream I had recurrently during my childhood, but which I no longer have. I would enter a house to wander through it, finding in an inner room a door through the wall that led not to another ordinary room, but to what I experienced as a secret room, or a special negative space inside the positive. I marvelled there at the mystery of that room, as much as Teresa did her Interior Castle, thought of it as 'incessant good fortune', like Thoreau, and detected there Bashō's 'hidden glimmering'. Then the dream would change, as I became frightened of a dark presence, down in the deepest corner of the room, so the dream ended each time in fear. From the perspective of later life, this dream gave me an experience of the spiritual, but warned me, by showing me my fright, that I would have to tame that ox nature, which takes fright in continuing contact with the spirit or spiritual level of the inner room. Meditators in the past have shown that such experiences can be induced meditatively. Patañjali and Teresa agree that this can be achieved through stages of successive development, and that the resulting experience bears truth. Teresa, now quoting from the section on the seventh mansions, says that the experience brings strength and healing: 'It is quite certain that, with the strength it has gained, the soul comes to the help of all who are in the Castle, and, indeed, succours the body itself' (p. 230). This belies the familiar contention that meditators withdraw from the world, indulge themselves, and do not make active, significant contributions to humankind. In fact, just the opposite occurs; they return to others struggling to enter the castle's interior, mature, powerful, and able to help. Further, their relation to the world changes, gaining in personal well-being, as Teresa notes: 'Once you have been shown how to enjoy this Castle, you will find rest in everything, even in the things which most try you, and you will cherish a hope of returning to it which nobody can take from you' (p. 234).

Though mystical ecstasy is but one of many ends which a person can serve through meditation, meditators who practise conscientiously will have these realms of experience opened to them. In the past, we have made too much of ecstasy's inaccessibility. It became associated with cloister and monastic, with wild desert renegades and heretics. This unfortunate misunderstanding results in tremendous distrust among most people today of mysticism, even to the extent that a prominent mystic, Agehananda Bharati, predicts in his book *The Light At The Center: Context and Pretext of Modern Mysticism* (Santa Barbara: Ross-Erikson, 1976), that mystics will soon suffer a new 'powerful Inquisition' which will decimate their numbers (see pp. 202–3). Perhaps Bharati's predicted 'criminal period for mysticism' will never come because no one can prevent any person from meditating, which is all one needs to do to enter meditative ecstasies. The unfortunate outcome of such misunderstandings and tensions within our civilization will involve not Inquisitions aimed against mystics, but simply that many people will continue to mystify mysticism, never thinking it may be an experience possible for themselves too.

Ox-Taming 6 *Riding the Ox Home*

What a wonderful scene this is, after the stressful prior moments in the transformation. Finally the boy, relaxed and playing his flute, rides on his ox, 'on the way back home'. The taming has put the ox's full force at the boy's disposal. His hands, no longer needed for the tether, can turn to the practice of other arts; here, he plays the flute. The ox prepares to cross by bridge over the waters without the boy needing to worry. One level of the training is over, inititating another, more advanced towards the goal of mental cultivation. He no longer attends excessively to the ox's behaviour, but has assimilated it to his new exploration of the flute, along with all the landscape around him. By not having to attend to an unruly ox, he can shift attention elsewhere, beginning his return home (the place of rest and contentment when being is natural and spontaneous and genuine).

The boy's previous efforts now bear fruit. He exists harmoniously with the ox, so no longer needs to lead or struggle with it. In fact, he has appropriated the ox's great power, to ride on it. Being in such harmony with his ox-nature frees him for other pursuits, symbolized by the flute. He turns his nature to the cultivation of skills more closely allied to spirit, as music is. The flute reminds me of Socrates, who, as Plato's *Phaedo* reports, had a recurrent dream during his last days telling him to compose and practise music, saying, 'Thou shouldst make more music', meaning that he needed before death to balance his rational side with more emotional or spiritual development. This the boy does, taking up his flute. Music symbolizes cultivating the art of feeling, and the deeper means of knowing. So the boy deepens his awareness of his nature in taking up the flute, following the way 'back home', that is, to his original voice, to his own sense of place in the total cosmos.

In spiritual traditions 'home' symbolizes returning to being able to hear the voice of one's inner self which our conscious mind has hidden among its self-deceptions, its rationalizations, its anxieties and its infantile adaptations to the world. The agony or struggle involves the battles one fights with oneself to overcome these obstacles to self-knowledge. When victorious we feel at home wherever we are, because that feeling arises from within, not as a result of a temporary successful orchestration of external circumstances. The inner self possesses its own inalienable happiness, not dependent on externals or conditions. Successful adaptation means managing one's challenges as best one can and then carrying on, realizing that all that can be done has been done. My own dream of the inner room brought me years ago an unforgettable presentiment of how as an adult I must train the ox of my being, so that I can appropriate its powers for my ride home, to the central inner mystery of my own being. Jung once told Aniela Jaffé (recorded in *Memories, Dreams, Reflections,* New York: Pantheon Books, 1973, p. 196):

During those years [of confrontation with the unconscious, as he approached his forties] ... I began to understand that the goal of psychic development is the self. There is no linear evolution; there is only a circumambulation of the self.

The self dwells in the centre of our being, the secret, inner room of the house we build, made of our genetics and ancestry, our experiences, experiments, mistakes, choices, predilections and acceptance or avoidance of responsibilities. Finally, as we begin to assume conscious life, at whatever age, we realize that we create the ox nature by our thoughts, actions done or postponed. The inner voice, however, cannot totally be silenced, for it speaks in dreams, in conscience and when released by fits of uncontrol (anger, regret). Conversely, the person who engages the ox to tame it eventually hears the still small voice of the inner sense, which knows what true home is.

I remember once seeing a Tibetan version of the ox-taming pictures which used an elephant (because Tibetan *glan* means both elephant and ox) to symbolize the great power of our sensory and motor faculties. Just as the boy, the monk in that series captured and disciplined an elephant until he could ride it, thus appropriating its great power. All people have such power as symbolized in the ox or the elephant, were they but to train and use it. In this picture, a major transformation has begun, for here, the boy no longer needs to occupy himself with the ox's unruly nature. He exists as a partner with the ox; I even imagine the ox to be listening to the boy's flute, incorporating its soothing notes and harmonizing with the boy's growing realization of spirit. The days when these developments happen are indeed joyous and fulfilling, when efforts to change produce the changes intended. Too many people abandon meditation long before this stage, thus never experiencing its bounties. But any great creation takes great effort, the greater the effort resulting in the greater creation. Everything in this picture seems to be coming into a harmonizing which should have significant implications for the next stages in the boy's transformation.

7

Science Studies Meditation

Today, science provides us with the most reliable empirical knowledge we have of the world and its workings. Naturally, it would interest us should scientists, for whatever reason, begin to study meditation. Only recently have they done so, but already the results of their studies have contributed to advances in our understanding and practice of meditation. Actually, like meditation, science is a way of coming to significant experience or knowledge. Science makes certain basic assumptions about reality; then, using these, it elaborates systems of knowledge (like biology, anatomy, chemistry) and practical applications of these (like medicine) to provide human beings with the power which they need to survive and improve their lives in the world which science studies. Meditation does much the same, but, starting with alternative assumptions, produces another experience of the world and, with it, as interesting and as significant forms of knowledge. We should not expect the knowledge produced by meditative assumptions to be like, or to be about the same experiences as, those produced by the scientists' assumptions, but by the same token the conclusions of one do not invalidate those of the other. Scientists and engineers create extraordinary and astonishing applications of their knowledge, such as skyscrapers and jet transportation, while, on their own terms, meditators have just as incredible results, such as their creation of forms of relaxation and inner states of contentment as well as 'psychic' ways of knowing which scientists do not deliberately develop or use and of which they remain ignorant.

Scientists have come to study meditation extensively only within the last decade, so much of their material is still either unpublished or present only in the scientific journals. The Transcendental Meditation group produced much of the early work, published in their collection called *Scientific Research on the Transcendental Meditation Program*, and H. Benson, a professor at Harvard, published a popular account of a secular form of meditation in *The Relaxation Response*. It remained for Patricia Carrington, a clinical psychologist and lecturer at Princeton University, to write the first, and to this date the best, scientifically based study of meditation, which she called *Freedom in Meditation* (New York: Anchor Press, 1978). Carrington's book exemplifies the best of the scientific tradition, since it is complete in its survey of the existing literature, and it is critical. The author practises and teaches meditation, and studies it as a clinical psychologist, so her book has the authority and objectivity which characterize good science. Though I will summarize some of her findings in this chapter, I heartily recommend that everyone interested in meditation should read her book in full. She writes from the point of view of a 'sound psychology' (p. 173), which corrects the imbalance brought into the study and teaching of meditation by some religious groups. Many such groups, though sincere and honest, do not take a critical, objective view of meditation; rather, they follow, often too blindly, the lead of their sect's teacher or tradition. Though this may satisfy people's needs for authority figures and inspiration, it does not wholly satisfy or serve the search for reliable objective knowledge about meditation. Hence, what we can learn from the scientific study of meditation becomes all the more important.

Still, some may ask the question, 'why should science study meditation?' First, I would say, because it exists as a phenomenon, as a little-known dimension of human experience which deserves investigation and description. Second, because meditators make interesting and challenging claims about meditation and its benefits, science should study it to determine whether such claims can be treated seriously or not. In this process of study, science, especially physiology and psychology, could discover what applications meditation might have in human life, and what its limitations and dangers are. Traditionally, meditators have claimed that their practice leads to better health, relaxation, happiness and especially valuable 'altered states of consciousness.' Scientists can investigate these claims in hopes of finding new avenues of solving some of our contemporary problems, just as ethnobotanists study and gather traditional herbal remedies to discover new, more effective drugs for allopathic medicine's pharmacological repertoire. Then, from the point of view of meditators, science should be encouraged to study meditation not only for the above reasons, but also for the benefits of increased knowledge which will enhance their own practice and knowledge of it. Reliable scientific know-ledge can 'de-mythologize' their practice, since over the centuries people with considerably less empirical understanding of meditation have created a mythology about it which may not accurately describe what is actually happening during meditation. If, for example, traditional Indian systems claim that *mantras* function as excellent meditative objects, scientists could investigate whether this is so, and which *mantras* empirically function best (on which see Carrington, Chapter 9, 'The "Mystery" of the Mantra'). Further, by describing meditative processes, we could expect to improve and rationalize both the teaching and the practice of meditation. Again, in traditional times, techniques for its teaching and practice have come about without the benefit of precise empirical knowledge, say of the brain wave patterns associated with various states of relaxation. The same advances that scientific technology has produced in the practice of agriculture or transportation could similarly be made for meditation. I personally think that the most significant effects of scientific study could so improve our ability to teach people how to meditate that meditative states could be made available to many more people.

Scientists possess a method of gaining knowledge which gives them certain advantages over those who traditionally have taught and practised meditation. I refer to religious groups and sects, which naturally place more importance on non-empirical doctrines and their own traditional ways than on objective investigation and elaborating new techniques. Hopefully, the two will not be in conflict, for science excels at producing empirical knowledge but all too often fails when it comes to using the information wisely, while religion uses information well but often adopts outmoded or imperfectly conceived knowledge to support its well-chosen values. In the future, science can provide accurate empirical information about meditation and religion can adapt it to the best human use. Science holds, to my mind, the greatest promise for meditation in its ability to study and understand the processes it involves, thus allowing meditators to maximize the results they desire. For example, Carrington cites evidence (pp. 150–2) which suggests that meditating in the early morning hours helps one to counteract the effects of the higher levels of adrenal hormones present in the blood then (which correlate with heightened physical vulnerability and emotional instability). Other studies show (Carrington, p. 287) that sensory deprivation, of which meditation is a form, most effectively produces alterations of consciousness when monotonous stimulation, rather than near elimination of all stimulation, occurs. This accounts for the effective use, in meditation, of meditative objects like the mantra or repetitive music; with scientific observation of this effect, we can rationalize the use of such meditative objects to maximize their effects. This sort of cooperation between science and meditators from various religions as well as from secular groups holds the greatest promise for future growth. Also as traditional religions lose their appeal because of their reluctance to break with their past doctrinal claims and forms of practice, we can expect other disciplines and groups to take their place. Today, the large enrolments in psychology classes on every college and university campus show how many students must turn to scientific psychology for guidance in personal growth and knowledge, for religion has failed to perform for them its traditional function, so important to their needs for maturation. Psychology, too, of all the branches of science, has made the greatest advances in understanding meditation.

For generations scientists did not study meditation, probably because there were no meditators to study. When European doctors encountered 'yogis' in India who seemed to be able to violate through meditative disciplines some of their basic conclusions about human physiology, their colleagues at home scoffed at the reports as fake 'Oriental wonders'. In the twentieth century, some preliminary studies occurred in India, where experienced meditators could be found (see for example, Kavoor T. Behanan, *Yoga, A Scientific Evaluation*, reprinted by Dover, which as a 'scientific evaluation' leaves much to be desired), beginning a tradition in the scientific study of meditation which continues today in a much more adequate form. As Carrington notes, however, this study did not begin to flourish in the West until several conditions allowed its rapid growth in the last two decades. Some of these new conditions included growing interest in altered states of consciousness, the presence of meditation groups which made meditators available to scientists, and advances in technology (such as brain wave monitoring devices which opened up many new avenues for such study). Suddenly the old reports that yogis could supposedly control involuntary autonomic responses began to be re-investigated when finally the technology could measure and make such control useful, as thousands who have participated in biofeedback regulation of heartbeat and other supposed involuntary body mechanisms now know. Also, I think that the contemporary climate which places vastly increased importance on therapy and self-transformation has given new impetus to the study of meditation, as has the great interest in forms of relaxation for anxiety- and stress-plagued people in all walks of life. Finally, the importation of meditation along with attractive ideas about it from Eastern religions has stimulated the study of their meditative techniques and claims about their benefits.

It is undoubtedly too early in this scientific study of

meditation to make any definite broad generalizations about it. Indeed, many of the early studies, such as those first brought before a large audience in Charles Tart's *Altered States of Consciousness* (1969), have now been eclipsed by studies using more sophisticated equipment and experimental design. Carrington notes that the critical spirit of science has begun to review the first generation of studies on meditation, especially those done by enthusiastic TM adherents, finding some confirmation but also some nonconfirmation of their results (see her Chapter 4, 'The Other Side of Research'). In fact, many problems present themselves to researchers, difficulties involving experiment design, placebo effects, and the positive effects of experimenters' expectations brought into the outcomes of their studies. Other problems involve the meditators themselves – such as whether they remain in the study, whether they all are meditating, in comparable states, whether control subjects are not meditating – which, ingeniously, scientists are now learning to minimize. We are a long way from having a relatively complete, adequate picture of meditation in the scientific literature, but within another decade or two, we should be on much firmer ground. Work has proceeded, on the physiology of meditation, both in Europe (see Th. Brosse, *Etudes instrumentales des techniques du Yoga: expérimentation psychosomatique*, Paris, 1963) and in North America. James Funderburk recently published a useful compilation of this data in his book *Science Studies Yoga: A Review of Physiological Data* (published in 1977 by the Himalayan International Institute of Yoga Science & Philosophy, a Swami Rama group). This book provides the most complete review of this kind of data, drawing from widespread studies, new and old.

Some of the first studies indicated that meditation reduces usual levels of bodily activity, like oxygen consumption, heart rate and respiration, as well as the electrical resistance of the skin, an indicator of stress. This confirms the claim that meditation relaxes and re-energizes a person.

Other studies indicate that even after a fairly short time of practising meditation, a person's central nervous system changes, and that a person can better handle stress. Meditation itself involves a low stress state, or what Benson calls a 'relaxation response' (which can be achieved, admittedly, through other techniques). Early studies noted changes in the patterns of the meditator's brain waves, especially in the alpha range. Recently, with more sophisticated equipment, scientists have found that probably the most important characteristic of brain waves during meditation is their 'hypersynchrony', a phenomenon which involves the coming into 'phase' of the two separate hemispheres of the brain. In 1979, G. Maxwell Cade, a British researcher, published his findings (Cade and Coxhead, *The Awakened Mind, Biofeedback and the Development of Higher States of Awareness*, New York: Delacorte Press, 1979), based on the readout of a new biofeedback device called the 'Mind Mirror'. This monitors both brain hemispheres on twelve frequency ranges of brain wave activity, from the slowest delta (1.5 cycles per second) to extreme rapid beta (40 cps), going through the middle ranges of theta and alpha which early researchers noticed especially active in meditation. Cade's book presents for the first time a well developed application of a biofeedback device to enhance the training in and practice of meditation. As in other studies, Cade's Mind Mirror demonstrates that hemispheric bilateral symmetry is a primary result of meditative practice. The brain wave pattern of a non-meditator, and a person who is not very calm, shows little right hemisphere activity, but does show high amplitude beta (characteristic of alert awareness or of an alarm reaction or anxiety). After meditative development, bilaterality develops, generally with reduction of beta, and much greater alpha present; with meditation over a period of years, this reduces in frequency towards the theta range (see Cade, Appendix A).

Science has much work to complete before it can contribute substantially to our practice of meditation, but I firmly believe that its impact will be great, just as it has been in the many other fields of human endeavour to which it has turned its attention. This does not mean that science will 'take over' meditation, because it remains for meditators to decide what to do with their practice of it, and how to direct its powers. The research focusing on the effects of sensory deprivation, for example, can tell us much about how to alter states of consciousness, and under what conditions various kinds of alteration occur. Further, with this information, we can make new sense out of reports of meditative practices, of how Lame Deer went up the mountain and into his vision pit, of the legends and stories of cell-dwelling yogis in the Tibetan tradition or desert-dwelling Christian hermits and of how Sufi whirling dervishes dance, twirling, into ecstatic states. Investigators from the University of Manitoba (Zubek *et al.*, 'Perceptual Changes After Prolonged Sensory Isolation (Darkness and Silence)', *Canadian Journal of Psychology* 1961 (15), 83–100) demonstrated that prolonged darkness and silence produced hallucinations, changes in emotionality and 'significant changes in EEG activity' (p. 97). They hypothesized with other investigators that the brain, to function 'normally', needs 'constantly varying *meaningful* stimulation'. Though psychologists may be interested in maintaining the normal functioning of mind, meditators may be more interested in modifying that 'normal' functioning in various ways, and thus could well benefit, when devising various ways of meditating, from studying what psychologists have found about various kinds of sensory deprivation. I suspect that many traditions already know, from direct experience, about some of this, as the Lame Deer example illustrates, and how in those contexts, what psychologists observe and interpret as the 'considerable disorganization of brain function' resulting from sensory deprivation can be given sufficient cultural cushioning to have positive rather than negative effects on the person experiencing the disorganization. One of the goals of meditative experiences is to initiate the mind into different realms of experience, which from the point of view of its organized conscious functioning may seem 'disorganized' but which can indeed be made meaningful by culturally induced expectation, special set and setting, and interpretations provided by more experienced elders after the unusual or 'disorganizing' experience. We can learn, partly from deprivation studies, how best to orchestrate such experiences which function as doorways to expanded or deepened consciousness.

Only the tip of the iceberg of science's study of meditation shows today. Still, it already reveals some tantalizing possibilities. Carrington devotes an entire chapter to the relatively new study of the cycles we go through each day (on which see *Body Rhythm: the Circadian Rhythms Within You*, New York, Harcourt Brace, 1979). Like everything else in nature our biological processes flow in rhythmical sequences (e.g. the Ultradian rhythm, daytime daydreaming cycles, the oral activity cycle, as well as other cycles tied to cosmic rhythms, seasonal, solar and lunar, which influence us). The question is: do these rhythms influence our meditation, and can they be used to further its goals? We can hope that scientists will investigate the effects of such rhythms on meditative practices. Another study cited by Carrington (p. 323, the full reference is Cohen *et al.*, 'Electroencephalographic Laterality Changes During Human Sexual Orgasm', *Archives of Sexual Behaviour*, Vol. 5, No. 3 (1976), pp. 189–99) claims that during orgasm changes occur in laterality and amplitude ratio. This may explain why explicit sexual imagery appears in spiritual and mystical literature. Indeed, some meditators have used sexual orgasm to induce such hemisphere function shifts, such as in Taoist sexual meditation, and in the Indian system of Tantra. Although sexual intercourse constituted only one of myriad Tantric rituals, it was used in late classical and medieval India (and continues to be so used there today by a tiny minority, see Bharati, *The Light At The Center*) to induce ecstatic states. Scientific investigation of brain wave states in ecstasy and orgasm may provide interesting new leads in the search for more effective techniques for meditative transformations.

Parapsychology presents another area of scientific research which promises to contribute greatly to the advanced development of meditation. Although still in infancy, the investigations now being pursued in this field follow the general rules of science, guaranteeing that their results, with the ordinary qualifications of adequacy of design and repeatability, can be considered reliable. Parapsychology studies the phenomena associated not with the physiology or psychology of the body/mind, but roughly with its psychic (or 'spiritual') dimensions, long considered beyond the pale of legitimate scientific investigation. Today, however, scientifically trained investigators increasingly turn their attention to the claims, usually considered anecdotal and unreliable, made for the psychic powers of the mind. This field particularly interests meditators, because meditation acquaints them directly with these psychic dimensions of mind, and has done so ever since the beginning. Patañjali devoted most of his third chapter to the psychic phenomena experienced in *samādhi*, or meditative ecstasy, detailing in verse after verse the subtle psychic experiences that meditators encounter when they expand the domains of their conscious awareness. Unfortunately, problems plague experiments and studies of psychic phenomena. Some day, should as much time and energy be spent in solving parapsychology's problems as has been lavished, say, on the study of sub-atomic particles, we can expect results as amazing as hydrogen and neutron bombs (but hopefully on the constructive side of the use of such awesome power).

Jeffrey Mishlove has recently written by far the best single survey of parapsychology in his book *The Roots of Consciousness* (New York: Random House, 1975). Though not directly about meditation, this book treats many phenomena associated with meditation, and gives much information of interest to meditators (for we all have to decide what to do with meditatively induced ecstasy, and this book describes what many have done, whether meditators or not). In effect, as soon as a person plans to enter meditative states, a decision must be made as to what to apply the special state of consciousness; many answers have been provided, as the next two chapters will show. Though some of the things associated with parapsychology (and 'occultism', a term which I dislike) may strike us as fringe phenomena in healthy human experience, we should not let the myths of the past, often perpetrated by outmoded world views which we now have shed, to colour our investigation of the potentialities of the mind. I recommend reading Mishlove's first section as a historical guide to some of these phenomena, and then his second section, called 'Scientific Approaches to Consciousness', to see what science has already accomplished in its investigation of psychic mind dimensions. In his third section, Mishlove investigates theories of psychic reality and 'practical applications of PSI', which should interest meditators, since these range from behaviour modification and gambling through archaeology, crime detection and on to healing and business administration. Since meditation takes a neutral stance on what the state of mind it produces could be used for, such surveys of what psychics have used their altered states of consciousness for can be instructive.

As examples of the sort of research scientists now undertake in this field, let me summarize three studies which interest me. The first, by D. H. Lloyd, published in the *Journal of the New Horizons Research Foundation* (Vol. 1, No. 2, Summer 1973), showed for the first time that an objective, physically observable event in the brain's cortex correlated with a telepathic stimulus. Thus, a brain correlate, monitored by EEG data, has been found for the psychic phenomenon called telepathy, suggesting that the brain actually does respond to psychic stimuli originating outside itself. This result may be a tiny first step in the processes of describing what Patañjali described from experience nearly two thousand years ago. Should one day we have an adequate scientific description of the objective processes involved in psychic or 'psi' events, like extra-sensory perception and psychokinesis, we could elaborate meditative procedures for sending and receiving such stimuli, producing as significant an advance for the powers of the mind as machines have accomplished for the powers of the body.

Secondly, an article published by a New York psychologist, Rex G. Stanford, called 'An Experimentally Testable Model for Spontaneous Psi Events, 1. Extrasensory Events'

157

(in the *Journal of the American Society for Psychical Research*, Vol. 68 (1974), pp. 34–57), shows that uninduced or non-deliberate psychic experiences have already attracted the attention of scientists. Stanford's paper attempts to understand the familiar experience, which we usually attribute to good luck or chance, of having a problem solved for us without, apparently, our conscious effort. The author considers this to occur by unconscious ESP, citing as an example the following account of a retired attorney:

One Sunday afternoon I was headed for Greenwich Village intending to drop in on my good friends and artists, Mr and Mrs P. I took an express subway train to 14th Street, where I would change to a local train to 8th Street. However, upon leaving the express at 14th Street, I 'absentmindedly' walked right out through the gate and half way up the stairs to the street before remembering that I had intended to take the local train. Not wishing to pay another fare, I decided to go on to the street and walk the additional six blocks south. I had proceeded along Seventh Avenue as far as 12th Street when I met Mr and Mrs P. walking northward, on their way to some appointment in the area. I was able to walk with them for a few blocks and receive credit for the call. Obviously I would have missed them had I traveled as planned.

(Stanford, p. 35)

In his article, Stanford does what science must do at the beginning of its efforts to understand a phenomenon about which it knows nothing. It gathers instances of it and then attempts to elaborate a model to explain it adequately. His model proposes that the organism spontaneously uses its psychic mind (its psi, or ESP) along with sensory means to scan its environment for solutions to its needs. For meditators, confirmation of this model could be important. It would show that such a dimension exists. Once confirmed, one could devise ways of intentionally directing and influencing this psychic dimension through meditation rather than relying on its spontaneous operation, guided by what experimenters find in describing and predicting the conditions and operations of these sorts of events. Too long have we dismissed the effects of this kind of mind function as being the result of 'luck', or 'chance', thus neglecting a powerful means of deliberately adapting to our environment. Shamanic accounts of the deliberate cultivation of this psychic mind show that its adaptive potentialities had long been exploited by our ancestors. But with the advent of sceptical science, directed by its materialist prejudice, everything without apparent material basis has been relegated to the realm of fantasy. The pendulum has swung too far in the direction of physicalism, counteracting the excessive non-physicalism of medieval Christian and Platonic views of the natural word. Now, it begins to swing back again, taking into account things previously dismissed, now seen in the new light provided by technological advances which can study the apparently very subtle phenomena and increasingly known physical bases of psychic phenomena. Meditation stands to benefit enormously from the balancing of the scientific paradigm of reality which accepts the psychic as a legitimate object for investigation.

Another early stage in scientific method involves describing phenomena. This makes them more amenable to inquiry. An example of such work comes from the *Journal of Communication* (Vol. 25, 1975), in William G. Braud's article 'Psi-Conducive States'. The author describes the characteristics of persons in states of mind which conduce to psychic phenomena, drawing from many diverse sources, including meditation. He seeks to show that a 'psi-conducive syndrome' exists, thus establishing the existence of something which many have doubted. This provides the first step in understanding. Braud says that persons in a psi-conducive state are physically relaxed; their physical arousal or activation and sensory input and processing are reduced; they have increased awareness of inner processes, feelings and images; they show decreased action of the left hemispheric functioning with increased right hemisphere functioning; they have a soft, accepting view of reality rather than a hard, realistic view; and, finally, their psi response 'would aid in fulfilling some important *need* of someone concerned in the situation' (p. 150), which Stanford also noted as being very important.

This list of features strongly resembles features of people who meditate, again linking meditation with psychic activity. This work of mapping the new field of psychic phenomena can substantially help meditators to enter upon these largely unexplored (in our culture, at least) areas of human consciousness, an important contribution which science makes to meditation. Somehow when phenomena can be described by our accepted means of achieving reliable knowledge about the world and the mind, they become acceptable realities, thus opening the door to many who otherwise would never think of entering. Science permeates our contemporary culture. We have accepted, unwittingly, the reality limits which early scientific theory defined for us, so, as science expands these limits, it will mean much greater acceptance of and knowledge about realms of experience which have been common fare for shamans and meditators for millennia.

Finally, the objective methodology of science has positively influenced another sort of literature about meditation, which also greatly benefits meditators. I refer to the humanistic investigations of meditation which scholars are now beginning to write in the disciplines of anthropology, philosophy, religious studies and the psychology of literature. I consider my book to be one such study, since I have tried to survey the subject of meditation using the data available to us from all these objective disciplines. Though most do not realize it, science has brought great improvement to our knowledge of other cultures, their languages, literatures and cultural achievements. Just read what Europeans and North Americans wrote about meditation and Eastern literature in the nineteenth century, and you will realize how inadequate the sources of our information about these subjects have been. The great formative minds of our century, including Freud and Jung, had so little adequate information about non-Western cultures and civilizations that their theories of human reality were compromised by being too culture-specific. Only in the last few decades have scholars been producing accurate translations of the classics of non-Western civilizations, many of which contain valuable information on meditative and deliberately altered states of consciousness. This includes translations from Biblical, Arabic, Chinese, and Indian sources. Further, only recently have anthropologists gathered methodologically objective, relatively complete information on the cultures they have studied, showing us how deeply involved other peoples have been in psychic ways of understanding reality, and how much meditative disciplines have shaped and created their world experience. Since the great wars of the century (the two World Wars, the Korean and the Vietnamese) and the independence movements they spawned, we have slowly realized that there are other people out there, in what we gratuitously call the 'Third World', with different ways of understanding and acting. One of the most salutary effects of the scientific spirit in knowledge has been its attempts to eliminate prejudices and cultural preconceptions in our view of other peoples. Science flushed away the prior spirit of exploitative colonialism and the culture-centric pride of Judaeo-Christian notions of cultural and religious superiority that plagued our relations with the rest of the world from the time when Columbus claimed the 'new world' for the Spanish throne and the Roman Pope.

Academic scholars have led the way in this new attempt to understand objectively what the rest of the world thinks and knows. Finally, scientifically minded scholars have begun to write about subjects relevant to meditation, thus increasing our knowledge of our human heritage. Within the last half decade, two major books appeared by leading academics who have brought this new critical spirit with them to the study of the Asian sources of our human tradition. Both focused on mysticism, a major phenomenon associated with meditation, and a major reason more and more people are interested in meditating. Both happen to be Sanskritists, but we can equally expect books from specialists in other traditions.

Frits Staal, a professor at the University of California Berkeley, published in 1975 his book *Exploring Mysticism* (Berkeley: University of California Press, 1975). During the course of his investigation of mysticism, Staal makes many observations about meditation with the clarity of a fine mind trained in languages, humanistic criticism and philosophy. In many respects, Staal defines mysticism as nearly synonymous with meditation (or 'yoga'), since mystics have been involved in meditation to reach the state or to teach it to others. The author knows the Indian tradition very well, so he can dispel much of the fuzzy information and many of the misconceptions that are paraded about as truth on the subject. Another critical spirit to enter the realm of mystic studies, and a practising mystic himself, is Agehananda Bharati, professor in the Department of Sociology and Anthropology at the Syracuse University. His book, *The Light At The Center; Context and Pretext of Modern Mysticism* (Santa Barbara: Ross-Erikson, 1976), speaks with authority from several points of view: experiential, in that he has had mystical experiences; scholarly, since he has studied mysticism, along with the ancillary disciplines of languages and linguistics, philosophy and anthropology; and personal, since he speaks from the position of belief (he is an initiated member of an Indian order of renunciants). Though oriented to the contribution of Indian mysticism, this book exemplifies the healthy, scientific critical approach which I think will contribute much to our future knowledge of meditation, mysticism and psychic states (which this author hardly touches upon – an interesting omission but probably related to his hard-line scientism). Also, Bharati claims that taking LSD, which he calls the 'exquisite product' of the Swiss Sandoz lab and Albert Hoffman, helped him to induce his fourth mystical experience, which, in true Tantric form, occurred after making love with a 'very beautiful woman' (p. 43). Unfortunately, Bharati does not tell us anything about his personal meditation, but compensates the loss with his astute observations of the flood of Indian gurus that inundates the West and his observations of the contemporary search for the mystical experience. He feels, for instance, that the popularity of some forms of Hinduism and Buddhism rests on their ability to provide the possibility of ecstatic experience (p. 233), which observers of the spiritual underground (like Theodore Roszak, Robert Ellwood and Bharati himself) emphasize is a major motivation in those who flock to new age prophets (and their many products).

The keystone of both Staal's and Bharati's works comes in their shared emphasis on reason. Staal argues convincingly against the alleged irrationality of mysticism and against irrational approaches to its study. Instead, he writes, we must study mysticism (and by implication meditation and religion) rationally. Bharati takes the same approach, going farther than Staal in calling for a 'rational mysticism' (p. 234) which, unfortunately, most would consider a contradiction in terms. He realizes, too, that few practising mystics exist anywhere in the world today, some in India, and some in Euro-america. But every civilization produces mystics, particularly prosperous ones, so I think that in the future, we shall see the study and practice of meditation and mysticism grow increasingly in Euro-america, but less rapidly elsewhere, until the rest of the world reaches an adequate standard of living and realizes that the Western-initiated craze for material possessions leads to a spiritual dead end. As Albert Camus noted, before persons can turn to spiritual or aesthetic satisfaction, they need enough bread to satisfy the elemental demands of the stomach. To the disgrace of science and politics, most people on the earth today barely reach the satisfaction of even minimal nutritional requirements, and can hardly be expected to become meditators. If meditation contributes anything to the future of our world-wide civilization, it probably will occur first in the affluent West, which is now not crippled by a 'retarding lead' in the field of meditation as the East is. Paradoxically, the decline of meditation in the East comes with its exportation to the West, which is the only region of the world today which possesses the cultural prosperity required for its practice. If Staal's and Bharati's books can be considered harbingers of the tenor of the West's response to the impulses arriving from abroad and internally from our own traditions (such as Hassidic Judaism, Quaker Protestantism and contemplative Catholicism), I have no fear for the future of meditation. It will be scrutinized, described and practised in the spirit with which Euroamerican rationalism has beneficially enlightened humankind, since, whether we blow up the world or not, it is better to have knowledge than to remain in ignorance, whatever the consequences.

Ox-Taming 7 *The Ox Forgotten, Leaving The Boy To Meditate Deeply*

At this stage in the self-transformation, the boy enters upon important changes which lead to a reversal of ordinary, immature consciousness. Naturally, the entire series sets out in firm stages what happens in much less of a logical progression. One can reach any of the stages and yet need to work on prior ones, too. Autobiographical accounts of such self-discipline (like those of Bashō or Carl Jung) indicate the process to be ever expanding; though gains can be integrated, particularly up to this point, one can exist simultaneously in all the stages in different respects. Here, though, a definite accomplishment is symbolized, for we can now no longer see the ox. Discipline has so integrated the ox back into the boy's consciousness that it no longer needs special attention. Released from the demands of such discipline, the boy leaves his rope aside. He has led and ridden the ox back home, where at peace he plunges deep into meditation, 'leaning on his armrest' (Chuang Tzu). Though the sun still floats in the sky above distant mountains, he is able to enter into the 'twilight' state of meditative liminality. All nature spreads before him, through which he meditatively 'wanders' (again, as Chuang Tzu describes it). He has reached 'home' again, not so much a physical home as a comfortable place in the cosmos, which Sino-Japanese civilization placed in nature. He dwells in utter solitude. The boundary between self and world gradually softens as he begins to go beyond the self whose animality is now tamed and integrated within.

This scene portrays the first moment of the 'self' forgetfulness which matures the boy by bringing him into a properly spiritual consummatory (i.e. not instrumental) experience of the Other (here, Nature). The difficulty in reading mystical texts about this experience is their insistence that one be 'self-less', or beyond ego, for this to occur. In fact, the meaning of 'self' in such contexts extends not to the entire conscious self but rather just to the anxious, self-preoccupied dimensions of self which exist because one has not tamed their immaturity or animality. Self-deception and self-preoccupied animality mitigate against our truly knowing and participating in the Other because, when motivation flows from such deeply conflicted structures, the immature self's gratification occupies the entire mental economy, blotting out real other persons and the world except as instruments of satisfying the anxiety ridden self's needs. This is the source of our inhumanity to fellow beings and the ecological catastrophe which we now visit upon creation. The boy takes another path by confronting the ox, that immature selfhood, correcting its nature until it can simply be 'forgotten'. This implies not its repression (which would never eliminate its effects in consciousness), but rather the clearing away and resolving of its complexes, animality, anxiety and self-preoccupation. A conflicted consciousness is brittle and subject to being thrust into anger or apathy by the slightest anxiety-arousing incident. The archaic fight-flight structure no longer functions adaptively in civilized conditions, no matter how apparently it leads to success and satisfaction. This the boy has dealt with, and he prepares in deep meditation for the ultimate experience of mystic selflessness (see Fingarette, *The Self In Transformation,* Chapter 7).

One can thus say that here the immature self has been tamed, rid of its unruliness, to be integrated into the deeper self's spiritual maturity, so that it no longer obscures that centre of one's being. The ox is no longer out of control; training has made it completely harmonious with the deepest self's wisdom, so that it serves that self, rather than concealing it. As recorded in the *Analects* (see Arthur Waley's translation, Book 2, 4), Confucius recognized this in himself as the crowning achievement of his efforts to 'correct his faults', remembering:

At seventy, I could follow the dictates of my own heart; for what I desired no longer overstepped the boundaries of right [literally, 'without transgressing the square'].

(Waley, p. 88)

The ox no longer rushes out into the world, beyond one's control, as it does for immature persons, those dependent upon the drugs of self-indulgence, tied to the world by the ox which constantly and habitually demands immature satis-

166

faction. After travelling recently during the height of the rice-growing season in northern Thailand, I realized the import of this extended image of ox-taming. I saw there many people riding their water buffaloes, magnificently graceful creatures which lumbered along shallow waterways carrying their quiet riders. The remembrance I have of those scenes portrays to me the harmony which people can achieve with beasts. This Oriental self-transformation myth uses the ox-taming image to dramatize its powerful lesson of bringing our infantile bestiality into harmony, by training it, with the deep self's true nature.

This picture shows a crucial turning point in the process of the boy's struggle for self-transformation. Without the victory over the ox (the infantile, animalistic self-nature), he will never be able to go outside that self (i.e. achieve ecstasy). When persons remain immature, they make other people and the world into instruments for their uncorrected self's gratification. Such a person sees everything as an opportunity for or as a deprivation of that fragile self's supposed fulfilment of habituated needs. He does not see other persons as people, but as potential things which can be exploited by the desiring self; the world too becomes merely the material source of products required by the self for its pleasure. Such people have no empathy, no sense of or concern for the feelings of others, or for the well-being of their mother earth. Everything merely exists to evoke inner-fantasy-oriented responses; everything is evaluated solely on the basis of how well it can serve as the instrument of the self's fantasy or anxiety gratifications. Everyone, the famous, the poor, the rich and the forgotten, must, to achieve maturity, fight this battle with the infantile self. Or, unfulfilled, they die having only known the world and other persons from the particularly narrow perspective of that self's needs. They remain for ever like children, but without their playfulness, the saving grace of childhood. Everything they plan has its starting point in what benefit it can bring them; each one is the single most selfish person in the world. When acting as groups or civilizations, motivated by the collective infantile self, they accumulate the *karma* which has condemned every civilization ever created to eventual senseless, painful destruction resulting from the exhaustion of their delicate ecological support systems through insatiable greed.

We can now realize what the boy has accomplished. He has eliminated what stands between him and Other, both cosmos and persons. The moment indeed eclipses all others (in importance), for the boy stands at the threshold of his own maturity, finally to experience reality as it is, without the narrow focusing lens of infantile self-preoccupation. Thus, he rests in immersing meditation, finally ready to present his deep psychic mind to the presence of Nature herself. He has reached the conquering of his faulted self when it sheds its final vestiges of immaturity, revealing the immaculate light within. Without the inner fantasy needs for gratification, he comes to nature consciously ready for the very first time truly to know what exists, which before was always just beyond the ox-self. This escapes most people to their dying day. The consequences of this readiness indeed reach far into the world. In the last three pictures, we can study these culminations of the boy's struggle.

8

'Meditation And ———?'

Undoubtedly, the most important question facing meditators today is what to use meditation for. Unfortunately, this also happens to be the least asked question about meditation. Almost universally among religious and spiritual groups teaching and practising meditation, the answer comes along with the training, provided without the question's alternative answers ever being seriously considered. For such groups, meditation aims at 'realizing God', or 'knowing the Supreme', or 'attunement with Creative Forces'. I have no quarrel with such goals, but wish to point out that they involve only one of many possible uses for meditative ecstasy. Even within groups which apparently embrace other goals for meditation, such as increased ability to deal with stress, and for relaxation and the everyday benefits of calmness, eventually, as one progresses to more advanced levels, religious goals begin to appear and be emphasized, revealing the underlying tenor of the training. Transcendental Meditation exemplifies this kind of progression, leading eventually to espousal of specifically Indian ideas about reality, deriving from its Indian *guru*, or leader, the Maharishi. Other groups begin with a remarkable personality, who speaks wisely to a small initial group of followers, which then grows, the leader's fame increasing, until he or she gains awesome charisma; people consider the person more than human, and then, particularly after death, divine. This happened to the

169

Buddha and most of the founders of the great religions, and the process repeats itself today. I have nothing against such spiritualizing evolutions, but only observe that they inherently limit the possible applications of meditative states, to the detriment of meditation as a whole. Further, such exclusively spiritual applications of this tool for mental training excludes many people, who could potentially benefit from meditation, because they do not wish to apply it to spiritual goals.

In fact, meditation has no inherent goal or aim. One can apply one's meditative states to the realizing of any goal one chooses. When your local dealer sells you a car, you possess all the mechanisms for you to drive it safely, but the car does not tell you where to drive it. If it did, it would be useless every time you wanted to go somewhere else. In much the same way, meditation is a means without a sole or exclusive end or goal. To consider that it has but one proper goal limits it so narrowly that more harm than good comes as the consequence. Today, we should reverse the tide of centuries to consider meditation in the broadest way possible, asking the question of what its uses may be in both secular and spiritual contexts. In the past, civilizations have made great advances when techniques originating in or practised by exclusionist groups came to be used outside these groups. Sanskrit, once the exclusive possession of the priestly class in ancient India, became in later times a powerful literary and scientific lingua franca for all the Indian elites. Meditation in the past two thousand years has come to be understood as being the exclusive possession of religious and spiritual groups, being considered to have little to contribute to the large majority of people who do not participate in the esoteric pursuits of these minority groups. Most Westerners express great surprise when they learn that hardly anyone meditates in the East, that even among monks, very few seriously meditate who are under fifty years old. The East has largely deserted meditation (or never practised it in the first place) just as surely as the secularized West has largely left the churches.

When certain groups with already chosen goals exclusively control the practice of meditation, it comes to be considered only in the light of those goals. This does not further its development, and consequently it must be freed from these unnatural restrictions. The history of meditation shows that it has become increasingly available to more and more practitioners, but this process needs to be greatly expanded. The first meditators, shamans and shamanesses, constituted a tiny minority of our hunter-gatherer ancestors. Then, after the advent of agriculture and civilization, around eight thousand years ago, meditation passed into the hands of priests and eventually monastic communities who allowed admission only to the few who dedicated themselves more or less exclusively to meditation's practice and the spiritual goals they affirmed. By and large, meditation has not secularized itself to this day (except perhaps in India, on the evidence of its tales of *yogin*-adventurers), but this should be its next step. Meditation must be freed from those who have married it exclusively to spiritual goals, to investigate and develop its uses along all possible lines and dimensions. When priests and monastics took meditation over, they specialized it to exclude many of the applications shamans put it to, bringing us where we are today, with an impoverished vision of meditation's possibilities.

We can learn much in this matter from the example of shamanism. These specialists in 'archaic techniques' for achieving ecstasy used this state for a great diversity of goals: some involved purely empirical matters of survival in the material world, such as finding game and improving hunters' skills, predicting weather changes and the outcome of actions, influencing the course of natural events and knowing things beyond the scope of the physical senses. Further, shamans healed illnesses and injuries. Another speciality involved the guiding of troubled souls, either of the sick and disturbed, or of those who had died. Later monastics and priests dropped, to a large extent, most of these functions of the psychic-ecstatic shaman, whose meditation on behalf of material and empirical concerns came to be the purview of popular religion, the rituals and ceremonies and magic characteristic of all peasant societies. Then, since the Industrial Revolution, these empirical concerns have increasingly been served by science and technology, with consequent eroding of popular religion (in Asia very few young people go to the temples or practise divination, etc., in the cities). So meditators have retreated into exclusively spiritual concerns, leaving all matters of daily life to the new priesthood of science and technology.

The consequences, as observers note, constitute disaster for the human dimension of life. In the field of medicine alone, we see an increasingly strong revolt against treating illness solely by medical science's technology, as if all healing requires is a better tuning of the body's 'machine'. We now realize that not only healing, but also preventing illness and becoming ill, intimately involve not only the body's machine but its mind, too. Suddenly, with this simple realization, the psychic dimension of the human being comes back into the matter of achieving well-being. And, as soon as this happens, meditation, which directly effects changes in the mind, becomes a good candidate for being one of the best doctors a person can ever have. Traditional wisdom recognizes that the person heals, not the doctor, though many have forgotten this with the over-confidence we have been taught in medicine's technology. Do pills cure disease? Apparently not without the cooperation, at least, of the person. Sometimes they 'cure' but are just placebos. Nor can they prevent disease, but rather (as in vitamin and mineral supplements) they can at times provide some of the necessary elements whereby the mind/body can maintain the body's well-being. Many observers go even farther. They claim that the mind permits all illness, and all accidents. If this is the case, even in part, it means that meditation, which directly affects the state of that mind, can be a most powerful instrument in maintaining our well-being, as indeed the shamans of old knew.

In the same manner, we must begin to ask how the mind, and hence meditation, can effect other changes in the various areas of our lives. Meditative techniques reliably produce, when properly practised, ecstatic states of mind not only for monastics but for anyone who practises them. Suddenly, therefore, we have a whole new set of possibilities open to us. This excites my imagination as much as I imagine the invention of the aeroplane did the Wright brothers. At least, the contemporary rediscovery of meditative ecstasy holds as promising and as far-reaching consequences as the great discoveries of the past. I do not think this exaggerates the case. Almost as suddenly as we had the atom split, or mechanical flight, or computers, suddenly we have meditatively altered states of consciousness that make available again the ecstatic powers of the archaic shaman. We need to discover what this new tool, the meditatively transformed mind, can be put to for good. Now, the secular and the spiritual components of our culture must look again at the meditatively activated mind, using experimental and experiential approaches, to discover how best – and most diversely – we can use what so rapidly we are rediscovering.

A few historical precedents exist for this new exploration which we must make. We have noticed that the ancient Taoist metaphors for the cultivation of meditative states used skills as examples, so meditation long ago became associated with being skilled, as also the Sanskrit term *yoga* indicates. I suspect that at least some meditators used their ecstatic states not only for spiritual goals, as I claimed above, but also for practical helping in their social contexts, for healing and other ends. The *Bhagavad Gītā* long ago claimed that 'yoga (results in) proficiency in actions' (2.50); its hero, Arjuna, Hinduism's model of the practical *yogin*, used his meditative skills in battle against the warriors of evil arrayed against him in ancient India's great civil war. The marvellous story literature of classical India (*c.* AD 300–1200) shows us that merchants and adventurers used the meditative disciplines of 'mind control' to achieve their goal of gaining wealth and surviving the rigours and dangers of travel in those days. Clearly we see merchant adventurer heroes using the techniques of meditation to gain access to the deep mind to extricate themselves from tight situations, indicating that the techniques which meditators applied to their spiritual goals also came to be used for other, more secular ends. (University of Chicago professor J. A. B. van Buitenen translated these wonderful fables in his book *Tales of Ancient India*, University of Chicago Press, 1969.) I have been interested in the possible applications of meditation ever since a friend of mine claimed that, after a large percentage of his lungs had been surgically removed when he was thirteen, he saved his life by practising meditative breathing taught to him by Yogi Ramacharaka's little book *The Hindu-Yogi Science of Breath* (London: Fowler & Co., 1960).

Already, some groups teaching meditation expand its uses to include, or focus on, other than spiritual goals and functions. I expect this to increase greatly in the decades to come as we learn more about the manifold possibilities of using ecstatic states in our daily lives. Many of these early groups take their applications of meditation from the example of the remarkable American psychic Edgar Cayce, who showed in well documented instances time after time how psychic mental states can be used for all kinds of tasks, many of which Cayce (or his moral sense) rejected. He would become weak, or ill, or lose his powers after using them to benefit others in a monetary sense, which raises an objection to my claim that meditative ecstasy could be used for secular purposes. But I have not claimed that they can be used for self-serving ends; in fact, the example of Cayce shows that the mind's powers function best when exercised for the benefit of others, or if used for one's own gains, if these gains also will help others. This requires simply that meditative ecstasy be used to serve or help other human beings. Cayce's psychic consciousness developed incredible forms of knowledge: he predicted accurately world events to come, he could follow the actions of individuals hundreds of miles away, he could determine their state of health and recommend ways of curing their illnesses, he found oil, predicted the outcomes of horse races and commodity market fluctuations, in addition to all the 'readings' he gave on more spiritual matters, such as past lives, *karma*, and the moral implications of our actions and dreams. Interestingly, Cayce did not develop these mental powers exclusively in meditation (though he recommended meditation many times in his readings). He could not gain access to his deep mind's psyche for the detailed work he did without someone (usually his wife) who would help him into the state and direct him with specific questions to the desired knowledge. Had Cayce been born into an environment more disposed to meditation, I think he would have reached the same states through meditation.

The US-based Silva Mind Control group (and its many offshoots) teaches meditation in a largely secular context instructing its students to use their meditative states for a variety of purposes. José Silva and Philip Miele documented the group's approach in their book *The Silva Mind Control Method* (New York: Simon and Schuster, 1977). Probably the title 'mind control' is unfortunate; for years I shied away from such mental training because its title suggests that someone else could control my mind. I failed to understand that just the opposite occurs, that the training teaches persons how to gain control over their own minds (the ox) and how to meditate without implicit spiritual goals. After studying meditation and Eastern religions from texts for fifteen years I still (like most of my professors and fellow students), only three years ago, had not learned to meditate myself, in part because I distrusted the religious groups teaching it, and in part because no other groups presented themselves as candidates to teach me. Finally, a friend suggested that I take a course offered by a group whose teacher had studied with José Silva, and she initiated me into meditative states. Such an initiation brings a person to experience directly the elusive state, which once experienced one can develop on one's own.

Although my teacher used 'spiritual' ideas from many religious traditions, but mostly the Judaico-Christian biblical version, she also integrated scientific findings into her teaching of meditation, and further, taught us how to apply the ecstatic states we entered in many diverse ways, most of them directly relevant to the concerns of our daily lives in secular reality. Speaking of graduates from his group's courses Silva says: 'Some use it for health, some to help them study, others in their business lives and family relationships, and many, who say little about it, use it to help others' (p. 155). The Silva course, as the book shows, teaches people to apply their meditative states to improving memory and learning, to learning how to use one's dreams for self-improvement (including healing) and self-control (say, of bad habits), to making one's marriage better (including meditative sex), and cultivating ESP. Miele adds chapters on psychiatric applications of meditative states, as well as on increasing self-esteem and using ecstasy in business. In the course I took, we also learned how to visualize or programme what we wanted to occur in our lives, how to de-programme old conditioning, how to avoid insomnia, remember our dreams, wake up without an alarm, stop bleeding, heal ourselves, to diagnose and to help others to heal, all with the meditative state into which our teacher initiated us.

I am often asked questions about such groups, many of them stemming from distrust or lack of understanding. Somehow, they evoke fears of brainwashing and adverse mind control. Many people still believe that meditation should remain in the monastery, and, with the rest of our culture, that to tamper with the mind could lead to dangerous consequences. Patricia Carrington's book *Freedom In Meditation* treats the dangers involving meditation very sensitively (see especially Chapters 14 and 15); from her survey and my own experience so far, I think our cultural apprehensions find support in ignorance rather than in fact. I am encouraged by the appearance of sensible, secular literature and groups which teach meditation and its everyday applications. Eventually, their 'graduates' will demonstrate that meditation can play a helpful, useful role in our lives, just as education, recreation and art do. The paranoid reaction of some elements today, as evidenced by the bill presented some years ago to the California legislature which sought to ban 'mind control' groups, and fed by the extremism of (largely religious) cults, presents a very real threat to the rational development of meditation and must be counteracted by goodwill and increased information flow.

Innovative approaches to healing and health maintenance have taken up meditative techniques to an increasing degree in the last decade. Though often called relaxation, or imagery exercises, they use familiar ways of reaching meditative states to focus the mind's activity on healing or preventing illness. Probably because health occupies such an important place in all our lives, this area has come early to meditation. Literally hundreds of clinics and groups use meditation-based techniques, for everything from self-regulation of bodily processes ('biofeedback') to handling pain (such as C. Norman Shealy's clinic in La Crosse, Wisconsin) and to combating such problems as high blood pressure, tension headaches, bronchial asthma, heart disease and even the dread plague of cancer which today occupies the attention of so many. As just one example, the book *Getting Well Again* (Los Angeles: Tarcher, Inc., 1978) by the Simontons shows how great success has come to some people with cancer who learn a basic meditative relaxation technique to enter a state in which they approach counteracting their cancers with positive images of healing and other forms of self-suggestion. The Simontons argue that stress and a person's reaction to stress play a crucial role in becoming ill, so that to reverse the stress-illness cycle one must take control of one's mental processes. This book shows the crucial role which the mind plays in our health, making a practical application of meditation to something which concerns all of us, not only sufferers of cancer but of all 'diseases'. Finally, at least in this all-important field of health, meditation is beginning to play its vital role, thanks to the revolution begun by such doctors as Shealy and Simonton. (For an objective report of Edgar Cayce's views, read Patrick Berkery's *The Edgar Cayce Guide to Self-Healing*, Contemporary Mission, Inc.: Westport, Connecticut 06880).

Researchers have discovered that meditation can substantially aid activities in many fields of endeavour. In Part III (on Personal Growth) of her *Freedom* book, Carrington lists the following applications that have already been studied: as an adjunct to psychotherapy; in combating physical illness (especially as a preventive measure, and in tension-related illness, one-half of all diseases); to counteract insomnia; in becoming more open to life; as ways of deepening self-awareness and gaining greater openness to others; as an aid to increased creativity, creative productivity and quality, and to increased stamina in creativity; to induce shifts in cognitive mode (left-to-right brain hemisphere functioning); in counteracting excessive ego concern; for energy increase; for its desensitization effects; in learning self-acceptance; and in other dimensions of self-education or ox-taming. In her concluding chapter, on the future promise of meditation, Carrington cites further possible applications in the realms of medicine, psychiatry, education, business and industry. In addition, Mishlove (*Roots of Consciousness*, pp. 300ff.) investigates psychic-meditative applications in the areas of gambling, archaeology, crime detection and business administration. I would add commodity market speculation to the list. Some of these areas may seem totally unrelated to meditative skills, but investigators take great interest in possible exciting applications. Mishlove cites studies showing that successful executives score much higher on ESP precognitive tests, a skill which can be cultivated in meditation. Already, the field of parapsychology in anthropological applications has been described in a published collection of articles (see Joseph K.

Long, *Extrasensory Ecology: Parapsychology and Anthropology*, Scarecrow Press, 1977) indicating that people in ecstasy can help archaeologists to determine what vanished peoples may have been doing with the artefacts which have survived their destruction.

Everyone can find some area of interest in which to apply meditation. This relates to meditation's ability to discipline the mind and to focus it on a task at hand. Everyone notices how sometimes action flows, and at other times blocks appear before our desired goals. Carrington cites a study of 'flow' by University of Chicago researchers (*Freedom*, pp. 239ff.) which shows that people who become totally involved in whatever they are doing exhibit the same characteristics which meditators systematically cultivate. These features which meditation and 'flow' share include total absorption, keeping one's attention on a limited stimulus field or object, self forgetfulness, self-control, and that the situation or problem be clear with the person involved having no goals or rewards external to the activity itself. Clearly, if these indeed characterize successful action, people who practise meditation can substantially contribute to their ability to act in such a flowing manner. Meditation can be applied to any activity we choose, primarily because it influences the state and focus of our mind, and the mind creates our reality. In this connection, I remember the words of one of China's greatest meditators, Chuang Tzu, who said:

If you can harmonize and delight [in the changes], master them and never be at a loss for joy, if you can do this day and night without break and make it be spring with everything, mingling with all and creating the moment within your own mind – this is what I call being whole in power.

(Watson, p. 70)

In recent times, many people have noticed the connection linking meditative states of mind and sports. A whole series of books has appeared on such topics as the yoga of running,

179

the yoga of tennis, and, also, the Zen of running and tennis. Tradition links them too, as in the martial arts of the Orient. A friend who was studying *aikido* in Japan told me that after he had been learning for some time his master told him to enter his state of *samādhi* (meditative ecstasy) before practising. Individuals who excel at their particular sports report that, at a certain point in their playing, they enter into another state of consciousness which facilitates their play. John Brodie, then quarterback of the San Francisco 49ers football team recalled such an experience in an interview published in the January 1973 issue of *Intellectual Digest*, pp. 19–21:

At times, and with increasing frequency now, I experience a kind of clarity that I've never seen adequately described in a football story. Sometimes, for example, time seems to slow way down, in an uncanny way, as if everyone were moving in slow motion. It seems as if I have all the time in the world to watch the receivers run their patterns, and yet I know the defensive line is coming at me just as fast as ever. I know perfectly well how hard and fast those guys are coming and yet the whole thing seems like a movie or a dance in slow motion. It's beautiful.

Brodie here describes an altered state of consciousness most often experienced by meditative mystics (or people experiencing an accident). Clearly, in the course of playing football, Brodie has learned some of the principles of meditation. He mentions being 'right there, doing that thing, in the moment', and 'here-and-now awareness, clarity, strong intention'.

Also in keeping with meditative experience, Brodie described the intuitional or psychic dimensions he experienced while playing football. Two instances are included in the following accounts. The first took place when he was in a tight situation:

We had to *make* something happen then ... With third down and one yard to go on your own 22-yard line in a close game – and a play-off game, which leaves you with no second chances – you wouldn't usually go with the particular call I made. After I came to the line scrimmage and started my snap count, I saw the defense shift into a position that might not happen in the game again. I gave the team a basic pass audible and gave Gene a little signal we had worked out, faded back and threw him that pass. When I threw it I *knew* it was going to connect . . . Even this does not finish the story. Somehow the ball eluded the defending player. Pat Fisher, the cornerback, told the reporters after the game that the ball seemed to jump right over his hands as he went for it. When we studied the game films that week, it *did* look as if the ball kind of jumped over his hands into Gene's. Some of the guys said it was the wind – and maybe it was.

But maybe, too, Brodie's meditative state somehow, psychokinetically, influenced the flight of the ball, to follow the 'certainty' he felt at the moment he threw it. Here, again, in another account, the meditative-psychic dimension of sports played at the peak of concentration comes out:

. . . it's a highly intuitive thing. Sometimes we call a pass for a particular spot on the field, maybe to get a first down. But at other times it's less defined than that and depends upon the communication we have. Sometimes I let the ball fly before Gene has made his final move, *without* a pass route being set exactly. That's where the intuition and the communication come in.

It follows that, were people so deeply involved in sports to practise deliberately, in meditation, some of these mind skills, their performance would benefit.

Everyone can practise meditation to improve some kind of action or important activity, quite apart from meditating for spiritual goals and general everyday meditative benefits, such as relaxation and visualizing positive set expectations. I have chosen to experiment with meditation as part of my gardening. For two years now, I have gardened, gaining health and vitality from the hard work, and from the fresh produce Livia and I have grown. However, I had not meditated as part of

the activity. With this Fall's garden, I have started to meditate, in part because of reading about the experiences of
members of the Findhorn community, as reported in their
book *The Findhorn Garden* (New York: Harper & Row,
1975). This describes how early members of the community,
particularly two sensitive women and one perceptive man,
greatly improved the garden's production by meditatively
communicating with garden 'devas', 'shining ones' and
'spirits', particularly of each plant, which cooperated with the
gardeners to grow exraordinary plants on land which had
held little promise of producing anything but brambles and
furze. Also, the man most responsible for the initial garden
maintained a meditative attitude towards his work and,
though he did not make contact with these garden spirits,
tried to be in harmony with them. In my work, I meditate to
attune myself to the needs of my garden, linking my deep
mind with its growing, and I listen for the voice of the plants,
so that they may advise me as to their needs. When I quiet my
mind, I take the first thing that comes to it as such communication; kale told me it would nourish me well, and chard told
me to fertilize and to use mulch under it. I also buried a
moonstone, traditionally the talisman of agriculturalists, in
our garden, to focus some of my meditative thoughts
through it into the earth, attuning my energy with hers.
Now, I feel much better about this garden than others I have
grown, and do not mind if all the 'effects' of my meditation
are just 'in my mind'. Then too, a good bit of evidence
indicates that plants do respond to our mental states, as
Peter Tompkins and Christopher Bird claim in their book
The Secret Life of Plants (New York: Avon Books, 1973).
Whether or not one thinks such research sound, centuries of
experience have taught us that one first has to believe something uncertain is possible for it to become so, so I steep
myself in the literature, hoping to be one of the explorers
on the new frontiers of the meditative mind.

Meditative techniques can be practised relating to any
activity, indeed, even in every garden, every occupation and

every recreation. Our images of what meditation can do derive too exclusively from one traditional application of it, from cultures far less secularized and quite different from our own. We need not perpetuate these limitations, however. Whatever the activity may be, it can become one's meditative object, the focus of the harnessing of the sensory and motor powers. Friends of mine, Ken and Penny, went to India several years ago, to study music and dance, but had no contacts prior to their departure. So, they used meditation. In Bangkok, they meditated on what they should do when arriving in Calcutta, and Ken saw an image of a shoe. Upon disembarking, a shoe salesman offered them help in finding a place to stay. After lunching in the hotel, again they meditated, and saw that they should leave that evening by train for Benares (Varanasi). Their host said that to obtain a ticket on a long distance train at such short notice was nearly impossible, but they went anyway to the station. The meditative direction was confirmed when they found two tickets still available. In Benares, after finding no teachers there for what they wanted to learn, meditation directed them to a town at the feet of the great Himālayas, where indeed they found congenial teachers and a good place to live and work. This seems an excellent way of using meditation, to mediate between an unknown and one's intention, not only with the intellect and its doors to the world, the five senses, but also with the deep mind's psychic reach, being open to the inner voice's advice. In this way one can bring all the mind's powers to bear on the self's journey through the world.

So I would apply meditation to any activity I wished to enhance by bringing more of the total activity of mind to bear on its success. Adventure and travel for me make excellent meditative objects. I discovered this the last time I went backpacking, hiking up from Lone Pine, California, over Whitney Pass into the remote eastern portions of Sequoia National Park. I decided to make my trek meditative, carefully setting up a meditative frame of mind. At the top of Mount Whitney I meditated, remembering that cultures everywhere consider mountain peaks specially favoured by spiritual forces. I identified with the mountain's presence, harmonizing with its being. That evening, as I set up my tent below, the sun reappeared from behind clouds on the horizon, lighting the park before me with a golden hue. I meditated on the scene as my welcome into this special place, and next morning, as I came upon the first mountain meadow, descending from the treeless high country, two pairs of mountain bluebirds met me. Perhaps many people would have noticed such things as a striking sunset and these birds as phenomena of nature, but to me, they entered my meditative set as special signs that Nature was welcoming and greeting me to her realm.

My application of meditative techniques accompanied me throughout the eight-day journey. I tried to establish every day a meditative set, opening my consciousness to the ever-changing scene along the trail. At special spots I sat for a while, using one or another sense to fix consciousness with its sensory modality on my meditative objects: hearing on the sounds of birds, wind, and stream; smell on the scent of things; sight on their surfaces. As the Zen tradition emphasizes, to meditate means to 'enter the quiet of one's mind', stilling one's ordinary thoughts and especially one's self-preoccupations, as Bashō wrote, going to the pine and the bamboo. Too often have I filled my head with thoughts of home or the bothers and trials of the trail as I made my way through the mountains. In this case, I tried to make my mind quiet in one-pointedness (*samādhi*); my meditative object was each tree I passed (I talked silently to ones close to my trail), each animal I saw, each stream I forded. Scientists find that after a period of meditation, and as one becomes more skilled at meditation, when one resumes activity, the meditative brain wave pattern can persist, so I worked on keeping the meditative mood as I walked. Morning and evening I kept fifteen or twenty minutes for special meditations, each time finding reward for my silence, a certain bird call, or deer grazing in the meadow. I tried walking *mantras* to alleviate the fatigue of carrying a heavy pack, and before I slept I massaged my body, telling the parts that hurt (shoulders, back, feet and sometimes head) to relax, to heal. I visualized my next day's hike and fell asleep fully expecting to awaken renewed and vigorous. To counteract altitude sickness (headache due to elevation and brilliant sun), I practised meditative deep breathing, especially as soon as I felt the first suggestions of pain. When my feet developed blisters, I cared for them (draining the liquid) and meditated on healing the surface irritation, visualizing blood going to that area and the skin not wearing off. Once, I slipped on a wet branch while crossing a wide rocky stream. The surprise was as much a shock as was the fall into the cold water. I immediately 'felt' like bathing my feet in the deeper but chilling stream nearby, without really thinking why; later, that evening, I noticed that I had sprained my ankle, but the cold water had already nursed it and my fall had not incapacitated me, when it well could have. At the time, I had found my body shaking from shock, and meditated then to clear the dangerous stress which flooded my body with excess adrenalin. Finally, on the last day, I reached to the top of the pass below Mount Whitney by 4 pm, so I had an hour to meditate, before going down the other side to camp for the night. As I gazed to the west over the country where I had spent a wonderful week, I thanked every being, from rock to bird to cloud, that had accompanied me. A large bird (a rare California Condor) sailed by above me, my sign that completion had come. I was ready to leave, the bird omen releasing me from the magic time and the special space which I had meditatively entered.

A thousand applications still remain, after all these I have mentioned, for other meditators to discover and elaborate. Only the imagination which accepts limitation can limit its uses, so no mind which recognizes its own intrinsic freedom will ever consider the question closed. On the other hand through the centuries one goal has led so many meditators to an ultimate kind of experience that I must devote the next chapter entirely to it.

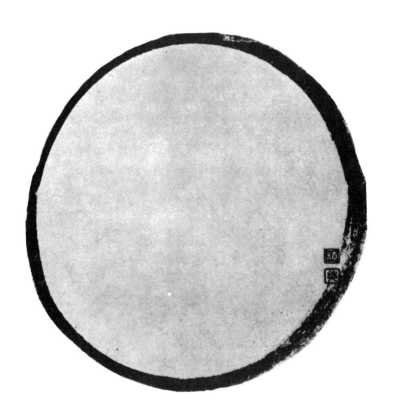

Ox-Taming 8 *Both Boy and Ox Forgotten!*

This picture presents the most enigmatic statement of the entire series, but since its subject is ecstasy, we should not be surprised by its lack of specific content. In effect, spiritual ecstasy transcends the ordinary, rational content of consciousness and plunges it into the fathomless emptiness of immaterial, spiritual reality. Ecstasy temporarily extinguishes all the separating blinders of individual selfhood (which is not to say that it is an unconscious state), removing the distinction they create between self and other in an ultimate sense (at least for this kind of self-transforming ecstasy, but certainly not all ecstasies). Ecstasy is experienced as unlimited, beyond past, present and future, an eternal now, beyond 'here-versus-there'; it is being everywhere. Traditionally, mystics have described this kind of ecstasy as an experience of oneness with everything (as light unites all diverse space, or as darkness does). The ecstatic episode may be short or long (from several minutes to days), but subject reports claim that it is timeless, beyond measurement by temporal and spatial rulers. As in Chuang Tzu's description of Tzu-ch'i's ecstasy, the body becomes like a withered tree, the mind like dead ashes; Tzu-ch'i reports to his companion, 'Now I have lost myself' (Watson, p. 31). This picture represents what the Buddha meant when he identified his ecstasy under the fig tree as a *nirvāna*, literally a 'blowing out' of separately conceived selfhood. Mystics who have this experience universally report that such selflessness is an ultimate experience, which transforms the experiencer in indefinable yet unalterable ways; not that the person automatically attains sainthood, but rather just that the person has an unforgettable experience of another dimension of 'self' or 'consciousness' which is 'selfless', quite unlike our ordinary identifications of these.

It would be interesting and helpful to be able to specify more about such a state, yet it resists such characterization. Rather, like certain other all-or-nothing experiences (such as orgasm), it either happens, or does not, and there can be no mistake. In my definition, many states qualify as ecstatic, but this particular one, which is so important in self-transformation, is distinct from others. These kinds of ecstatic states occur when individuals loosen their desires for things and their clinging to life (which is why many traumatic and near-death experiences produce them), when they surrender (or are forced to do so through intolerable situations, disease, extreme stress or the threat of death or execution), when the anxious self gives up or 'dies', allowing an alternative condition to flood the consciousness. A wholly new perspective comes to be adopted by consciousness, which is not extinguished (though the anxious self is, hence *nirvāṇa*) but expanded, witnessing rather than acting, feeling oneness rather than perceiving duality or multiplicity, being light rather than adopting a particular content or time-space identification. All of these meanings come in this empty circle; it is the mind resolved back into its absolute spirituality, the polar opposite of the fight-flight, kill-or-be-killed animal mentality, the archaic heritage of our ancestry and infancy. Being spiritual or immaterial, it accepts no such designations as 'mortal', 'limited' or 'conditioned'. One still has to interpret this, and the many interpretations of this kind of ecstatic experience are just that – interpretations borrowed from one's culture, and usually one's religious training. The best alternative to interpretation is experience, and meditation can lead, especially in conjunction with other disciplines, to such experiences.

This eighth picture represents a specialized kind of ecstasy, which is at times achieved by meditators, at times by non-meditators, technically designated as 'mystical' ecstasy. I have specialized the general term 'ecstasy' (see Introduction) to indicate excursions out of ordinary consciousness, especially those meditatively induced or aided. There are many altered states of consciousness which are not in the subclass I intend here (see diagram opposite, upper part), and in the sub-class of potentially spiritual ecstasies are included many which are not mystical. For example, dreams can be ecstatic, in fact are much more likely to be so than ordinary experience, because of the freedom of dream consciousness from the normal limitations of matter. An ecstatic dream is sometimes the easiest access to the experience of ecstasy. It has clear imagery and can demonstrate transcendence, be a concrete experience of it, not 'unreal' in the least. Trauma of all kinds, severe illness, chronic suffering, accident, or near-death experiences, all also seem able to induce ecstasies, many being of a spiritual nature, and some becoming mystical. Visionary experience must be another type along this continuum, as well as all special, meditatively entered consciousness forms, including the realm of psychic experiences, experiences of light and immateriality, and ecstatic flights and mergings. Many other forms might also be included in this sub-class of ecstasy (indicated by the etc.). Then, specifically mystical ecstasy may be placed at the other end of the whole spectrum of consciousness, its polar opposite being ordinary consciousness:

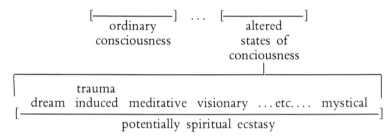

(Diagram not drawn to comparative scale but to indicate isolation of potentially spiritual forms of ecstasy.)

The defining feature which distinguishes or separates mystical from other kinds of ecstasy is the characteristic learning it gives. In many forms of ecstasy, one can gain self-knowledge, but in mystical ecstasy, one is initiated into the spiritual knowledge of one's identity. Ordinarily before such an experience, a person identifies 'selfhood' by its physical or mental localization in matter. In mystical ecstasy, one passes outside that usual identification to experience, as spirit, a second identity, the force of the experience being initiatory (hence the symbolism of death and rebirth, surrender, willingness to give up dependency). As Bharati properly argues, the transformation brought about through the experience of mystical ecstasy only changes this awareness of one's true identity, so the person who has had the experience may not be changed in any other respect (Bharati has met mystics who remained 'stinkers', and so have I). The ox-tamer thus accomplishes two ends by the taming, first preparing for all kinds of ecstasy by controlling the animal mind, and second, making this specialized mystical ecstasy possible by clearing up the anxious mind so that it can re-identify its 'self' with the spiritual. Otherwise, with the ox untamed, the person remains hopelessly bound to what the animal is dependent upon, which is an identity, but one which does not participate in the spiritual. Lame Deer, to take one example, experiences this transformation when Mrs Elk Head initiated him into it by showing him the most sacred Buffalo Calf Pipe (*Lame Deer Seeker of Visions*, p. 262):

That Buffalo Calf Pipe made me know myself, made me know the earth around me. It healed the blindness of my heart and made me see another world beyond the everyday world of the green frog skin.

Similarly, beginning in early life, Carl Jung distinguished in his experience a No. 1 (ordinary) and a No. 2 (spiritual) personality. He described the earliest experience of this re-identification in *Memories, Dreams, Reflections* (pp. 32–3):

I was taking the long road to school ... when suddenly for a single moment I had the overwhelming impression of having just emerged from a dense cloud. I knew all at once: now I am *myself*. It was as if a wall of mist were at my back, and behind that wall there was not yet an 'I'. But at this moment *I came upon myself*. Previously I had existed, too, but everything had merely happened to me. Now I knew: I am myself now, now I exist. Previously I had been willed to do this and that; now *I* willed.

Both Jung and Lame Deer, on the basis of such experiences, re-identified their ordinary 'I' consciousness with another spiritual selfhood, beyond and outside ordinary perception (the green frog skin world, referring to money, the being willed or conditioned in the ox-dependency on things, referring to the senses). Though it took both of them many years to solidify these intuitions of another, more important, spiritual identity, it began in the initiatory experience of mystically ecstatic de-identification with the ordinary self, symbolized here in the eighth ox-taming scene of 'self-forgetfulness'.

Thus this experience of mystical ecstasy conveys a special learning. In the process of self-transformation, this learning is crucial; it occurs in both eighth and ninth stages, for the next picture should be viewed with this one, giving as it does the Sino-Japanese interpretation of transforming ecstasy as a return to the source (a basic theme in Taoism which strongly influenced the Ch'an/Zen Buddhist tradition). Any report of the experience must occur within a tradition, although the experience itself is common to all humanity. I borrow one such description from Imakita Kōsen, a Meiji era Japanese Zen master (as reported in Dumoulin's *A History of Zen Buddhism*, Boston: Beacon Press, 1969, p. 273):

One night when I was engaged in zazen [seated meditation] the boundary between before and after was suddenly cut off. [He enters the timeless realm, the void of this eighth picture.] I entered the blessed realm of the exceedingly wonderful. I found myself, as it were, on the ground of the Great Death, and no awareness of the being of all things and of the ego remained. [Selflessness attained.] I felt only how in my body a spirit extended itself to ten thousand worlds, and an infinite splendor of light arose. After a short while I breathed again. In a flash seeing and hearing, speech and motion, were different from every day. As I sought the supreme truth and the wonderful meaning of the universe, my own self was clear and things appeared bright. In the excess of delight I forgot that my hands were moving in the air and that my feet were dancing.

Teachers and students of Buddhism should carefully read this passage because it clearly establishes that the famous doctrine of *anātman* ('no self') applies to the 'ego' (anxious self) and its instrumental perception of things, and not to the total selfhood. This latter, the master says, extended infinitely (as a spiritual dimension of consciousness), and, in ecstasy, he saw both self and things as clear and bright. The passage reveals the transformative impact of such an ecstasy, for suddenly the meditator's consciousness slipped out of time (the before and after), dying from the old, immature selfhood to be 'reborn' into the self's true spirituality. Once one has gone through such an episode, a new component to one's experience is added to consciousness. No, it does not magically cleanse immaturity away; we have seen that the ox-taming comes before this. It does, however, give an unforgettable initiation into spirit, the basis for a new being in the world.

Meditators, who take self-knowledge as their ultimate goal, eagerly seek this spiritual initiation (see the discussion in the next chapter). Once one crosses this invisible boundary or threshold, the world and other human beings become real, more than just fantasy objects for one's secret desires or some hidden agenda. Participating in the spirit dimension of the other is a consummatory experience valuable in and for itself, rather than an instrument for some immature need gratification. The learning which makes a person mature comes from such moments. This 'great going out' figures as the goal of manifold human hero myths; the hero struggles to learn what is beyond the immature self. This fulfils the promise of self-transformation; the heroic encounter with, taming and loss of 'self' allows the ecstatic participation in the 'self's' spirituality. To understand this superficially paradoxical claim, one need only realize that the two uses of 'self' describe different levels or dimensions of consciousness, one the ground of animal immaturity, the other the basis of spirituality, well-being and a mature adaptation to life.

9

Meditative Achievement of Self-Knowledge

The most striking goal to which meditation has been applied involves the gaining of deeper and deeper degrees, levels and dimensions of self-knowledge. After all is said and done about the other uses to which meditation may be put, gaining increased self-knowledge remains for many its ultimate application. Shamans possessed their 'power' to help and heal because they had achieved deep knowledge of the inner self, and thus could draw from its calmer, superior grasp of reality. We have all known remarkable individuals who impress by their presence alone, exuding sympathy and wisdom; Maslow called such people 'self-actualizers', while others have designated them saints or great heroic leaders of humanity. They laugh easily and love deeply; they have secret inner springs of fortitude and endurance, they know while others wonder, they see when others remain blind. These people somehow, through various experiences, have come into possession of what tradition labels 'self-knowledge'. Socrates thought such knowledge constituted the basis for all human wisdom and action. According to Xenophon's remembrances of Socrates,* he thought it 'madness' to be ignorant of oneself, and that 'people derive most of their benefits from knowing themselves, and most of their misfortunes from being self-deceived' (p. 191). In answer to Antiphon, who identified happiness with luxury and

---

*All quotations except when otherwise noted are from the Penguin Classics translation *Memoirs of Socrates* by Hugh Tredennick.

extravagance, something many people do today as well, Socrates said:

I have always thought that to need nothing is divine, and to need as little as possible is the nearest approach to the divine; and that what is divine is best, and what is nearest to the divine is the next best.

(Memoirs of Socrates, p. 62)

I do not think Socrates here teaches that the best path denies life; rather, he points out that to be dependent for one's happiness on material luxuries and extravagance reduces one's happiness to the availability of the objects of one's dependence. But what, then, in the human realm is the real object of happiness? As Xenophon reports, Socrates believed that the self *(psyche)* is that which 'more than anything else *that is human* partakes of the divine'. Thus to know self means to be in contact with that part of ourselves which most fully participates in the divine, the contact which brings enduring, essential happiness. To turn attention to and care for the *psyche*, Plato reports in the *Apology* (his remembrance of Socrates), ranks as far more important than achieving fame or fortune. Religious elites (by which term I mean to exclude the many who practise a 'popular', ritual form of religion in an attempt to increase life's fortune and avert misfortune) have practised meditation almost exclusively to pursue this goal of gaining self-knowledge. I do not think this applies to the earliest religious elites, such as the Egyptian pharaohs, who attempted by their pyramids to build themselves into the happiness of immortality, nor have most priests used meditation in this manner. But in every age for which we have fairly complete records, some of the most remarkable literary documents come from individuals who immersed themselves, through meditation and allied disciplines, in knowledge of the deep self within. Socrates himself listened to his 'inner voice', with which he had made contact at an early age in his natural ecstasies. Monastics, mystics, prophets, diviners, saints, saviours and seers all sought for this deep participation in the inner quality of our human being-ness, the self which possesses or has the quality of being 'divine', whatever that term designates.

Undoubtedly, when people experience ecstasy, they touch deeper aspects of themselves (as well as deeper dimensions of the world), unimagined during ordinary waking experience. Knowledge of self may be one-dimensional, as in the majority of people who consider valid only what they know when awake in good and sound mind. Others enlarge this definition of valid self-knowledge by considering different states of mind also to reveal reality. While most consider dreams mere 'fantasy', some take them as contact with other, deeper dimensions of themselves. Still, many other special states of consciousness exist, which also can help establish deeper self-knowledge. Highly emotive aesthetic and religious experiences lead to such deepenings, as do the alterations of consciousness which occur when we travel, or even simply as we grow older. Fantasy and visionary experience, though distrusted or dismissed as being 'unreal' by our materialistic presuppositions about reality, may lead to significant self-perceptions, too. But these do not come every day; nor do the more specific attempts to gain self-knowledge through deliberate psychological techniques of intensive self-exploration (including psychotherapy, reflection, deliberate self-examination). Finally, meditation opens another major path to enhanced self-knowledge for some by its peculiar ability to induce consciously sought after ecstatic states.

Usually, we consider our 'self' to be relatively uncomplicated, the object of our waking consciousness, consisting of everything that we do and think; the self exists as that of which we are conscious, our public and private *personae* as gardener, lover, mother, grandson, artist, worker, skier. 'Self' possesses recognizable characteristics (our 'personality traits'), experiences feelings, expresses aspirations, suffers traumas, all the while enduring as the central focus of our being. Furthermore, we ordinarily consider that of all that we know, we know our own self best. In his *Memoirs of Socrates*, Xenophon (iv, 2, 24) reports that Socrates asked

Euthydemus whether he had heeded the Delphic temple inscription enjoining 'Know Thyself', to which Euthydemus replied 'surely not', explaining, 'I was certain that I knew this, for I would hardly know anything else if I did not know myself' (Anna S. Benjamin, from the Bobbs-Merrill translation *Recollections of Socrates*). Socrates goes on to point out that our usual assumption that we know ourselves does not withstand careful examination, an observation confirmed repeatedly by therapists who very quickly can help to remove certain inner blinders from the understanding even of people who declare themselves problem-free and in good possession of self-knowledge, revealing beneath their personality surface a wholly different, hidden self.

This recognition of deeper, inner, ecstatic aspects of self can come from many different experiences which alter our usual consciousness of self. Psychologists, particularly those identified with 'depth psychology', recognize that 'self' designates a multiplicity of identities and part-identities, rather than the singleness we assume the single word indicates. Even though we say, 'myself', or 'the self', we should not make the false extension of the singular noun to the actual reality of the total human being we are. The early scientific distrust of dreams, fantasy and the imagination as not giving verifiable information about the 'real', physical, external world, came, incorrectly, to be applied also to non-tangible, inner realities of the psyche, an unfortunate extension of the model of empirical science into the realm of introspective self-observation. If we ever decide to explore the real depths of the psyche, we must utilize the many ways of ecstatic knowing available to us.

Accepting the 'reality' of so-called fantasy experience opens the door to a total selfhood which we all possess. Taking dreams as an example, commonly we all consider dream experience to be 'unreal', ephemeral, night-time fantasy which tells us absolutely nothing about anything real or important. As an alternative, we could easily consider the content of dreams to reflect a part of our real self (what else could it be – part of our unreal self?), betraying a part of what we really are. By this slight shift in our reality definition, we can throw open the doorway to a wholly different way of knowing the self, one which has profound implications, as students of dreams know, for our self-knowledge. To restrict our knowledge of self merely to what we know in conscious, non-fantasy experience amputates whole portions of the self from our understanding, alienating them, so that we exist, iceberg-like, with consciousness focused solely on the very tip, while the deep psyche lies mysteriously, sometimes threateningly, below the water line or threshold of awareness. Or, to take another example, should we understand visionary experience as pathological, as a 'break with reality'? Such an evaluation makes nonsense of the long-standing human tradition, attested in every known culture and tradition but our own, that attributes important meaning to visions of all kinds. (It was acceptable in biblical times, but not today). Though we may not want to interpret visions in the traditional manner (as messages from spirits, or the divine), we should not dismiss them as pathological aberrations of consciousness. Rather, we could look at them as reflexes of different dimensions of our selfhood, erupting into consciousness not with a message from the divine but with information about previously hidden aspects of ourselves.

The Swiss depth psychologist, Carl Jung, for one, understood visions and dreams as eruptions into consciousness of the unconscious contents of the self. Thus, he used such material in the process of elaborating his self-knowledge because he did not consider it alien or unreal but a part of his actual selfhood, thus accepting it into his total experience as meaningful and self-revealing. The wholeness of the 'self' derives not from its being a unified, one-dimensional selfhood, reliably known only in conscious, non-fantasy waking consciousness, but from the perceived fact that all these experiences, dream, vision, fantasy, imagination, and perception, constitute the experience of what we think of as 'I'. 'I' am the subject of all my diverse experiences, thus, in some sense, they all reveal to me aspects of my multi-dimensional self. What depth psychology stresses today, ancient Indian psychology discovered centuries ago when meditators observed the psyche's productions in meditative ecstasies to formulate the postulate of the Hindu-Buddhist notion of reincarnation. The biographical myth of the Buddha memorialized this for all Asian thought when it portrayed his first enlightenment vision as being the remembering of *all* his past lives, or in our sense, the multiplicity of his self. Because we disagree with India in our understanding of time and personal identity, we reject its interpretation of this multiplicity of selves as reincarnation of previously lived multiple selves, but find our psychologists now claiming that we indeed have many 'incarnations' (multiple selves) in this one lifetime. I experienced some of my 'incarnations' in dream, others in fantasy, or vision, or imagination. I can 'remember' my past lives by focusing on the dimension of my psyche which contains – or creates – their memory traces, the things which come spontaneously to mind when I ask it for such 'recollection'. I wish here to avoid the ontological issue as to whether I actually 'lived' those past lives in Rome and medieval Europe, to focus on the undeniable fact that when properly accessed, my psyche 'images' them spontaneously and on its own, for its own reasons. Whatever those reasons may be, I trust my psyche; it is part of me, my 'self', my reality. I choose to accept, in the same manner, my dreams as a form of genuine life-experience. I expand my 'self' to include dream experiences of flying, incredible transformations, wondrous fascinations with unearthly beauty, adventures and terrors, mysteries and discoveries. By remembering and gaining insight into the symbolism of my dreams I integrate these experiences into the total selfhood which I am, rather than shunning them as being without significance.

At the end of each chapter of this book, I have discussed another picture in the classical Ch'an/Zen Buddhist series of ox-taming pictures. My interpretation of these focuses on them as a portrait of how a person comes to maturity, first through gaining self-control (knowing and controlling the ox-self) and then by transcending the ox and immature boy-self, through ecstasy to return to life as a self-possessed person of mature power. Though many techniques exist for achieving such a maturation, meditation can play a major role in it, and has done so for generations in all world civilizations. Since meditation directly accesses deep, as well as surface, dimensions of mind, it not only is itself a powerful means of coming to knowledge of 'self' but can enhance and be used in conjunction with other techniques, such as dream recall, fantasy production and imaginative identification with meditative objects which expand the self's boundaries. Often while meditating in the morning, my last night's dreams well up into my meditatively opened mind. Notoriously ephemeral, dreams actually just come from and exist in a subtler dimension of self, to which one can gain access through meditation. Fantasy, guided imagery and non-pathological vision (being experience to which no physical world object corresponds), can all be enhanced and developed through meditative means. Imaginative identification with meditative objects can similarly expand and deepen one's knowledge of the self's potentialities. This is illustrated by the example of the Christian tradition of the imitation of Christ, and in that of Tibetan Buddhist meditation, in which the monk identifies with the god whose power he wishes to incorporate into his own self-structure, so as to use it for the benefit of others in ritual and healing actions performed for them.

I have learned from my own personal experience, as well as from my reading in the history of religions, that the urge to gain deeper self-knowledge usually does not come until one has gone through both the challenges of emerging from childhood dependency into the adult world and those associated with establishing one's identity and position in that world. Physiological maturation makes possible successive stages of learning; as children, we cannot learn to walk or talk until a certain stage of physiological maturation arrives. Somehow the same applies to achieving deep self-knowledge. After sufficient world experience and the physiological changes which 'slow the body metabolism down', one becomes more able to incorporate into one's knowledge aspects of the deeper self, and one begins to experience the desire to do so. For some, this comes much earlier, as in the case of Socrates, or the need motivates such activities as our great artists and writers exemplify. The history of religion shows, however, that the critical age begins around one's thirtieth birthday. At twenty-nine, the Buddha left the palace, to be enlightened at thirty-six; Jesus Christ's ministry occurred at around the same age, Muhammad did not begin the visionary activity of receiving the Lord's *Koran* until the age of forty (after, as a successful merchant, he had begun to meditate), Japan's poet-mystic Bashō began serious meditation with a Zen master around the age of thirty-six, retreating from the 'floating world' of Tokyo's city superficiality to his banana hermitage, which he also left, at the age of forty, to become a fully-fledged wanderer in the Sino-Buddhist tradition. Although he experienced his power vision at sixteen, Lame Deer did not become a great healer until after he had raised hell, womanized, and gone to jail during his second and third decade. St Teresa of Avila struggled with the trauma of her mother's death and her own highly sensitive physiology from the age of seventeen until around forty, when she finally integrated the mystical eruptions of her deeper self into the frame of the Catholic theology which (especially in Inquisition times) taught her explicitly to distrust such unitive experience. When one participates in the deep inner self, one considers it to be divine, but monotheistic theology teaches that one does not become or think oneself God. Mystics from all branches of Western Asian religion (Judaism, Christianity, Islam) have suffered mightily because of this theology, many being executed or condemned to ostracism because of their response to the calling of the divine within.

Around the age of forty, Albert Camus wrote 'The Sea Close By' (*Albert Camus, Lyrical and Critical Essays*, New

York: Vintage Books, 1968, pp. 172–81). He begins this reflective essay by using the sea to symbolize his emerging desire for deeper self-knowledge. About to embark on a long awaited sea-voyage, after the postponement caused by World War II which had ended Camus' youthful innocence and interrupted his plan to re-trace by boat Odysseus' wandering around the Mediterranean, he uses the sea to describe the longing for the self which had become alien to him:

I grew up with the sea and poverty for me was sumptuous; then I lost the sea [at the beginning of the war period] and found all luxuries gray and poverty unbearable. Since then, I have been waiting. I wait for the homebound ships, the house of the waters, the limpidity of day. I wait patiently, am polite with all my strength. I am seen walking on fine, sophisticated streets, I admire landscapes, I applaud like everyone, shake hands, but it is not I who speak. Men praise me, I dream a little, they insult me, I scarcely show surprise. Then I forget, and smile at the man who insulted me, or am too courteous in greeting the person I love. Can I help it if all I remember is one image? Finally, they summon me to tell them who I am. 'Nothing yet, nothing yet ... '

(Lyrical and Critical Essays, p. 172)

Camus grew up on the Algerian coast of the Mediterranean, poor but in a land bathed in warmth and sunshine. He left the paradise of his youth, drawn beyond his power into a dark, war-ravaged northern Europe. Two decades later, he confesses to be waiting for 'homebound ships' (home = self, ship = means of transformation), for the 'house' (= self) 'of the waters' (= the primal innocence of his youth, his true inner state). Everything seems superficial – action, accomplishment, fame, and insult. He has but one longing, 're-members' only one image, that of the 'sea' (= inner self) which holds his sole true identity.

Many people experience this longing, particularly in middle age, but, unfortunately, few know how to respond to it. Our culture discarded the traditional religious avenues for aiding such response several centuries ago. The rising tide of sceptical rationalism declared such concern for inner experience and the attainment of deep self-knowledge to be tantamount to self-indulgence and participation in near-morbid self-preoccupation. Major establishment institutions today continue to affirm this value commitment, such as our universities which shy away from meditation and depth psychology. All the while, psychology departments grow enormously, fuelled by the renewed interest in the psyche, shunned as it is by our secularized religious institutions. What groups or institutions can persons turn to when the inner longings for increased self-knowledge arise? Unless their implications involve pathology, thus calling for some kind of therapy, one can look long and hard for a suitable context in which to develop one's response to them. Some artists, writers, and some other independent spirits do follow the call, integrating it into their vocation or avocation, while some fall into the fortune of discovering the few therapeutic or meditative or self-realizational contexts which exist to further these desires, but I personally am distrustful of many of these because they so often appear to be crippled by cultish ideas and worn-out spiritualisms. Perhaps my distrust is unfounded, as one person's spirit may be another's devil; I fervently wish for the development of rationally based, doctrinally neutral groups and institutions which will honestly and impartially initiate seekers into the rich realm of deepened self-knowledge.

The experience of Carl Jung demonstrates how radically our contemporary culture has cast the seeker after self-knowledge adrift in a sea of ignorance and distrust. Though he was visionary from childhood, Jung's world, dominated by empirical science, determined that the only respectable educational path open to him required that he study medical science. As he remembered in his book *Memories, Dreams, Reflections*, he completed his medical training, and became a professor and a psychiatrist, working with mentally disturbed patients. By that fateful age of around thirty-six years (in 1911–12), however, as he describes in his chapter entitled

'Confrontation with the Unconscious', he became increasingly drawn into contact with his 'inner images', finally allowing them to come forth from the deep psyche for a disturbing but highly creative period of five or six years. He entered the 'dream-like' atmosphere of the unconscious psyche, disturbingly dream-like to the medical scientist trained exclusively in rational, empirical procedures for knowing 'reality'. But to do this, he had to oppose everything in his scientific training, fearing personal psychosis and professional ostracism; further, he had no precedents to follow, and no people to help him, though he previously had hoped that Freud would do this. In this sense, his act provided the pathfinding example of such a self-analysis for the Western world as the Buddha's vision quest did for the Eastern, some 2,500 years before. Tradition considered Gautama *svayaṃbhū*, or 'self-created', in the sense that what he did had no apparent precedent and he had no teacher to guide him through his encounter with the psyche. We should consider Jung one of the major explorers of our century for this courageous response he made to the inner calling of his psyche.

Essentially, Jung decided to consider the inner psyche real ('Therefore my first obligation was to probe the depths of my own psyche . . . '). With this decision, he proceeded to explore what flowed up from the unconscious in 'fantasy' (or what I have called vision). Unfortunately, he did not have available to him the vast human tradition, both Eastern and Western, which used meditation and guided imagination in just such self-explorations, so he invented his own ways. One was to use play: he built, childlike, a miniature stone village on his lakeside land. He adopted unknowingly an important meditative principle when he decided to try to control his fantasy life by focusing his inner attention on one fantasy at a time, taking it as his meditative object instead of allowing a whole flock of unconnected fantasies to well up and confuse his exploration. He recounted that in December 1913 he took this 'decisive step', continuing:

I was sitting at my desk once more, thinking over my fears. Then I let myself drop. Suddenly it was as though the ground literally gave way beneath my feet, and I plunged down into dark depths.

(Jaffé, p. 179)

A vision followed, one of many which took him years to understand (or make part of his self-understanding). He later called this method 'active imagination', teaching it to hundreds in his later therapeutic career. Just as Buddhist monks teach Gautama's techniques, Jungians now do the same in their practice of Jungian psychotherapy. I would call it meditation, since it requires that the person make a conscious decision to take the visionary contents of the deep psyche (whether in dream, play, or imaginative fantasy) as the meditative object and follow them through to their final implications. Another example of this deliberate meditative technique which he used we now call guided imagination:

In order to seize hold of the fantasies, I frequently imagined a steep descent. I even made several attempts to get to very bottom. The first time I reached, as it were, a depth of about a thousand feet; the next time I found myself at the edge of a cosmic abyss. It was like a voyage to the moon, or a descent into empty space. [He then describes the vision which followed.]

(Jaffé, p. 181)

Tibetan Buddhists made similar explorations (see S. Beyer, *The Cult of Tārā*, Berkeley: University of California Press, 1973) using meditative techniques and devices, including the maṇḍala, which Jung also re-invented during his quest, calling it the expression of the self which restores 'inner peace' (i.e. by providing a meditative object which balances the psyche by externalizing and helping to resolve intrapsychic conflict and anxiety). Also, Jung mentioned the use of some other meditative techniques to allay the anxiety released in this process, but his remark is too vague to make much of ('I was frequently so wrought up that I had to do certain yoga exercises in order to hold my emotions in check, Jaffé, p. 177).

This difficult five- or six-year period of self-discovery gave Jung a lifetime of value, as it does to anyone who is willing to undertake its trails and struggles. He recalled:

The years when I was pursuing my inner images were the most important in my life – in them everything essential was decided. It all began then; the later details are only supplements and clarifications of the material that burst forth from the unconscious, and at first swamped me. It was the *prima materia* for a lifetime's work.

(Jaffé, p. 199)

Jung had achieved in those years what most never suspect possible, but which can hold the entire success or failure of our efforts toward achieving personal happiness. Gaining deep self-knowledge is crucial to a life worth living, as Socrates instructed our largely unheeding Western civilization. It can be a major goal of meditation, used in conjunction with other techniques of self-discovery. Jung recalled that his achievement of self-knowledge distinguished him from others more than anything else, writing, 'The difference between most people and myself is that for me the "dividing walls" are transparent. That is my peculiarity. Others find these walls so opaque that they see nothing behind them and therefore think nothing is there.'

What Jung observes in this passage pertains to the experience many report of being two selves, personalities, or aspects of self, one conscious, the other usually hidden deep within. Jung associated this second inner personality with what I have called the 'psychic' dimension of mind, observing it in his mother and others as well. Probably, one of the primal human achievements of knowledge involved coming into touch with this inner dimension of self. Historical religions consider it the soul, spirit, or self (*ātman* in Sanskrit), and Lame Deer became aware of it and its power during his vision quests, indicating it played a central role in prehistoric religion as well. The first evidence of religion comes from middle Paleolithic times when Neanderthal man became aware of this human innerness and began to pay special attention to disposal of the dead. Their burials prepared for the continuance after death of this inner spirit either by providing grave-goods for life on the 'other side' or by trying to prevent in some way or another its return as a malevolent ghost. Like children, primitive people often could not handle this growing awareness of an inner dimension of self lying below the surfaces of consciousness; projected on to the world, at times they feared it, at times considered it malevolent, especially after dark. Jung had the same experience as shamans where the dividing wall of the threshold of consciousness disintegrated to become porous to the contents of this deeper psyche. Humanity has matured considerably since the days of the Neanderthals, and ever since the advent of civilization and the world's major religions, human beings have been able to work through their fears of such deeper contact, integrating the psyche's contents into their total self-conception, rather than externalizing them as 'real' gods, demons, or ghosts. The Buddha, like the other 'saviours', also resolved the disturbing intrapsychic conflicts and anxieties of his surface consciousness, allowing him to make contact with the deeper aspects of his awareness.

One of the most constructive developments within the world's religions has been their refinement of the process of coming to deeper self-knowledge. This occurred not in the religion concerned with magico-religious rituals (festival, yearly agrarian rites, cults of saints, protection ceremonies, pilgrimages and the like) but in elitist, esoteric religious subcommunities, particularly among monastics and mystics. Whereas Socrates exemplifies a kind of natural self-knowledge, achieved at a very early age and preserved from youth, and Jung shows how someone quite independent of any established tradition can gain such access to the deeper self, the great mystics of the world's religions show how man has learned how to cultivate such deeper self-knowledge primarily through meditative means. Of everything which religions have developed, their elaboration and systematization of means for achieving this spiritual knowledge will probably contribute most to the future evolution of human consciousness. Far more people have matured into fuller self-knowledge following these procedures than through any other of man's institutions or activities.

Remarkably, no one religion or set of religions developed these meditative techniques of self-realization to the exclusion of others. Probably this came about because mystical intuitions urging toward deeper self-knowledge are a feature of all human consciousness, as are the major means of realizing these goals. As an example, I often compare the lives of two individuals so separated by cultural context and geography that they must be considered (in anthropological terminology) as examples of independent, convergent evolution. St Teresa of Avila lived as a Catholic contemplative in medieval Spain; Matsuo Bashō was a poet and a lay disciple of Zen Buddhism in medieval Japan. Neither culture by that time had significant contact with the other, but Teresa and Bashō achieved their self-knowledge in similar ways. Both experienced psychological dislocation as a result of the death of someone close during youth (Teresa her mother, Bashō his companion), both struggled during their second and third decades to balance the adult world with their longings for inner self-knowledge, and both achieved a relatively stable resolution of their conflicts by the age of forty through meditative disciplines. Teresa practised the prayer of quiet, spent long hours in contemplative reflection, and eventually made sense of her ecstatic flights into the psyche's depths by interpreting them in the terms of Catholic theology (see her idealized map of the path in her memoir, *The Interior Castle*, New York: Image Books, 1961). Bashō never became a monastic, as Teresa did, but cultivated the art of increasingly spiritual poetry; by the age of thirty-six, he began serious meditation with the Zen Buddhist priest, Bucchō, deepening his access to the deep self so that he could write exquisite *haiku* poetry, as Teresa could write equally exquisite medieval Spanish inspirational literature. By the age of forty,

Bashō had sufficient self-knowledge to know that he could only be happy by accepting his own form of 'monasticism' in becoming an itinerant wandering poet following the manner of old China. (See his memoir, translated as *The Narrow Road to the Deep North and other travel sketches*, Baltimore: Penguin Books, 1966.)

Bashō and Teresa both experienced the fears and trials that shook Jung during his period of struggle (the classical term for which is 'agony', or contest with self, as in Christ's agony in the Garden), but had traditional meditative ways of responding to the challenges, as Jung did not. Thus, we who like Jung lack such means, can learn from the example of these older meditative traditions, just as we can learn, too, from what science is beginning to elaborate about meditative approaches to consciousness development. A fascinating model life in this transcultural tradition of meditative self-transformation became available to us when Burton Watson arranged and translated a hundred poems by the Chinese T'ang lay Buddhist poet Han-shan in his book *Cold Mountain* (New York: Columbia University Press, 1970). Han-shan's poems portray a life whose ultimate meaning derived from the poet's practice of meditation in the Ch'an school (the Chinese form of Japanese Zen). Since Ch'an meditation practices derive largely from Taoist forms, with an overlay of imported Buddhist ideas, we can consider the example of Han-shan's life a genuine Sino-Buddhist model for meditative achievement of self-knowledge. Like Teresa and Bashō, Han-shan's poems give autobiographical information about his life and experience, which I find preferable to biographies and the accounts of followers, which usually so idealize the Master that we lose the reality of the person in the aura of the admiration he inspires.

Han-shan, who lived around the early ninth century AD, started off, as many do, in relative comfort, well enough provided for by his family inheritance. Married, with a child, he lived as a country gentleman, but with a difference: he tells us his bed was 'piled high with books' (poems 1 and 2), and his poems show us how he became aware of the transience of his youthful experiences of beauty and pleasure. Now anyone who piles the bed high with books should not expect an uneventful life. After adventuresome youth, Han-shan's life took a turn towards poverty (he mentions his being part of a company of 'poor scholars'), his heart (inner sense) became restless, his wife and friends turned away from him, leading to his breaking 'ties with the world of red dust' (poems 31–5). Looking back on his youth, he saw how he lacked self-awareness during that time (a common regret of people who become more conscious as they mature) living with a deluded view of existence, and:

> Then, before I knew it, things went to pieces.
> Now who would bother with an old man?

> (Watson, p. 53, poem 35)

Though the poems do not tell us how old Han-shan was at this point in life, I imagine he had reached or was approaching his fourth decade; he says (poem 43) he divined and decided to live in the T'ien-t'ai mountain range, sacred to Buddhists and a refuge to many who had decided to withdraw from the red-dust world of anxiety and contention.

In the language of self-transformation, Han-shan had decided to take responsibility for his states of awareness and lack of self-knowledge, just as Jung did during mid-life. In self-transformation symbolism he decided to 'go home' (come to deeper knowledge of the inner self), writing:

> And today I've come home to Cold Mountain
> To pillow my head on the stream and wash my ears.

> (Watson, p. 56, poem 38)

As translators have noted, 'Cold Mountain' means both a place and the state of mind which Han-shan achieves through meditation; his image of pillowing and washing at the stream indicates he takes nature as the meditative object to purify his consciousness of intrusive elements, very much in keeping with the organicism and naturalism of Taoist meditative practices. The time, as usual, comes fraught with the stormy emotions associated with major personality reorientation; again, Han-shan uses the symbol of taking his body home to describe his solution:

> Why am I always so depressed?
> Man's life is like the morning mushroom.
> Who can bear, in a few dozen years,
> To see new friends and old all gone away?
> Thinking of this, I am filled with sadness,
> A sadness I can hardly endure.
> What shall I do? Say, what shall I do?
> Take this old body home and hide it in the mountains.
>
> (Watson, p. 54, poem 36)

'Cold Mountain' symbolizes Han-shan's taking refuge in the calm and inner security of meditative ecstasy. He records 'I lie alone by folded cliffs ... My mind is clear and free of clamor' (Watson, p. 60, poem 42) – the clear mind being the goal of Buddhist meditation (clear of anxiety and self-preoccupation), the 'freedom' in meditation which provided Patricia Carrington with the title of her book. 'Since I am mindless, who can rouse my thoughts?', he writes (poem 49), and holds fast to his inner reality, as opposed to the external aging of his body:

> Though face and form alter with the years
> I hold fast to the pearl of the mind.
>
> (Watson, p. 73, poem 49)

What Han-shan did gave him the key to his life's happiness; he took responsibility for his inner development, for his own states of consciousness, and through meditation came to peace of mind, as many of his later poems indicate. The achievement rested upon the deliberate action of making the choice for meditative self-cultivation. In a marvellous metaphor, he describes this as 'opening a business of one's own':

> In the old days when I was so poor,
> Night after night I counted other men's wealth.

Recently I thought it over
And decided to open a business of my own.
I dug a hole and found a hidden treasure –
A store of crystal jewels.
A blue-eyed foreigner came in secret
And wanted to buy them and take them away
But I only answered him,
'These jewels are beyond price!'

(Watson, p. 77, poem 59)

Here, Han-shan describes turning inward through meditation as digging a hole to find a hidden treasure (the psyche) which exceeds all material value, the discovery of which makes one far richer than any of one's own possessions or the fortunes of others. He 'thought it over', that is, observed his ways and values, deciding to change them to be more inner directed, to value self-knowledge more than material wealth. This value reorientation opened the door to new happiness through meditatively enriched self-knowledge; though Han-shan remained a mountain-dwelling recluse, whatever one's material fortunes are after making such a decision (most live simply, sharing in another wealth), the happiness one treasures most derives from coming to knowledge of the inalienable self.

True to his Buddhist doctrine, Han-shan stressed the emptiness of the meditative mind. He compares mind in ecstasy to a pool of clear water, sparkling like a crystal, which one can see right through, to the bottom (i.e. to the deep psyche, poem 86, p. 104), concluding:

> My mind is free from every thought,
> Nothing in the myriad realms can move it.

This definition bears the distinct imprint of India (recall Patañjali's definition), but we should not fall victim to misunderstandings that can flow from the peculiar Buddhist interpretation of the meditative experience (or, for that matter, from any other, Christian, Hindu, Jewish, Taoist or Muslim). Each meditation system will describe the goal in

211

terms of its own theological interpretation of ultimacy; what remains, after we consider all these systems is what the essence of meditation consists of, namely, self-knowledge. As Han-shan himself saw, many ask for *the* (one) way: 'People ask the way to Cold Mountain', to which he replies, puzzled, 'Cold Mountain? There is no road that goes through', concluding that what defines all the separate paths is the centre, the self, for which they all search:

> If your heart were the same as mine,
> Then you could journey to the very centre!

> (Watson, p. 100, poem 82)

In our contemporary Western culture, we have rediscovered the notion of the deeper self as the centre or orienting reality of our total selfhood in the world. Many have shared in creating this rediscovery; it incorporates something almost so essential to human happiness that it could not be excluded for ever from our intellectual and emotional horizons. Pathfinders such as Freud and Jung have provided new outlines of human reality along with those who took the journey to the East (as Jung himself did, almost dying in Calcutta in the 1930s) and who responded, like Maslow, to the void they found in contemporary psychology along with the impoverished theology of secularized Judaism and Christianity. Once Jung dreamed of Liverpool (the name he interpreted as symbolic, since the liver is the source of life as is a 'pool' of water), where he found a blooming magnolia on a sunlit island in the middle of the dreary, rainy city. This dream brought to a close the period of his raw self-exploration, after which he gradually understood over the years what had flowed forth from his inspiration. He gave this interpretation:

This dream brought with it a sense of finality. I saw that here the goal had been revealed. One could not go beyond the centre. The centre is the goal, and everything is directed toward that centre. Through this dream I understood that the self is the principle and archetype of orientation and meaning. Therein lies its healing function. For me, this insight signified an approach to the centre and therefore to the goal. Out of it emerged a first inkling of my personal myth [i.e. his 'self-knowledge'] ...

(Jaffé, p. 198–9)

Everyone can come to this point by attending to the inner work; for me, meditation sometimes provides a centralizing activity, around which dream, therapy, work, travel, play and the seeking for visions organize themselves, building the experiences out of which I shall create my personal myth, which I hope will lay bare before my death, my 'selfhood'. My desire to lead as creative a life as possible makes life into an adventure.

I dreamt recently, in Calcutta, at the end of a journey through Sikkim and Nepal, that I was under a large tree with thick limbs. I reached up to find one limb quite rotten, and very light; I pushed at it and it came off, on to the ground. Of the eight or so remaining limbs, I did the same to five or six, each one surprising me with its pliability to my hand. I noted the pile, and also that the remaining limbs had a few leaves still on them, which assured me that the tree would continue to live, and be able to regenerate itself. I interpret this tree to be my being, which I am now clearing of the dead wood (*karma*) of my past (which surprisingly is lighter than I think). The action I took in the dream symbolizes my current efforts at self-transformation. Upon returning home, I dreamed that I went outside my house and found there, again to my surprise, that bushes close to it had begun to flower; I discovered one kind of flower after another, marvelling at their colour and beauty. To me this means that what I seek is coming closer; it is just outside my house (conscious self), and I am becoming more able to reach that world's beauty. Meditation cannot alone bring me to my goal, but it can be a powerful means of transforming that mind which seeks to know itself, at all levels, in all the dimensions which constitute its 'reality'. I no longer define that reality narrowly as that of which I am immediately conscious. I turn to dreams, divinations, imaginings and fantasies; like a child I accept everything I experience in these modes as interesting, confident of not being betrayed by the jewel of my own consciousness.

Ox-Taming 9   *Return To The Source*

In this scene, ox and person are still forgotten, but something has appeared: plum blossom, rock and squat bamboo, beside a gently flowing stream. The subject, like the last, remains mystical ecstasy proper, but here is given its Sino-Buddhist interpretation, which in effect is highly Taoist in tenor. Chuang Tzu emphasized in his accounts of mystical ecstasy this characteristic of its being a 'return' to the spiritual source of all phenomena which constitutes a person's true identity. This, in whatever context, is again what defines mystical ecstasy, the identification with the spiritual, and the refusal to see 'self' in anything particular, especially not in either ox or person. So both these are still 'forgotten' in the mystic selflessness; but the Ch'an and Zen tradition shows, in this second interpretation of the ecstatic crux around which self-transformation turns, that this being beyond or de-identifying with the material or mental self involves a sense of being a part of or a oneness with the cosmos itself, in its spiritual essence. This the artist symbolizes in the favourite Chinese 'Three Pure Ones', rock, plum blossom and bamboo, all three of which stand beside the waters of universal change, the Tao itself. There is here no sense of separate individuality, or self identified with any material locus, but rather the purity of spirit itself pervades, as it does in mystical ecstasy. This is just how one tradition symbolizes this ultimate transforming ecstasy wherein one learns the proper, spiritual identity of the self. This scene then represents the 'correct' self-knowledge which all spiritual traditions teach or point to, from Socrates and Confucius to all those (including secular mystics like Arthur Koestler) who have reached and spoken of it. Maturity in its spiritual sense flows from this re-identifying experience, which the next, final picture tries to illustrate. By showing for the second time neither person nor ox, the series emphasizes again that mystical ecstasy is an experience of transcendence.

Mystics of all civilizations report that this experience occurs outside time and carries with it a sense of being one with, or not separate from, the source of life. Chuang Tzu (see Watson, *Basic Writings*) emphasized the unitive character of this timeless moment, in such phrases as 'he merges himself with things' (p. 42), '. . . in utter freedom he dissolves himself in the four directions and drowns himself in the unfathomable . . .' (p. 108), enjoining that one should 'Leap into the boundless and make it your home' (p. 44), and 'Let your mind wander in simplicity, blend your spirit with the vastness . . .' (p. 91). But I do not think, by identifying this ecstasy as a mystical state, that we should imply that it can be attained only by the rare few who seem able to allow the blinders to drop away from narrowly focused eyes at will. Mystical ecstasies and their consequent 'self-knowledge' have come to many people throughout human time, in many diverse types of experience and brought on by as many different ways as humans can experience or invent. Their crucial feature is to reverse the prototypical separation which caused anxiety to arise in our consciousness in the first place. Although tradition reports many sources for such self-transforming experience, from unseekable grace to unsought initiatory illness, like any other features of possible experience, anyone can learn it, so one may have to develop into this consciousness. It can derive from the skill of entering meditative ecstasy, which can be learned, just as previously in life, we have learned equally astounding skills, such as talking, walking, riding a bicycle, being able to calculate, or write intelligibly, or translate from one language into another. To people who have not learned, for example, how to speak several languages, the task indeed feels impossible, but all who know another language realize on the contrary that it is just a matter of learning by application and practice.

This picture represents a transformation of one's consciousness or the reach of one's knowledge, the most important learning experience, according to traditional values, that one can undergo. I think this accounts for spiritual traditions having universally called this transformation a re-birth. It does not suffice to be born of the womb; for that, as Christ told Nicodemus (John 3) is but the physical birth into life, and does not guarantee that one shall know the kingdom of God. 'Unless one is born anew,' he warned, that is born into Spirit, one remains for ever outside the kingdom, locked (in my interpretation) in the infantile immature self's view of the world. To those gathered at Capernaum, Jesus taught: 'Do not labour (only) for the food which perishes, but for the food which endures to eternal life' (John 6), by which he could only have meant such an experience of 'spirit' which this picture portrays.

In part, the value which arises from this experience comes from learning 'one's place in the cosmos', thus knowing how one relates to that which transcends one's separate individuality. Am I related to something more enduring, more infinite, than the span of years clearly allotted to me in this life? Such a 'return to the source' answers this important question once and for all. One finds truth in mystically knowing this relation, for then one indeed knows of the kingdom, whether it be of Brahman, God, the Tao or just Nature, or however one wishes to describe what has within the last century appeared, astounding to the imagination, in our electron microscopes and in the giant mirror and radio telescopes that scan the cosmic night-time vastness. Once the discipline of meditation effects its changes in one's awareness, 'cleansing the doors of perception', forging a link with one's source, then desires, values and attitudes change, becoming more appropriate to the total reality in which our life exists and finds (or fails to find) survival and meaning. We have only begun to spin out, as Carl Sagan does, the new mythology which will give us an adequate sense of the meaning in the cosmos which science has just recently revealed to our senses. I fully expect that among the forefront of the mystics of the future – and this future is just round the corner – will be meditator-scientists, who will lead the rest of us, by virtue of their explorations, into the worlds which are the source of life, our life and all life, from the atoms to the stars. This is what our hero, no longer a boy, experiences here in the mystical ecstasy of the 'Three Pure Ones'.

The key which opens the window to this vision, this mature feeling for the source of life, finally derives from resolving the conflicts which arise out of the self as it develops from childhood. The self, as immature child, can never know the world without working through its own acquired sense of limitedness to step outside it, into the vast profusion of creation. And in knowing this, we realize finally that each person is a unique combination of limited and infinite dimensions. The rebirth comes only to those who break and tame the stubborn, immature ox, giving life to the mature spirit, the total selfhood which exists, finite yet a spiritual portion of the enduring whole, the source.

10

Meditation's Prospects, Today and Tomorrow

Meditation offers much to Western civilization, which today badly needs the balancing of the psyche; this it can aid in accomplishing. This makes meditation's prospects excellent, both for its own creative development and for its ability to contribute significantly to our growth as a civilization which now exports its science, culture and technology all over the world. Just as Euroamerica has sent abroad everything from its languages, jazz music and blue jeans to oil drilling technology, computers and jet aircraft, eventually we may even be able to contribute a reasonably developed knowledge of meditative states to a world which desperately needs spiritual rejuvenation. I have argued, in the course of my chapters, that Euroamerican value choices have resulted in immature ways of seeking happiness, with disastrous consequences for the entire world's population and environment. These unexpected results of our boisterous technology threaten the lives of every human being alive on earth today. Even worse, other countries, taking up the technologies we export, but with less consciousness of their dangerous consequences and much less ability and money to protect their environment, will tragically fare much worse in the coming decades than we will. Finally, patterns of direct or indirect exploitation undertaken by Western governmental policies and the closely allied multi-national companies will continue ruthlessly to exploit third world peoples and lands unless the whole tenor of world civilization turns towards more humanistically oriented values and overall goals. I fervently hope that meditation will further the changes which could transform the world as we know it today; hopefully, too, we may even export renewed and renewing forms of meditation to help to cure and mature our ailing, immature world civilization.

My main concern in this book, however, has not been to argue this case about our cultural immaturity, but to describe meditation, largely from historical and contemporary materials. I should now try to project meditation's prospects for today and into the future. As our knowledge about meditation increases, more and more people will realize that it offers much for little. In the current dilemma of world-wide inflation, practising meditation is non-inflationary; it requires no expensive equipment, buildings, training or travel; it can be done anywhere, at home, on vacation, at work (in the office washroom, if nowhere else be provided), alone, in groups or families. It can be taught in existing facilities (schools, churches, public buildings, homes, clinics and hospitals) with no additional capital outlay. Meditation invests no expensive capital, nor does it require extension of credit or expanding the money supply (causes of inflation), but rather it invests a person's free time in something that he or she already owns. The product of meditation is a state of mind rather than a costly material object, which sought by many with increasing money supplies naturally goes up in price accordingly. Meditation seeks to discover the ineffable innerness which everyone has, not some external possession for which many others compete; all of us already possess the ability to achieve what one can gain through meditation. Further, meditation belongs to no one group or organization or company; it is democratic, doctrinally neutral, unpatented and not copyrighted, applicable in any situation to which one dares apply it. As a non-religious, scientifically elaborated practical activity, meditation can be made available to as many as wish it for their own life-enrichment, with little or no expense to anyone.

The climate favourable to meditation will rapidly develop

in the near future on all sides. Cultural institutions formerly hostile to meditation (churches, business and industry, schools, universities, health services) will discover that it can legitimately be taught and used with benefit within their confines, without conflict with their ideals. Public acceptance will increase, particularly as meditation sheds its exclusive association with cultist and sectarian aims, and as education and scientific knowledge about it enhance its acceptability. As university scientists study and develop practical, secular forms of meditation, like Benson's work at Harvard, Carrington's Clinically Standardized Meditation from Princeton, and Cade's work in England, they will be suitable for adoption by many diverse groups and individuals with as many different goals to pursue. These developments will be accelerated even more by trends in the culture itself, summarized by some as the 'small is beautiful' movement, along with those which Theodore Roszak has described in his book *Person/Planet, The Creative Disintegration of Industrial Society* (New York: Anchor Press Doubleday, 1979), and which Stavrianos notes in his book *The Promise of the Coming Dark Age* from the point of view of the Third World. Meditation's time has arrived. As we all mature into the world-embracing culture of the future, meditation will transform humankind perhaps even shifting our value choices to accept inner, non-material forms of happiness cultivated by it, creating a sense of fairness to all beings. As science investigates and describes meditative phenomena, it can begin to present meditation in a form more suited to our materialistically inclined culture; in fact, science will create or provide the impetus for the most innovative new developments in meditation practice. This can only enhance its ability to respond to our contemporary needs and interests. Further, I personally believe that science will eventually describe and explain all the puzzling features associated with meditative ecstasy, including the currently unexplained psychic phenomena which meditators have known about for centuries. As scientific explanation further enlightens us on the subject, meditation will itself mature as an activity and become more acceptable and more useful for those who choose to use it.

Few observers have as yet noticed that some cultures have now entered a period of post-agrarian civilization; peasant societies, such as those all our grand-parents lived in, no longer exist in most of Western Europe and North America, having been replaced by urban, industrial cultures. The religions which peasant cultures evolved specifically for their own needs no longer respond to the new needs created by our new environments. We must reinvent 'religion', or, avoiding even the word, we must create our own spiritual culture which fully responds to our new situations in life. The religions taught today largely originated out of the experiences of shaman-priests and prophets who led peasants living in villages and towns, none having ever set foot in a large, urban, living complex such as those which most of us live in today. We have now replaced magico-religious attempts to control and exploit the environment for survival with science and technology. We no longer need to celebrate festivals for agrarian success, or perform rituals for the city's well-being for the coming year, or to stop epidemic diseases. Secularization and science have undercut much of the past's religious concerns and methods. We need to preserve and re-establish the spiritual culture which is rightly our best heritage from religion's past, so as to further the evolution of our current industry-based means of survival, increasing its spirituality, refining its values and suiting us to its require-ments, in order that we may survive its dangers and exploit its usefulness. The core of this new culture could well include meditation, with the new sensitivity to life and human values that it can bring, not contrary to scientific knowledge, but in harmony with its best insights.

Meditation can become a powerful force in the future evolution of human consciousness. We should not assume that consciousness as it has evolved so far exhausts all its possibilities for the future. Consciousness can never cease its growth. Imagine how rudimentary consciousness was when proto-human beings domesticated fire, or began paying attention to the disposal of the dead, or started making notation of the passage of time by scratching on bone. At one time in this evolution, consciousness evolved so that its possessors could produce diversified tool-kits of stone and wood, making them superior to those whose mental capacities could not imagine anything beyond one basic form of stone tool. Hundreds and thousands of years accounted for minute advances in human awareness, until fairly recently, for the last hundred or so years, we have suddenly undergone an incredible expansion of knowledge. Today, our position in the drama of survival is constantly being redefined by expanding consciousness. Yet, despite what we know, for diverse reasons, we continue to follow outmoded and immature survival patterns which eventually will inevitably lead, unless changed, to destruction. The balance of consciousness has been so unsettled that we need innovations as influential as the advent of sceptical rationalism to fill out the complete set of inherent possibilities for consciousness development, and thus the ability of consciousness to remain our most important means of evolutionary survival. I think meditation can contribute much to this essential process. Perhaps eventually very advanced forms of human conciousness will be transferred to an as yet unimaginable generation of computer-like devices to migrate into space (silicon-chip versus water-based consciousness matter); yet few today think that meditatively transformed psychic consciousness may be an essential dimension of this awareness which we shall contribute to the cosmos. Furthermore, contact and communication with 'extra-terrestrials', if indeed any such exist, perhaps will require psychic forms of communication (besides the possible use of psychic teleportation to traverse the vast distances of space). We should not assume that other beings which have evolved consciousness would be able to communicate as we do, nor should we expect that rational, left-brain reflection would be the only or dominant form of consciousness that others would possess.

The current impetus for meditation's development incorporates several motivations which we can expect to contribute to its further growth. The secularization of Western Asian religions (Judaeo-Christian-Islamic) has resulted in many people turning to those from South and East Asia (some forms of Hinduism and Buddhism, Zen, Sufi mysticism) for the access they promise to non-secularized approaches to spiritual consciousness, mostly meditative ecstasy. Asian imports have brought, along with the inevitable riffraff, both leaders and followers, some *swamis*, *lamas*, and *rōshis*, who are excellent meditation masters. They have established indigenous meditation traditions, training the first Euroamerican teachers. This transmission culminates a long process whereby Western civilization has finally become aware of Eastern meditation (Robinson and Johnson, *The Buddhist Religion*, Chapter 12, 'Buddhism Comes West', describes part of the process from its beginnings). Long ago, Greeks and Indians met – perhaps even Plato borrowed ideas from India (doctrine of knowledge as remembrance, his notion of reincarnation) – and Western monasticism may have been influenced by Indian practices. But today, how different our contact with the East has become. We travel to Asia, learn in its monasteries, and already have independent Asian teaching lineages established on Euroamerican soil, building institutions, teaching students and publishing vigorously. Valuable contributions can come from these groups to meditation's growth. Furthermore, our own religious institutions have taken up meditation, such as in Catholic monasteries.

Another reason for our heightened awareness of meditation's attractiveness came out of the early acquaintance with psychedelic drugs. In the late 1950s and early 1960s, before government restriction, many people thought that psychedelics might provide the access they were looking for to spiritual ecstasy. Certainly this motivated Aldous Huxley to experiment with mescaline and LSD. Suddenly, many thought that chemical means could be used to 'cleanse the doors of perception' (as Huxley wrote in his little book whose title borrowed this phrase from William Blake). What Aldous Huxley was unable to accomplish, Carlos Castañeda completed in his series of four books reporting the teaching of the mysterious Yaqui, don Juan. Suddenly the psychedelic gospel, in an appropriately alluring form of a pseudo-shamanic secret teaching, became extraordinarily attractive, especially to young people (and some academics, who thought the book a form of spiritual anthropology). I doubt that anyone will ever be able to assess the impact of these books on popular culture of the last decades of the twentieth century. Nearly everyone overlooked the fact that Castañeda, in his third book, *Journey to Ixtlan*, recanted the implication of the first two that psychedelic experience equates to spiritual awareness or meditative ecstasy. In fact, the third and fourth books both claim just the opposite; all of the crucial experiences in Castañeda's maturation, as he reported (or invented) it, involved non-drug related, meditatively induced altered states of consciousness, the first 'breakthrough' experience coming when he talked with the coyote at the end of the Ixtlan book. At that time, don Juan told him to go into the desert and wait for a vision. Just wait, quietly, he was told; no peyote, 'magic' mushroom or jimson weed was needed.

The experience of the last twenty years indicates that psychedelics can be used to alter consciousness, but does not bear out the contention of their early proponents that psychedelics give a short-cut route to spiritual consciousness. In effect, for the duration of the state they directly induce, some (but I suspect few) people experience ecstasy identical to that brought on by meditation, but as soon as the effect 'wears off', the person must again induce it with the chemical means. This indeed is possible, but two consequences result. First, in the interim, one is just about the same as one was before (i.e. the self-transformation does not carry over to normal states of consciousness), and secondly, one depends on the psychedelic agent to induce the ecstasy once more. In circumstances some would deem symbolic for our age, Aldous Huxley died still dependent upon psychedelics for his ecstasy. His nurse wife, Laura Achera Huxley, reported in her memoir (*This Timeless Moment*) that she heeded his request to receive intravenous LSD as he expired. True to the ideal of spiritual aspirations, Huxley wanted to die in ecstasy, but he had not learned how to enter into it through his own mental ability. Asian meditators regularly die in meditative ecstasy, as the Buddha did, but do not depend on any such substance for its attainment, as perhaps their less mature shaman ancestors did (see Wasson on paleo-Siberian *Amanita* use, and Waley's *Nine Songs* which shows that the earliest record of archaic Chinese shamanism preserves many references to herbs and 'spirit' plants).

Apart from the issue of dependence, does psychedelic ecstasy sufficiently imitate meditative ecstasy? I think the answer to this must be a qualified 'no'. For some people it does, during the short period of the psychedelic's action, but once exhausted, the person largely remains the same person, unaffected by the ecstasy. The crucial features of meditative ecstasy are two: first, that one learns from it, which only a few who take psychedelics do, and second, that one can induce it repeatedly, to use the ecstatic state for whatever one's goals may be. To remain dependent on an active placebo to induce the ecstasy, when other, as reliable, safer and much more repeatable means exist, seems wasteful and irresponsible. Huxley did not have a chance, or did not choose, to learn meditation, and so remained dependent to the end on the chemical means whose short-term effects had not given him reliable access to ecstasy.

The reports of people who have experimented with psychedelic ecstasy indicate that eventually the dependence becomes intolerable, a dead-end in the path of personal maturation. Even Lame Deer concluded this, after six years of participating in the Native American Church's peyote sessions. He told his biographer,

I found out that it was not my way. It was a dead end, a box canyon, and I had to find my way out of it ... And if you take a herb – well, even the butcher boy at his meat counter will have a vision after eating peyote. The real vision has to come out of your own juices ... You have to work for this; empty your mind for it.

(Lame Deer Seeker of Visions, pp. 64–5)

Or, take the case of (for or against) LSD. I remember how Albert Hoffman, its discoverer, recounted in a lecture in San Francisco in 1978 (and later in his book *LSD My Problem Child*) that though he had taken LSD a limited number of times, today he recommends that even scientists devote a regular period of time (he suggests an hour) to meditation every day. Apparently, LSD has initiated him into a state of mind which he finds more satisfactorily attained in meditation. His recommendation for those who somehow do not achieve ecstasy through meditation was that, after meditative cultivation, they use LSD once to initiate them into the state, but only if so required. (The same applies to its adjunct use in therapy.) As to the North American prophets of LSD, one, Timothy Leary, remains adamant, still apparently seeking solace in drug experience, while his ex-Harvard partner, Richard Alpert, now Ram Dass, speaks against it, condemning it for the dependency its use involves. The popular press (as for example the article 'Ram Dass, Nobody Special' by Calvin Fentress in *New Times,* 4 September 1978) reports that after three hundred 'trips' depression overtook Alpert, which he himself described as 'a very gentle depression that whatever I knew still wasn't enough' (p. 41).

The same article quotes Tom Wolfe as writing, 'It is either make this thing permanent inside of you or forever just climb dragged up into the conning tower for one short glimpse of the horizon.' This properly critiques the impermanence of psychedelically induced ecstasy; but, as Bharati counters (in *Light at the Center*), no ecstasy can be permanent, no matter how often Asian gurus claim it to be so. The real difference is that meditatively induced ecstasy arises because a series of karmic tranformations (or 'ox-taming') occur which permit and lead to ecstasy. Though not a 'permanent' state itself, the being in whom the states occur is permanently changed or matured, for the better. Because most of the prophets of psychedelic ecstasy did not undertake the requisite self-transformations, they failed to realize their most cherished goal, losing even the benefits which chemically induced intiation into ecstasy could have brought them.

Meditation will increasingly replace psychedelics as the favoured means of achieving ecstasy as these lessons become apparent to more and more of those who desire the experience. In fact, meditation should begin to be seen as an attractive alternative to all forms of consciousness alteration which depend on mind and mood altering substances, like alcohol, cocaine, coffee, tobacco, tea, other drugs and pills of all kinds (the so-called uppers, downers, anti-depressants, etc.), all of which have negative side-effects and all of which promote intolerable dependency. Meditation could promote our collective maturation concerning these chemical crutches, freeing us from their domination, along with the massive miseries they have brought to our families and friends. Reliance on other sorts of escapist activities, everything from decadence, pornography and legitimate but hardly edifying television programming to glamorous expensive sports (and brawling spectator sports), addictions and violence could also be lessened by the wider practice of meditation.

In many ways the problems we face today, those crucial to the very survival of our civilization, stem from our very beginnings, when on the basis of agrarian surpluses, urban civilization originated. Buddhism, the one world religion which systematically developed meditation, arose as a response to one of those urban civilizations (the Indus-Ganges complex) and had its greatest success in city culture, as if its meditation had something which urbanized people desperately needed. Psychologists have demonstrated that rats, in conditions of excessive crowding, become violent and turn against each other. We see this drama playing itself out in every major city in the world today, unable to heed our own past and science and to learn from them. The great concentration of peoples in expanding urban centres (Mexico

City, Calcutta, London, Los Angeles, Lima, etc.) correlates with rising urban malaise, violence, addiction and escapism. We all feel the distress which such conditions create, however successful we think we are in trying to insulate or isolate ourselves from them. If we do not take up remedies soon, they will never have a chance to take effect before our cities turn in upon themselves in fits and orgies of self-destruction. I have in this book proposed one means which could work with many others for the spiritual rejuvenation and healing we all need for survival and to continue our creativity. We need to do everything possible, including the teaching of meditation to our children and our grandparents. As parents and adults we should care, not only for ourselves, but for the Other in all its forms.

Thus, in the broader view, meditation could become a major source for healing on a culture-wide scale, in conjunction with other disciplines and activities. Few understand the deepening malaise we experience today, but all respond to it, by necessity, seeking to survive. Something in our contemporary urban, industrial ethos or cultural outlook has cut us away from the deepest roots of our consciousness, our humanity, and from nature, the very source of our livelihood. We need to heal this spiritual wound before it kills our collective spirit and brings our civilization to nought. In terms of our meditative possibilities, we need to rediscover spiritual adventure, the spirit's ecstatic ability to enrich our lives through non-material, non-competitive goals and achievements. Spiritual action's motivations respond to our needs for consummatory rather than instrumental experiences, rewards and goals. They seek something gained in and for itself, as in play, rather than to be an instrument to other ends, as self-preoccupied, anxious striving is. Their satisfactions derive from immaterial rewards intrinsic to the experience and not something gained as an additional possession at the expense of another's loss or to the detriment of our world's environment. We need ways of reaching for such adventure through non-competitive spiritual agony and ecstasy. Meditiation can provide this, thus leading us to an experience realm of fulfilment which we have only begun to realize is available and free to anyone who will sit for a moment, closing the eyes and breathing calmly so as to enter into that 'empty chamber where brightness is born', in whose silence fortune and blessing gather.

Ox-Taming 10 *Meeting Pu-tai on Life's Playful Road*

This last scene in the set of ten presents ambiguities which demand careful interpretation. The traditional commentary gives this picture the title 'Entering The City With Hands

Hanging Down' (Fontein and Hickman in *Zen Painting & Calligraphy*, p. 117), or, in Suzuki's translation, 'Entering the City with Bliss-bestowing Hands' (*Essays in Zen Buddhism, First Series*, p. 376). We see the boy, or rather the mystically matured person, still beyond the projected ox, but in this case, he meets a figure well known in Chinese iconography as Pu-tai, the 'hemp-bag monk' of Ch'an or the 'laughing Buddha' of popular religion. The traditional verse speaks of 'his' (whose?) going into the city, and returning home, having visited 'wineshops and fish stalls', and considers something which happens here as miraculous and beneficial to others. Certainly both figures are smiling and playful, Pu-tai with his hemp-bag full of everything and in his other hand a gourd, full of nothing. The ox-tamer meets the saviour on the road, on his staff a fish (for dinner?), a symbol of plenty.

I have interpreted the prior two moments as maturing mystical ecstasy, so it follows that this scene shows the result of the self-transforming re-identification with the spiritual. In his own time, meeting with Pu-tai, who actually supposedly lived in China in the first half of the tenth century, would have meant in itself a challenging encounter with an enigmatic enlightened master. In later legend, this perplexing old monk came to be identified with Maitreya (as a 'pre-incarnation' of that Buddha still to come), and thus with the saviour of the new age. In either case, such a meeting signified encounter with the spiritual enigma and fulfilment of existence, here the fruit of all the ox-tamer's steadfast discipline and effort. To come upon Pu-tai means to have commerce with and to be among the enlightened; both, as agonists who have passed through the self-transforming process, recognize the other, exchanging smiles on the road.

Such encounters indeed have the savour of the miraculous, and such people benefit others. Here the entire human spiritual tradition speaks in rare agreement, by ascribing to those who have achieved such self-knowledge and maturity the capacity to help others. It was Jesus Christ's ability to answer people in terms of their own need, to heal and to transform, which served as the seal of his ministry; the same may be said for the other saviours and great individuals of history, remembered simply for their mature, knowing, spiritual perspective on life, both profound and, at the same time, playful. It may be only the formulaic presentation of a set of ten stages that sees this maturity as something which at a certain point one finally achieves, as opposed to what probably actually happens, that it is gradually realized. The portrait of the process simply posits the ideal, the goal, of self-transforming action, however often one must go through all the stages to realize it in greater and greater degrees. Meditation and other disciplines conduce to the achievement which may be defined as the broadening of responsibility. First, one must take reponsibility for oneself, one's own actions and livelihood. Then, not in narcissistic self-serving, but in a temporary (however long drawn out it may be) agonistic process, one transforms the very basis of one's life and choices to the extent that a whole new relationship to the Other begins to be created. The infantile and fight-flight responses come to be replaced by more open, perceptive, realistic and caring attitudes and consciousness forms, until, as Teresa noted, 'It is quite certain that, with the strength it has gained, the soul comes to the help of all who are in the Castle, and, indeed, succours the body itself' (*Interior Castle*, p. 230). Such ability comes from spiritual sources (the 'heart' in traditional symbolism), serving both self and Other. Teresa noted its converse too, when she wrote, 'Once you have been shown how to enjoy this Castle, you will find rest in everything, even in the things which most try you, and you will cherish a hope of returning to it which nobody can take from you' (*Interior Castle*, p. 234).

So not only does initiatory mystical ecstasy awaken a person to spirituality, as we saw in the last picture, but it also brings about a new relation to persons, oneself and others, and to the conditions of life and its environment. Responsibility and empathy define this new relation, this being with others not on the basis of one's own narrowly perceived needs, but in terms of all our needs as a human community. Such a person, such a mature adult, seeks to preserve the environment which is the very source of all our lives and takes an active, helping, healing part in the everyday life of family and community and world. Perhaps the process of correcting one's nature never ends, but at a certain point, represented in this picture, it adopts a new basis in spirit, and, taking the new perspective, relates to others and the world from a spiritual point of view. Part of the new commitment is to help others who seek to enter into or to further the process (the agony and the ecstasy) in themselves. Socrates thought of himself as a midwife because he attempted to help others give birth to themselves. He aided their agony, their contest with the mean ox for eventual self-control, ecstatic experience and enhanced adult maturity. Because he had already healed himself of the illness, he could be above the anxiety and the struggle of those still confronting the monster of the uncontrolled, uncorrected self. Like the ox-tamer on the road, his playfulness derived from maturity, not immaturity; in the fullness of the human spirit it is a joy to help, because finally it has really become possible, fulfilling William Blake's hope (expressed in *Milton*):

To cleanse the Face of my Spirit by Self-examination
To bathe in the Waters of Life, to wash off the Not Human.

Appendix 1

Johnsonian Stanzas on Meditation

1 Now some new mnemonic stanzas on meditation.

2 Meditation disciplines and develops the mind, deepening its knowledge and experience.

3 Practised regularly, focused on a meditative object, for a fifteen- to thirty-minute period, once or twice a day.

4. Difficult to begin, unpromising, frustrating, not apparently going to the goal, meditation is easy to give up.

5 The alternative leads to the beginning of a new consciousness.

6 This new consciousness brings a subjectively deepened awareness through softening of the threshold or limen of consciousness, permitting inner images and knowledge to well up to attention directed inwardly.

7 Attaining subjectively altered, meditative states of consciousness becomes easier as practice brings increased skill in 'entering the quiet' of the mind.

8 The ultimate goal of meditative practice is to achieve ecstasy.

9 The ecstatic state allows one to step outside one's ordinary consciousness to learn.

10 Ecstasy is a temporary, non-temporal, spatially un-delimited set of consciousness states in which, through the activation of the deep psyche, additional mental abilities and activity become activated.

11 Meditators decide how they will use these mental skills cultivated in meditative ecstasy.

12 Human history indicates that shamans and others used these powers for purely empirical knowledge and goals, as well as for healing, and for guidance in matters of the spirit (including the after-death journey of the soul).

13 For self-transformation, ecstasy provides learning which matures a person's outlook on the world and other people, leading away from the self-preoccupied viewpoint of youth to the more accepting openness of adult maturity.

14 One achieves meditative ecstasy through disciplining body, breath, and mind.

15 These disciplines pertain particularly to the beginning of meditative self-development; later, one may take the meditative state so cultivated into action in the world.

16 First, achieve a relaxed, comfortable body position for your meditation.

17 Keep this position fairly standard each time you practise as your cue for entering your quiet.

18 Learn to maintain this position, with minimal movement and negative body feedback for a comfortable twenty minutes or so at a time.

19 Then, once so stabilized in body position, pay attention to your breath; be conscious of the in and out breathing; to initiate the deepening process, take a few deliberate quiet deep breaths; you may want to count your breaths, one to ten, for a period of several minutes or longer.

20 Or, practise other ways of focusing on the breath.

21 When the breath calms and becomes regular, you may proceed to the next meditative stage.

22 Discipline of mind comes when you focus it using either its inner sense, or one or more of the external senses, on a suitable meditative object.

23 The defining feature of a meditative state is that it (usually) arises by the focusing of the mind on a meditative object over a period of time.

24 This meditative object could be the incoming and outgoing of the breath, or a set of syllables which can be repeated over and over (Sanskrit *mantra*), or a meaningful word or phrase, or an idea, or a visual image or imagined environment or experience which one creates on the inner screen of the imagination.

25 Or, the meditative object can be focused on through the physical senses singly or in combination, as when one takes a sound or music as the object of the auditory sense, or an icon

or image or drawing for the visual sense, or a total experiential scene, involving all the senses.

26 Practise this discipline of the senses and mind regularly, once or twice a day for twenty to thirty minutes.

27 This will lead to experiencing and being able to enter into meditative ecstasies.

28 Or, thinking from the point of view of brain wave studies, the functioning of the right brain hemisphere develops and brain waves increase associated with relaxation in both hemispheres; at times both come into synchronous activity.

29 From the perspective of knowledge experienced in meditative ecstasy, greater access to the contents of the deeper self can be developed, including dream, fantasy, imagination, vision and creative thought; and the psychic powers can be activated and consciously controlled to reach beyond the sway of the physical senses.

30 Or, one can apply these mental potentialities reached and developed in meditative cultivation to any of the goals one chooses to try to attain in life.

31 Meditative ecstasy has no intrinsic meaning or goal; meditative states and practices exist devoid of doctrinal content; their practice is non-inflationary; being neutral, they can be practised in any system of thought applied towards any goal.

32 Particularly as scientifically and humanistically minded individuals practise and develop knowledge about meditation, greatly increased options and opportunities for meditative growth will become available.

34 Every person and every culture requires balance to live harmoniously within the bounds and limits reality sets; meditation balances the mind's bicameral functioning, deepens self-knowledge and self-control, matures, strengthens and calms those who practise it, offering the prospect which most will contribute to our collective human future, namely the further evolution of consciousness.

35 By integrating a meditative component into the evolution of human consciousness, its wholeness, wholesomeness and compassion will increase and be fulfilled, for the benefit of all concerned.

Appendix 2

How to Begin Meditation; How I Meditate

Many people, learning that I have been writing this book, which I describe to them as a trans-cultural history and description of meditation, not a 'how to meditate' book, respond by saying, 'Well, but are you going to tell us how you meditate?' When I answer no, they indicate disappointment, so I tell them 'it's no big thing, my own experience'. Keeping that in mind, I include some information of a more practical nature in this appendix. Actually, I have written a descriptive account of meditation because I consider that many books and groups already exist which teach how to meditate, but few know much about the total picture of meditation and how it has figured in past human experience. Further, I think that anyone already meditating or thinking about beginning or just interested in understanding what others are doing, can benefit greatly by knowing the sorts of information I have presented in this book. So that is the book's primary goal.

However, I recognize that many of the people who read this book may be interested at some time in learning how to meditate, if they do not know already, so in this appendix I will present some basic information, drawing from my own experience and research.

First, how could someone who has read this book learn to meditate? Strangely enough, finding the proper way to learn probably is the most difficult of all – far more difficult than meditating, as far as my experience goes. Our society does not have the mechanisms or institutions set up to teach meditation; until the demand increases, this will be a problem, just as two decades ago, one could find only a few tennis teachers, while now they abound. I remember when I was a graduate student at the University of Wisconsin, during the spring of my second year there (1966), I and others had learned enough about Asian religions to want to learn how to meditate, but no one group existed to teach it. Perhaps we did not scour the community sufficiently for opportunities, either. So one night we persuaded our professor to have a meditation session at his house, and went there in the evening. But no one, including the professor, really knew what to do, though he had a PhD in Oriental thought, and some of us, later to become PhDs in such esoterica as Tibetology and Sanskrit, and professors ourselves, had already tried meditation but failed to continue it. It was 'in the air' but no one knew quite what to do.

This must be the situation of many who would like to try meditating but do not know where to go for preliminary instruction. The story of my own experience continued to be one of frustration for many years, until well after I had completed my PhD and had taught about World and Asian religions for over seven years. I distrusted most meditation groups I came across, then greatly increasing in number, for the religious or cultist impression they conveyed to me. This removed me from the major form of access to learning meditation available in our culture today. I found no way of learning a standardized, secular form of meditation, in keeping with the doctrinally neutral character of meditation which I had learned to respect from my study of the transcultural nature of meditation.

Finally, a friend told me about a group in my home town of San Diego, California. I resolved to try it out with an open mind. The class took a week of evenings, plus a Saturday. Happily, our teacher was able to initiate me into meditative states and a standard way of entering them within that period of a week. The most important event in my meditative life had taken place – she had initiated me into meditative experience. Before such an initiation, one can try all one wants, but largely it just does not work. You need, first, then, to find someone, some group, or person, who knows not only how to meditate, but how to initiate you into meditative states. This crucial step suffices, because from that point on, you can develop meditation in whatever way or direction you choose. Our teacher did the one thing I needed to start meditating; for several nights she led me, step by step, into the special altered states of consciousness induced by meditation, so I could identify them and know them for certain. From then on, I could develop the states on my own. Naturally, I found it also a help to meditate with the group at the class (as well as others) as the group shares psychic-meditative energy, especially at the beginning; I also was greatly helped by two friends who meditated with me during the first months after my initiation, reinforcing what I had learned, and I then went back to our teacher's class for two additional week-long trainings, identical to the first, deepening the initiation.

Based on my experience, then, I recommend to people seeking to learn meditation that they find a group or person who can initiate them into meditative techniques and states. They do not have to agree necessarily with all the group's or individual's ideas about meditation or its goals; the essential feature is that the experience initiate them into achieving meditative states so that they can break the barrier which keeps them from carrying out their own desires to learn how to meditate and thus to be able to experiment, however they choose, with meditative states of mind. Without mentioning the names of any groups which teach meditation, nor recommending any or not recommending some, I suggest that people attend a trial session, ask other participants, or discuss meditation with various people or groups which propose to teach them to make their own decision. Particularly in large urban centres, and university towns, many varied groups exist which instruct in meditation. If you desire to find a meditation teacher, you will eventually find one.

If there is no meditation group or instructor available to you, there is one suggestion which I can make wholeheartedly. Patricia Carrington, whose book *Freedom in Meditation* is the best available today on the subject, has originated what to me is a useful form of meditation, which she calls Clinically Standardized Meditation (CSM) for use in her therapy practice and in her experimental work. Even better, she has made her system available to anyone, by recording a series of three hour-long tapes and writing a course workbook to accompany her recorded instruction, using which, anyone can learn this style of meditation within nine days, personally taught by Carrington (on tape) and self-regulated by the student following the step-by-step procedure outlined in the workbook. The course costs a reasonable $49.95; it can be ordered from Pace Educational Systems, Inc., PO Box 113, Kendall Park, NJ USA 08824. Extra copies of the workbook (which includes forms to complete as you learn) can be ordered for $12.00 (discounts for over twenty-five), so that the course could be used by an entire family or group of friends who are interested in joining together to learn meditation. Professor Carrington's course to my mind fills the need for a doctrinally neutral, scientifically based, standard meditation instruction, one which provides that crucial initiation a person needs into meditative states. From then on, one must choose whether to participate in a meditation group for additional practice and to try out the goals which that group puts meditation to, or to develop it on one's own. I also recommend the reading of some of the different books available on meditation, particularly those to which I have referred in this book, since the more one can learn about it, the more informed one's practice will be. I particularly think that people should try to form a regularly meeting meditation group to develop the advantages of meditating together with like-minded people, sharing energy and ideas as each session builds the group spirit. You could decide on a ritual procedure for the group, and share experiences after each meditation session. Families could do the same, especially with members (grandparents, brothers and sisters living away from home with their own families, etc.) who do not ordinarily come together except for the usual yearly festivals. By coming together regularly for meditation, families could release much constructive energy, including healing powers to maintain the collective health of the entire extended group, as have generations past.

Now, how do I meditate? Well, almost any way I can. I do not use a rigid invariant system, but modify it to fit opportune time and place. Most regularly, I try to meditate in the early morning, my preferred time, since I am most alert then. Many times, when I have had a good night's sleep, I will meditate even before rising, after waking and reviewing my dreams. The environment then conduces to meditation, the room being quiet and darkened, my mind being clear of most intentions, distractions and anticipated actions. I take some deep breaths, then focus on a series of meditative objects, the subjects for my meditation. These could include a review of my ideals and goals, visiting people psychically who need healing or comforting energy, or focusing on quiet, deeper states without specific content by repeating a *mantra* or by focusing on my breathing. Otherwise, I try to meditate as soon in the morning as I can find twenty or so minutes, usually outside the house, when I do the same things, or focus on external sounds (especially bird songs) or sights (trees, the sunrise).

During the remainder of the day, I meditate occasionally when an appropriate moment comes, as when I am waiting for someone or for something to happen, or when I have a chance to break what I am doing to refresh myself, or at the beach, or in the garden, before or after my work for the day there. I also (sometimes) meditate on Monday night with my wife, at the time when a group meditates in her home town, as we have both meditated with them. At times other friends join us for this session. At other times we invite a friend who has health or other challenges to meditate with us, using the programmes devised by C. Norman Shealy MD in his book (*Biogenic Health Maintenance*, order from Self-Health Systems, Rt. 2, La Crosse WI, USA 54601) or programmes we write ourselves. These allow one to guide a meditation in the direction where the help is needed; you can write one specifically designed for your own use, or for your relatives or friends. Include general suggestions for relaxation, and positive directions to the deep psyche to stimulate energy flow in the needed avenues. As I have described elsewhere in this book, I have used meditation in gardening, during travel (hiking in the Sierras, while travelling abroad, before teaching classes, and such). While I led a study tour to Asia, I meditated early each morning, focusing my positive thoughts on each participant, striving to knit the group together and to protect it from disease and injury.

In my regular daily meditation, I generally sit in a comfortable chair or against a backrest, close my eyes, initiating and closing the meditation period by sounding a pair of Tibetan cymbals. I generally use a few other devices (see following Appendix). Then I focus on my breathing for a while, and say a *mantra* I learned from an Edgar Cayce reading which I have chosen as my own. For the rest of the period I go through my meditative objects, and complete the meditation when I feel that I have reached that inner quiet which defines for me success in my practice. I arise then from my seat smiling, ready for the day and my creativity to unfold.

Epilogue

... how you labor in vain!
if you don't understand
that the mind is Buddha!

That is truly like riding an ox
looking for one.

> Pao-chih, a sixth-century
> Chinese wonder worker
> (translation: K. Tsai)

Ch'ang-ch'ing Ta-an (793–883), one of Po-chang Huai-hai's Dharma-heirs, gave this account of his master's *kung-an*:

I lived with Isan more than thirty years. I ate Isan's food, I excreted Isan's excrement, but I did not study Isan's Zen. All I did was to look after an ox. If he got off the road, I dragged him back; if he trampled the flowering grain in others' fields, I trained him by flogging him with a whip. For a long time how pitiful he was, at the mercy of men's words! Now he has changed into the white ox on the bare ground, and always stays in front of my face. All day long he clearly reveals himself. Even though I chase him, he doesn't go away.

> From Isshū Miura and Ruth Fuller Sasaki's *Zen Dust*
> (New York: Harcourt, Brace & World, 1966), p. 319

Selected Bibliography

You can find the books I have mentioned in the course of this book from the short or long reference there. In this bibliography, I want to single out certain of these books, giving my opinions of them. I do not mention any of the numerous books which teach how to meditate, but rather include those which provide information about meditation in some significant way or another.

By far the single best contemporary work on meditation, firmly based on secular, empirical studies, is Patricia Carrington's *Freedom In Meditation* (New York: Anchor, 1978). This book is comprehensive, easy to read, suitable for beginning and advanced meditators, packed with up-to-date scientific knowledge about meditation. Anyone interested in meditation or in meditating should read this book first. Carrington's book excels especially in sketching out meditation's possibilities for today, and in fairly sorting through the many claims for it made by its competing proponents.

Since most living meditative traditions come today to us from Asia, we need some reliable books to help us sort through the flood of information which so often is flawed by sectarian presentation and its consequent short-sightedness. I am frankly not very impressed by most of the books which try to present the diverse Asian systems of meditation (Zen, which leads the pack, Theravāda, Tibetan, Hindu and so forth), particularly because they present materials which derive from alien contexts which make little sense to us. This probably will be remedied when Euroamerican interpreters of meditation adapt these systems more fully to our needs. In the meantime, for Indic systems, the best scholarly work remains Mircea Eliade's *Yoga, Immortality and Freedom* (Princeton: Princeton University Press, 1969). This book presents a complete survey of yoga's development in Indian civilization, joined to an exhaustive bibliography. This book can be supplemented by Jean Varenne's *Yoga And the Hindu Tradition* (Chicago: University of Chicago Press, 1976), though it is less complete and less knowledgeable about the Indian scene than Eliade. For a quick survey, Mircea Eliade's *Patañjali and Yoga* (New York: Schocken Books, 1975) can provide interesting reading, a few good photographs, and some hearty laughs. Some editor must have produced the visuals, for one picture of Indians resting and sleeping in a large hallway (a common sight) is labelled 'Indifference to property and ambition', apparently in reference to yoga ideals, but totally off base, since no one here pictured is a *yogin*. Varenne falls into the same trap of cultural myopia by describing beggars and *sādhus* (not generally *yogins* either) as 'appalling emaciated beings by the roadside or even ... lying dead of hunger on the sunscorched ground' (p. 228). All this just goes to show that we must separate personal observations from scholarly, objective, informed views, of which both of these writers are capable.

Taoism, the Chinese system which specialized in meditative discipline, is still almost impossible to become acquainted with, although Isabelle Robinet's *Méditation Taoïste* (Paris: Dervy Livres, 1979) significantly remedies the situation for readers of French. As you know from reading this book, I have adopted the approach of using extensively the well translated early Taoist masters, Chuang Tzu and, to a lesser extent, Lao Tzu. Their writings derive from meditative experience, and often speak of it, albeit indirectly, requiring considerable interpretation; furthermore, a considerable secret oral tradition went along with the textual tradition, making it even more difficult to understand many of their esoteric references. Still, Burton Watson's translation (the shorter *Chuang Tzu Basic Writings*, and the longer *Complete Writings*, both from Columbia University Press) provide a major access to Taoist meditatively inspired thought, as well as to how Taoists thought about meditation.

Speaking of texts related to meditation, I have used various works from diverse contexts to talk about the pan-human meditative experience. These have included Bashō, Carl Jung, Thoreau, Teresa of Avila, Lame Deer and others. The list could be expanded, but each person will be attracted to different such sources. One of the most striking (and you see how I favour autobiographies) is the translation by David Snellgrove entitled *Four Lamas of Dolpo*

(Cambridge, Mass.: Harvard University Press, 1967). This fascinating work reports the life story of four Tibetan lamas who lived in the fifteenth and sixteenth centuries, clearly showing how meditation provided the central transforming activity of their lives and gave them access to both salvation and power to serve others in the world. To guard against misconceptions of the place of meditation in Asian religious life, B. J. Terwiel's incisive anthropological account of the 'Monastery of the Crystal Sky' in *Monks and Magic* ('An Analysis of Religious Ceremonies in Central Thailand', London: Curzon Press, 1979) is very instructive. Here, at the empirical level, Terwiel shows us that meditation's chief goal (as perceived by the eyes of the farmers which the monastery serves) is to generate beneficent power to support life, fertility and good fortune, and to ward off misfortune and evil spirits.

Turning to textual sources, Patañjali's *Yoga Canon* comes to us in several fairly slanted versions (I omit those which are totally slanted). The theosophical entry is I. K. Taimni's *The Science of Yoga* (Wheaton, Ill.: Theosophical Publishing House, 1968), which, despite its interpretive baggage, does manage to present a decent translation and fairly helpful commentary. Another commonly available translation and commentary is Rammurti S. Mishra's *Yoga Sutras* ('The Textbook of Yoga Psychology', New York: Anchor Books, 1973). Anyone who becomes deeply interested in Patañjali must also consult the traditional commentaries, the two most important of which were translated by James Haughton Woods in *The Yoga-System of Patañjali* (reprinted in 1966 by Delhi's Motilal Banarsidass). Though difficult to read, this is the genuine textual tradition.

As for the recent books commenting on matters relating to meditation from a secular, scholarly point of view, few as yet have come out to counter the flood of lesser works on the subject. On the perennial fascination we have with whatever mysticism is, out of the morass we have, apart from the older works by W. T. Stace, two entries which I have commented upon briefly already. First, from the University of California at Berkeley, Frits Staal wrote *Exploring Mysticism* (Berkeley: University of California Press, 1975), which one critic dubbed 'Avoiding Mysticism'. In fact, Staal spends as much time commenting on various facets of Indian yoga as he does on criticizing inadequate approaches of studying mysticism, but fails to extend his account into a constructive elaboration of the subject itself. Another professor, Agehananda Bharati of

Syracuse University, wrote a contentious but more revealing book on mysticism, *The Light at the Center* (Santa Barbara: Ross-Erikson, 1976), with the rather inappropriate subtitle 'Context and Pretext of Modern Mysticism'; he should have specified that he really talks mostly about Hindu mysticism from his analytic-anthropological perspective. Bharati also makes revealing comments about yoga, as Staal does, and excoriates mercilessly the foibles of contemporary religious proponents of what Henry Miller called 'all the flapdoodle that blows in from the East like a breath of the plague'. The advantage of both of these books lies not so much in what their writers have managed to say, but in how they go about saying it, introducing readers to the rational consideration of our subject.

I could mention many other books somewhat related to these matters, but this would extend the discussion too far. I think anyone interested in a good philosophical analysis of self-transformation from both a Freudian and an Asian data base should read Herbert Fingarette's classic *The Self In Transformation* (New York: Harper, 1977). For an adequate survey of the one world religion which originated in the practice of meditation, refer to Richard H. Robinson and Willard Johnson, *The Buddhist Religion* (Belmont: Wadsworth Publishing Company, third revised edition, 1981). Finally, for some unusual materials on meditation and its uses, I recommend the two volumes of Edgar Cayce's collected readings on meditation, *Meditation Part I: Healing, Prayer and The Revelation,* and *Meditation Part II: Meditation, Endocrine Glands, Prayer, and Affirmations* (Volumes II and III in the *Edgar Cayce Readings* series published from Virginia Beach by the Association for Research and Enlightenment, 1974 and 1975 respectively).

Finally, for those interested in reading more on the ox-taming pictures, the following books have interesting presentations. Jan Fontein and Money L. Hickman's *Zen Painting & Calligraphy* (Greenwich: New York Graphic Society, 1970) presents the basic set held in Japan's Shōkokuji temple with a short but fine commentary (pp. 113–18). Suzuki's most complete presentation came in his *Manual of Zen Buddhism* (New York: Grove Press, 1960, pp. 127–44), while M. H. Trevor's *The Ox and His Herdsman* (Tokyo: Hokuseido Press, 1956) gives a longer account. Zenkei Shibayama, in *The Flower Does Not Talk* (Rutland: Charles Tuttle, 1970) comments on a beautiful set of six pictures: the last one (where the ox-tamer meets Pu-tai), entitled 'Playing', gives the essential meaning of the transformation's spiritual outlook.

Other books I have mentioned in passing are:

Anderson, Charles, *The Magic Circle of Walden*. New York: Holt, Rinehart and Winston, 1968

Benjamin, Anna S., translator, *Recollections of Socrates*. New York: Bobbs-Merrill Company, 1965

Benson, Herbert, *The Relaxation Response*. New York: William Morrow and Company, 1975

Castañeda, Carlos, *Journey to Ixtlan*. New York: Simon and Schuster, 1972

Cavell, Stanley, *The Senses of Walden*. New York: Viking Press, 1972

Long, Joseph, *Extrasensory Ecology*. Metuchen, New Jersey: Scarecrow Press, 1977

Millard, Joseph, *Edgar Cayce, Mystery Man of Miracles*. Greenwich, Connecticut: Fawcett Publications, 1967

Moody, Raymond, *Life After Life*. New York: Bantam Books, 1975; *see also* the follow-up study by Kenneth Ring, *Life at Death: A Scientific Investigation of the Near-Death Experience*. New York: Coward, McCann & Geoghegan, 1980

Neihardt, John G., *Black Elk Speaks*. Lincoln: University of Nebraska Press, 1961

Prabhavananda, Swami, and Christopher Isherwood, *How To Know God*. Hollywood: Vedanta Press, 1971

Sagan, Carl, *The Dragons of Eden*. New York: Random House, 1977

Stavrianos, Leften, *The Promise of the Coming Dark Age*. San Francisco: W. H. Freeman, 1976

Suzuki, D. T., *Essays in Zen Buddhism*, First Series. London: Rider & Company, 1949

Tredennick, Hugh, translator, *Memoirs of Socrates*. Baltimore: Penguin Books, 1970

Waley, Arthur, *The Analects of Confucius*. London: George Allen & Unwin, 1938; *The Book of Songs*. New York: Grove Press, 1960; *The Nine Songs*, A Study of Shamanism in Ancient China. London: George Allen and Unwin, 1955

Woods, James Haughton, *The Yoga-System of Patañjali*. Delhi: Motilal Banarsidass, 1966

Index

Note: This index is a guide to the book's meaning and contents, analytically listing its major concepts and themes, along with events and interpretations; also, all authors and major proper names, people, titles and places, along with foreign language terms (in italics) found in the text. These latter have a brief definition in parenthesis or reference to their English translation equivalents where more information may be found.

Another feature of this index is its inclusion of a bold-type glossary of terms used in my interpretation of the spiritual tradition which accompanies meditation's development in human culture. Since my interpretation is but one of many possible ways of describing this subject, as an abstraction from the actual phenomenon of meditation, I have developed a system of interpretation or hermeneutic which serves to guide my overall view of it. Its key terms make up the glossary items defined in their meanings special to my hermeneutic.